Culture Industry

Culture Industry

Heinz Steinert

Translated by Sally-Ann Spencer

polity

Translated with the support of a grant from the Austrian Ministry of Education, Science and Culture.

First published in 2003 by Polity Press in association with Blackwell Publishing Ltd.

Editorial office:
Polity Press
65 Bridge Street
Cambridge CB2 1UR, UK

Marketing and production:
Blackwell Publishing Ltd
108 Cowley Road
Oxford OX4 1JF, UK

Published in the USA by
Blackwell Publishing Inc.
350 Main Street
Malden, MA 02148, USA

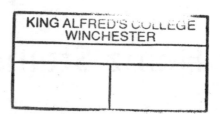

ISBN 0-7456-2676-9
ISBN 0-7456-2677-7 (pbk)

A catalogue record for this book is available from the British Library and has been applied for from the Library of Congress.

Typeset in 10 on 12 pt Palatino
by SNP Best-set Typesetter Ltd., Hong Kong
Printed in Great Britian by MPG Books Ltd, Bdmin, Cornwall

For further information on Polity, visit our website: www.polity.co.uk

Contents

Preface

These days we like to believe that we live in and write for one Western World culture, unified, and dominated, by the United States. Some people think of this (and not without justification) as cultural imperialism. But many of us, like the author of this text, who had to grow up in post-fascist Europe, view American cultural imperialism somewhat generously: it can be highly liberating. Billy Holiday and Elvis Presley, Miles Davis and Gerry Mulligan, Hemingway and Kerouac, Marlon Brando and Lauren Bacall did as much to save my youth from authoritarianism, philistinism and sheer boredom as Schopenhauer, Marx, Freud, Brecht, Camus and Sartre – or Adorno. Anglo-American culture, including, of course, Tony Richardson, Bertrand Russell and Mick Jagger, became part of our own world and helped us to deal with the German, European and world catastrophes of the twentieth century and their legacies.

The scholarly culture of the social sciences is even more international. But even after long stretches of time in London and teaching and research in Melbourne and New York, the process of translating this book surprised me at how deeply my thinking is steeped in a European, even Viennese background. At the same time, it is not possible to assume that people in London or New York know as much about this background as we know about theirs. Here we strike another facet of cultural imperialism: the transfer is inevitably asymmetrical.

Translating a text to do with cultural scholarship is thus of necessity more than transposing words and ideas from one language into another. The exercise is actually an attempt and invitation to engage in cross-cultural dialogue. In the course of working with my gracious translator, Sally-Ann Spencer, the text underwent a series of many small but necessary adaptations. It remains, though, a very European text, about a deeply European philosopher, written by a European social scientist, on an eminently Anglo-American topic: culture industry. It therefore explicates a particular perspective on culture industry that may be unfamiliar and perhaps even unpopular: a reflexive approach in the best tradition of European social theory. It asks the Anglo-American reader to be curious about that theory and open-minded about how it can help us to understand, and appreciate, contemporary culture. Under these conditions the reader and this book should be right for each other.

I have been very fortunate in being able to research and discuss culture industry matters with friends and students (some are both) in Vienna, Frankfurt, Münster, Hamburg, Berlin, Leipzig, Basel, Paris, London, Cambridge, Durham, Keele, Sheffield, Tel Aviv, Washington, New York, and not least Bundoora, Victoria. With some of them I have co-authored analyses and theoretical treatises in the field. With some I have shared cultural experiences and their interpretation. With some I have had disputes. Some I have taught. Some have contributed to producing this book materially. I am grateful for the support I received from each of them, knowingly or not.

Fiona and Nicolas, who both work in the field, will, I hope, like what I have made of our (more or less immediately shared) experience of the recent decades.

HSt

Acknowledgements

The author and publishers are grateful for permission to reproduce the following copyright material:

Extracts from Max Horkheimer and Theodor W. Adorno, *Dialectic of Enlightenment*, trans. John Cumming (Allen Lane, 1973), reprinted by permission of the Tanja Howarth Literary Agency.

Commentary from CD liner notes for Broadlahn, *Broadlahn* (The Fab Records, 1990), reprinted by permission of Reinhard Ziegerhofer for Broadlahn.

Extract from CD liner notes by Mary Katherine Aldin for Doug McLeod, *Come to Find* (Audioquest Music, 1994), reprinted by permission of Valley Entertainment.

Introduction: the pleasures of criticism

How do we make sense of the barrage of culture industry products that constantly assails us from every direction? Despite the hype, contemporary cultural criticism has proved to be of limited assistance. Generally, it leaves us more confused than enlightened: while some commentators greet a particular product with wild enthusiasm, others are scathing in their condemnation. Ascribing 'popular appeal' to a product is high praise in some circles, but a euphemism for crass vulgarity in others. Conversely, the civilizing influence of some culture industry offerings is lauded by some, while the same product or genre is dismissed for its apparent elitism by others. As all those who follow culture industry know, a fair standard of evaluation is hard to come by. This makes life particularly difficult for novices. The main aim of this book, therefore, is to provide a guide for the perplexed. It is designed to help the willing student to understand and master skills in critical evaluation. This ambitious undertaking becomes, in time, its own reward. Informed critical awareness allows us to experience the deep satisfaction that is to be had from reflexive engagement with cultural products and productions.

This book adopts a two-pronged strategy in pursuit of the pleasures of criticism. First, it offers an exposition and re-evaluation of one of the key sources of critical thought: the European tradition that culminated in Critical Theory. In particular, it examines one of the Frankfurt School's core ideas, the theory of culture industry. Introducing students to this theory equips them with a feel for the language of analysis, including the rich vocabulary of interpretation and criticism. But while knowledge of this important theory sets us on the right path, it is not enough. We also need to be able to scrutinize our own daily experiences with culture industry. The book therefore provides teachers and students with a method and with the techniques to help us record and analyse our own close encounters with culture and its products. It actively builds skills in interpreting and evaluating culture industry.

This task, however, is not as easy as it sounds. Criticism is inevitably a subset of culture industry, and so media commentators are caught up (often unwittingly) in the very vortex of culture industry that they purport to critique. To be effective, our own analytical tools must be understood as part of the mode of cultural production itself. In part, this insight can be achieved through a detailed examination of the founding text on 'culture industry' written around the middle of the last century, namely the 'Culture Industry' chapter from Max Horkheimer and Theodor W. Adorno's *Dialectic of Enlightenment* (1944/1947).[1] Horkheimer and Adorno were philosophers and social scientists, and Adorno was also a composer and pianist. A close reading and analysis of their text is still the best introduction to an understanding of the contradictions inherent in 'culture industry'.

Together, Horkheimer and Adorno set the standard for critical thinking for the postwar decades. (This is true of the reconstruction of post-World War II Germany but it is equally so for philosophical and critical subcultures all over the world.) These days, it is fashionable to dismiss their work as too old, too boring and too elitist, along with a host of other charges that now fall too readily at the feet of any work by dead white European males. However, the disillusioned distance afforded by Critical Theory offers us some unique perspectives that are otherwise missing from what passes these days as 'critical' discourse.

More specifically, the theory of culture industry:

- rejects the glib dichotomy between 'high' and 'low' cultural forms and 'serious' art and 'pop' culture. Ironically, commentators who dismiss the theory of culture industry as being 'no longer relevant' often do so on the grounds that the theory is confined to high culture and is therefore elitist. In fact, the opposite is true. Adorno and Horkheimer's theory is a sustained critique of intellectuals and their own self-absorbed immersion in the industry. It does not look down on 'stupid' audiences, but criticizes a cultural production that does not provide them with the challenges and entertainment that would otherwise be their due. It shows that the high–low distinction is itself produced by the sales imperatives of commodity culture.

- eschews the cult of novelty and newness. Artists as well as cultural theorists try to make their reputation through the apparent originality of their insights. The theory of culture industry, by contrast, holds that this emphasis on the 'newness' of cultural products (among them concepts and theories) is nothing more than culture industry's fashion mechanism, applied to the field of social criticism. Of course, Adorno and Horkheimer were not familiar with the internet in 1947. Yet, their historically informed analysis of the basic mechanism of 'commodification' has nevertheless been vindicated by the industrial mode of cultural production that we now take for granted.
- grounds itself in a materialist reflexivity. The theory locates the basis of culture in the mode of production (whether intellectual or other) and its dominant characteristic, the commodity form. Unlike postmodernism, Horkheimer and Adorno's theory does not accept that all positions are equally valid. According to the theory of culture industry, social and cultural criticism is possible – provided that the analysis is conducted in a reflexive manner. Critical theory resists the temptation to dissolve truth into diversity. On the contrary, it analyses the appeal of such extreme relativism as a consequence of a specific formation of the academic and intellectual market-place.

The book is divided into seven chapters. The first sets out the historical context of both the 'Culture Industry' text and the phenomenon of culture industry itself. The second chapter is methodological: it deals with how we should read texts (including philosophical works) and cultural artefacts. The next three chapters develop key aspects of the theory of culture industry, looking at cultural commodities and their implications, entertainment and its relation to advertising, and the instrumentalization of the audience. A short chapter on culture industry politics, based mainly on the writings of Horkheimer, follows. The last chapter reflects on the effect of culture industry on our understanding of intellectual activity, as well as on the role of the intellectual, past and present.

The key sections of the text provide an outline of the conceptual lexicon developed by Adorno and Horkheimer in their analysis of culture industry. However, the text goes beyond mere explication of Adorno and Horkheimer's ideas and analytical approach to demonstrate how critical analysis can be applied to current concerns. Inevitably, though, historical texts have to be criticized and updated. I have chosen to do this by drawing on psychoanalytic categories – by using 'countertransference' as an analytical tool, as well as (and most importantly) by calling upon the idea of a 'working alliance' to describe the relationship between cultural products and their audience. This makes it possible, for example, to reconceptualize and to reorder the main phases of the cultural history of the twentieth century. What is more, it allows us to locate Critical Theory in this line of succession. It can also help us to sketch out new research programmes, including audience research 'from an audience perspective'.

The method employed to help us understand cultural texts, artefacts and events also allows us to apply Adorno and Horkheimer's sophisticated theories to our own experience of contemporary life (and not least, to our diverse encounters with culture industry). Alongside the study of the 'Culture Industry' text, readers are encouraged to engage with all kinds of culture industry products, including those that may initially appear to be offensive or politically unacceptable. Training the mind for critical thought requires regular exercise. We can learn to take advantage of all the available opportunities. This means abandoning not only the stock distinction between high and low culture, but all the loose and limited labels routinely used to assess the value of cultural products (like 'this painting is eternal art' or 'this movie is suitable entertainment for a first date'). This book treats the most sophisticated (and high-class) products with the same irreverence as products that are ostensibly trivial, crude and rude (and low-class). Effective critical analysis seeks to understand both kinds of product with equal seriousness.

Acquiring the habit of recording and learning to analyse our daily experience in the world enables us to apply theory to interpret culture as we live and experience it. Throughout the book, therefore, sample 'field notes' are used to demonstrate the possibilities of applying Critical Theory in order to:

- arrive at new interpretations of the cultural terrain, even when it seems to have been covered exhaustively. (See field notes I on the *Mona Lisa*, field notes VI on exoticism and music or field notes VIII on clowns.)
- highlight the hidden connections between apparently unrelated commodities. (See field notes III exploring the relationship between the marketing of telephone sex and heartburn pills, or field notes V on insulting the audience.)
- derive counterintuitive interpretations and revisionist readings of cultural products. (See field notes II, IV and XII dealing with movies by Clint Eastwood and Woody Allen, and field notes IX, which discusses movies that invite us to 'laugh at Hitler'.)

- apply critical theory to a range of media and genres, as well as to the products of both traditional high and low culture. (See field notes VII, which analyses performance art. See also field notes XI, which examines the public hysteria surrounding the Princess of Wales's fatal car accident.)

This approach to culture industry studies is the result of teaching Critical Theory to students in the social science department of Frankfurt University – the department that is most directly heir to the approach developed by Adorno and Horkheimer in the 1930s, tested against their experiences during their exile in the US in the 1940s, and then brought back to Frankfurt and Europe during the 1950s and 1960s. It is also the result of my own experience of the rebellious 1960s and 1970s pop culture and the mass-mediatization of former elite culture in the 1980s and 1990s. Throughout, I draw on examples from US culture and its 'cultural imperialism' (although today we prefer to speak of 'globalization') because they constitute an instructive and engaging source that moderates the austerity of European cultural pessimism. At the same time, my approach remains faithful to the rigour and high standards of European culture and cultural analysis. This provides the necessary antidote to the insulting diet of trash that seduces us with a false promise of pleasure that is never realized. Real pleasure is mostly achieved vicariously through learning how to interpret these unsatisfactory offerings in unusual and interesting ways. This book, then, is the result of respect for, as well as distance from, both the European tradition and US-dominated commodity culture. It is committed to understanding both traditions, yet in an ironic mode that matches the media sophistication of contemporary audiences and consumers.

By this time, it should be clear that our two 'dead white European males' who are often accused of being cultural snobs were, in fact, responsible for producing a theory that is still relevant to contemporary concerns – if only we take their work seriously and apply it to current historical circumstances. Critical Theory, in the true sense of the term, is far from an exercise in high culture and intellectual one-upmanship – on the contrary, it is a guide to deep understanding and enjoyment. Contrary to popular perceptions, intellectual analysis does not deaden sensual pleasure. In fact, an intellectual appreciation of what we experience actually heightens our enjoyment. But a satisfying intellectual life also makes personal demands on us. Compensating for the trivialized and routinized state of culture industry requires razor-sharp wit, patience, and, perhaps most important of all, anti-authoritarian, indeed, even subversive sensibilities. As Adorno's and Horkheimer's life work attests, insight and intellectual pleasure are possible only if we stretch ourselves to the limit.

1

Approaching culture industry: recommended equipment

Tools 1 The text: Horkheimer and Adorno's 'Culture Industry' of 1944/1947

This book is based upon the seemingly ludicrous suggestion that we should approach 'culture industry' using a text that is now over fifty years old.[1] In studying this text, we will also tackle one of the themes of Critical Theory and thus get to grips with Critical Theory itself – an area of study that is generally considered to be 'difficult' and even a little outdated. Adorno's article on culture industry is almost always mentioned in the various anthologies and text-books on 'mass communication' and 'cultural studies', but it is usually dismissed as an 'elitist' work. Adorno's rigour makes him seem something of a spoil-sport. His unpopularity is only increased by the fact that he knew nothing of the internet and very little about TV. (By way of compensation, he wrote on Schoenberg, Berg and Webern, but these are 'difficult' composers whose music continues to challenge us today.) These days, it seems as if culture industry as described by Adorno is a thing of the past – now everything is much bigger, brighter and diverse, while we ourselves have become far more sophisticated in our dealings with the excess of cultural goods available. How could we possibly learn anything from such an ancient text?

The fact that we will be approaching culture industry by way of the very first text ever to deal with that topic means that we will be working within a very sophisticated theoretical structure.[2] By using Adorno and Horkheimer's historic text, we will be studying culture industry within the context of social history. This means that we will consider each text about culture industry (including Adorno's own) as the result of a writer's experience of cultural phenomena. In so doing, we shall dispense with the delusion that such theories offer any 'eternal truths'. While analysing such texts, we should also remember that every writer's experience is determined by their position within society. Thus we should acknowledge that Adorno's experience was determined by his status as a highly educated and cultured man. Taking an early text on culture industry as our starting point has the inbuilt advantage that its historical status will help us to see that 'culture industry' is a relational concept: the term describes the difficult relationship between educated individuals and the vast field of commodified culture. The relational nature of culture industry is more difficult to spot in contemporary texts, for this would mean confronting our own hang-ups and fixations. We find ourselves much less involved in texts written in historical and social contexts that are easy for us to categorize. Such texts can help us to learn how to exercise reflexivity, a reflexivity that should also and primarily be applied to our own position.

In any case, Critical Theory has always been the most reflexive of all sociological theories.[3] It is for this reason that Critical Theory provides us with a far more productive way of thinking than the strategies offered by many of the more recent sociological texts. Critical Theory should be read on its own terms – as an intellectual's reflection on his or her experience of society. If successful, this reflection reveals to us the structure of the relationship between the intellectual and society, as well as the structure of social relationships in general.

My analysis of the 'Culture Industry' text is conducted in different ways within the different sections of this book. In some sections, I work systematically through an excerpt from Adorno's text, analysing it in great detail. In others, I group together passages from different places in the text that are thematically linked, and describe the new constellations and interpretations that then arise. There are also sections in which I resolve the text's apparent contradictions and illogicalities, and others where I refer back to the experiences and models of thought that underlie it. I did not feel obliged to provide an exhaustive interpretation of Adorno's text. Instead, I chose to analyse those sections that are relevant to the text's central themes, leaving much unchartered territory for the reader to navigate alone. (Thus there is, for example, only scant reference to sport – a topic that Adorno discusses toward the end of his text – despite the fact that this activity has become quite central to culture industry today.) In each instance, the analysis of Adorno's text is complemented by excursions into contemporary phenomena, by references to contemporary sociological theories and by allusion to related themes and issues that remain to be explored.

The primary aim of analysing a theoretical and philosophical text in these ways is to explore and understand the meaning of the concepts that it draws on. However, the task of reconstructing these concepts is not made easier if the words that are used have multiple meanings. This problem can be aggravated if the process of translation blurs distinctions that are apparent in the original language. Both of these difficulties occur in the case of the term 'culture industry'.

Horkheimer and Adorno use the term in two different senses:

- In the first instance, 'culture industry' refers to commodity production as the principle of a specific form of cultural production. 'Commodity-form culture' stands in contrast to the bourgeois idea of art as something that is exempt from all practical interest; that is self-contained; that is 'useless' for any instrumental purpose; that forms a universe for itself; and that represents 'l'art pour l'art', as some writers and artists in the nineteenth century proclaimed.
- Secondly, 'the culture industry' denotes a specific branch of production, comprising film studios, recording facilities, CD factories, giant printing machines disgorging daily papers at an unbelievable rate (an image that crops up in countless movies), radio and TV stations with global coverage, and even the Times Square conglomerate of theatres, clubs and stage shows. 'The culture industry' makes us think of factories for cultural goods.

The two senses of the term are certainly connected, but not as closely as we might think. The artist or scholar working alone in an isolated studio can think and produce in terms of what will enhance sales and improve relations with the critics and the powers that be. On the other hand (although this is something that Adorno would not have accepted), the jazz musician in a commercial dance-band and the pianist playing in a bar for the patron are right in the middle of culture industry, yet they can play solo passages in which all that counts is the logic of the music and the expressivity of the person playing, no matter what the audience does and regardless of any external considerations.

It is also important to remember that 'culture industry' is not in any way identical with 'the media'. The principle of 'commodity-form culture' also extends beyond the media into architecture, design, art exhibitions, journalistic 'muck-raking' and 'scandal-mongering', the conventions governing dating, affairs and marriages, corporate culture, the composition of 'serious' music, our notions of the 'ideal' body (and our attempts to combat any discrepancies), religious and national rituals, self-help literature, philosophical and sociological thinking, and so forth. The study of 'culture industry', therefore, is not a subspeciality of economic or industrial sociology, or of management studies. Instead, it involves analysing the subsumption of diverse kinds of intellectual production under commodity principles.

Clearly, it is necessary to distinguish between the two different meanings of the term 'culture industry'. In the original German text, this is done by the definite article: 'the culture industry' refers to the media and their factories, while 'culture industry' stands for the principle of commodity-form cultural activity.[4] In English, the term has been unified into the usage of 'the culture industry', probably because this sounds more familiar, but also because the distinction between the two meanings was not recognized. (The use of the term without the definite article may sound slightly unfamiliar. Philosophical terms can, and sometimes must have this effect.)

In this book, a conscious attempt is made to re-establish the primary meaning of the term 'culture industry' as indicating 'commodity-form culture' (as distinct from 'the media'). Thus, where appropriate, the unfamiliar form without the definite article is used. Readers should be aware, however, that this distinction is not made in the only translation of the 'Culture Industry' chapter that exists in English. A simple test that can help with this problem is to try replacing the term 'culture industry' by 'factories' and then by 'commodity-form culture', and to see which version makes more sense.

Tools II   Cultural experience: Analysing the products of culture industry

In order to understand culture industry, we must also be familiar with its products. This requires us to go out and experience the whole range of goods that culture industry has to offer. At the same time, however, we must refrain from making our habitual aesthetic and/or moral judgements about the quality, usefulness, interest value, wholesomeness, suitability and so forth of these goods. We must move away from our everyday attitude towards culture and abandon our quest for cultural 'highs', in which we simply ignore anything that does not seem to fit those requirements.

There are valid practical reasons for taking a selective stance towards culture. For one thing, while the range of cultural products on offer is almost unlimited, our lifespan is certainly not. In any case, we are accustomed to selecting different cultural events for different purposes. We use big sporting events or pop concerts to provide us with safe thrills; we seek civilized, cultured entertainment by visiting a museum with a new partner or friend; we use the cinema to warm up for a big night on the town with our mates; a good book serves to provoke our thoughts, while the TV helps us to relax or fall asleep. It is for this reason that we are keen to discover which cultural event is best suited to each purpose. We are anxious to avoid nasty surprises, not wishing to condemn ourselves to hours of boredom, nor to become responsible for any nasty social gaffes.[5] We often use the media to combat our loneliness, but the media also play an important role in our social lives. Either way, we select a media event in order to create for ourselves the attitudes and relationships which that particular event offers and at the same time presupposes. This is why we like to know in advance what form these will take. It is on this basis that we select the event. We are helped in our decision by our backgrounds, which shape our preferences for certain genres of cultural products. In individual instances, we are aided by the numerous discussions that take place about current cultural events. Finally, the selection process is further facilitated by professional critics and advertising agencies – two groups of people whose activities often appear strangely similar.

For those with an academic interest in culture industry, this selective and evaluative approach to culture provides us with a first substantive finding. However, social scientists are not concerned about establishing whether any of these aesthetic or moral preferences can be justified. They are not interested in trying to 'rationalize' (I use this term in all its possible meanings) why it is that some products might be better than others, nor are they intent on explaining why all such products might be worthless. Such matters are frequently examined within the field of media studies. Indeed, there is a marked fascination with the effect of the media on society (Is it television that makes children restless and easily distracted? / Does filmed violence make (male) youths aggressive? / Can pornography lead to rape? / In short, does exposure to the media result in people losing their sense of reality?).

Such questions are part of a noble tradition that also has its roots in the arts. (See, for example, Cervantes' *Don Quixote* (1605), Flaubert's *Madame Bovary* (1857) and Woody Allen's *Play it Again, Sam* (1972).) These are also questions for which there is no real answer. It is extremely difficult to examine in isolation any one of the many factors that contribute to the make-up of our lives within society. There is, however, still less chance of successfully separating out one causal link from the other factors that affect events that are in any case interconnected. The link between violent young men and their consumption of violent films is, for example, complicated by further factors such as the lower-class origins of these men and their class-bound notion of masculinity – a notion that privileges physical strength. Moreover, this understanding of masculinity is also linked to the type of work that these men are able – and are required – to engage in. Given the complexity of this web of factors (whose threads we have only just begun to number), how could we possibly establish a direct connection between any one violent act and the viewing of violent films? Even if this were possible, what purpose would it actually serve? Above all, of course, it would provide us with a justification for censorship. However, if we then examine who it is that would support censorship, we will find that studies of violence and the media are often initiated by the media in situations of intense competition between different types of media. Thus the censorship of sex, violence and explicit language has become a point of conflict in the ratings struggle between state and private television. Indeed, censorship would deprive the private channels of the opportunity to win over viewers by using sensational and taboo material that the state channels are unable to use. Of course, it is not always so easy to identify the relevant political factors, but in some cases they are clearly apparent.

In any case, in the spirit of intellectual inquiry we shall distance ourselves from the factors that influence our evaluation and selection of cultural material. If we fail to distance ourselves, we will necessarily become enmeshed in the struggles between those vying to impose on us their own criteria for evaluating and selecting cultural products. Instead, it is our task to treat the struggle of interests (including its effect on us) reflexively, and to withdraw from it for the time being. In order to understand culture industry, we must take an active interest in all its products: from Barbie to basketball, from John Cage to the comic-book, from Goethe to the garden gnome, from home appliances to Hundertwasser, from classical music festivals to the cinema, from *Macbeth* to mass marathons, from sports stadiums to strip clubs, from tourism to talk-shows and from Westerns to Wagner.

We will not allow our curiosity to be limited by our personal preferences (which form an important part of our own self-image), nor by the good taste which all of us, of course, possess. It is possible that we will even come across a few things that were previously unknown to us. Quite apart from that, our drive for comprehensive cultural knowledge provides us with a marvellous excuse to examine those politically incorrect, tasteless, smutty and generally dubious cultural products that we do not usually allow ourselves to approach. Admittedly, we will also have to come face to face with some cultural products from which we would rather keep our distance. We will be forced to encounter products that disgust us (this is often the case with horror and porno films – worse still, such films can limit our nocturnal activities and impair our love life), and products that frighten us (as may be the case with the more or less fascist subcultures of machismo). It will not always be easy to find the right way of approaching some cultural objects. In any case, we will have to overcome our fear of confronting the unknown. This is not to say that we must brace ourselves to act as heroes – it is possible to observe certain things from afar. Nevertheless, it is a basic characteristic of the social scientist to exhibit as much curiosity as possible, even with regard to the most diverse of cultural phenomena.

We will be in particular need of this kind of uninhibited curiosity in order to explore the different avenues of high culture. I mention high culture because I do not wish to give the impression that our task consists solely in seeking exotic experiences and questionable pleasures. At this point, we should remember that it is reflexivity that constitutes our most vital concern. Such reflexivity will be particularly difficult to achieve when dealing with cultural products that we have come to admire. We will have to work hard if we wish to deal reflexively with those cultural products over which we have gained mastery and in whose glory we have learnt to bask. Of course, a certain degree of expertise is necessary when dealing with any cultural activity. As our cultural knowledge increases, so we learn to perceive the subtle differences that exist. (An obvious example of this would be the way in which many football fans learn to observe their game with the utmost precision, acquiring a vast knowledge of its history and players.)

Nevertheless, there is one area of culture that seems to require us to be particularly learned – traditional high culture. If we wish to discuss high culture, we must at least appear knowledgeable, if not witty. If we want to seem 'cultured', we must always have a trenchant opinion to hand. Most readers of this book will consider themselves to be 'cultured' and will therefore be subject to the pressures that this entails. Our status as 'educated people' is the result of a considerable investment that we have made. (Bourdieu calls this 'cultural capital'.) It is, therefore, only natural that we should wish to see this investment honoured. However, we frequently have to face situations in which our status is questioned, or in which we are forced to face the competition of others. In such instances, we must put on a suitable 'performance', in order to prove our credentials. (Thus it is that every time we are asked to give our views on an art show or concert, we are being invited to perform. This is a test situation, even if all we are required to do is to fill out a sociologist's questionnaire.) Of course, having to perform in this manner is not always enjoyable. Sometimes we prefer to avoid exposing ourselves to such pressure. Sometimes we would prefer simply to 'let ourselves go' or to 'let it all hang out'. (In the past, this had to be done in private, but now this is not necessarily the case.)

Nowadays, if we want to appear 'cultured' (or, in today's terminology, 'culturally sophisticated'), familiarity with high culture, its tradition and its highbrow avant-garde is not enough. (This area of culture is now relatively difficult to define. What is more, its practitioners are now frequently subject to the suspicion of charlatanism.) These days, we must also know all about popular culture. We have not yet entirely escaped the influence of the established canon of art (as composed by the dictates of good taste and cultural elitism). Nevertheless, in contrast to the nineteenth century (when the notion of the cultured citizen was in its heyday), it is now much easier to deal with it reflexively. This capacity to view the canon reflexively is to some extent also the result of sociological research, and in particular Bourdieu's analysis of the 'distinctions'. We now have a more tolerant attitude towards cultures which privilege particular cultural products – we simply see them as being different from our own, regarding the cultivation of exclusive tastes as a way of attempting to secure group identity. We no longer believe in a fixed hierarchy of cultural values. In contemporary society, cultured people have particular respect for those who possess a great range of cultural knowledge and who are able to deal reflexively with a multitude of cultural products. For us, knowledge of Schoenberg's music is no longer enough: if we want to appear educated, we must also be able to discuss cultural phenomena such as motor racing. This requires more than simply being able to embark on a critique of the sport. Mere critique would make us appear rather old-fashioned and provincial. In any case, motor-racing is a very easy target – after all, even the fans are well aware of the sport's threat to the environment, as well as of its promotion of macho ideals. These days, the 'culturally sophisticated' are able to criticize all forms of culture, but are also able and willing to enjoy the whole range of cultural products on offer. Cultural studies offer an excellent opportunity for guilt-free indulgence in such intellectual 'slumming'.

It has often been said that Cultural Studies (in particular the American variety) consists solely of intellectual slumming. If this were the case, then our endeavour would not seem especially worthwhile. At this point, we must encourage ourselves to take traditional high culture just as seriously as the cultural products offered by MTV or the net. We can aim to gain at least as much expertise in the field of high culture as we exhibit when we are able to distinguish between the different brands of pop music from yesterday and today. The best way of dealing with the intimidating amount of learning required by high culture is to compare it to the knowledge required for the understanding of popular culture, and to resolve to acquire both. In our dealings with both high and popular culture, we will encounter the problem of 'pseudo-culture'. This is described by Adorno in 'Theory of Pseudo-Culture' (1959) as the inability to experience the phenomenon in question properly and deeply, due to the surplus and unnecessary knowledge of labels and genres with which we surround it. However, the ideology of immediacy (a theory of cultural pedagogy that is directly opposed to the knowledge of labels) does not provide us with any solutions either. Experiencing art is not simply a question of 'opening ourselves up', so that art may speak to us – such naïve approaches to art are of little use. In fact, in order for us to understand high or popular culture, we must work hard and learn to mobilize all our social knowledge and insight. This will be necessary whether the product in question appears transparent or encoded, and regardless of whether it seems to demand us to be 'learned'. Those who believe that cultural knowledge and reflexivity can be acquired without effort have fallen for culture industry's ideology of 'fun'. Yet those who do not know how much pleasure can be derived from such effort have also been duped.

Tools III   Reflexivity: Writing field notes

Keeping a notebook will help us to consolidate our cultural knowledge. It is advisable that we jot down notes about our own reactions – as well as those of others – to particular (cultural) events. We should keep a record of our insights and our discussions, and then experiment with different ways of interpreting the various phenomena. Indeed, we should take every opportunity to write about and comment on culture industry. There is a big difference between thinking something to yourself, discussing your thoughts with others, and giving your ideas the definitive status of writing. In any case, our memories are in fact much shorter than we usually like to assume. If we preserve our experiences in writing, then we will be able to continue to work with them, looking for comparisons, trying to get different responses and interpretations, and seeking other events that we would like to add to our collection. If we then go back and read our earlier attempts to interpret events, we will often find fascinating evidence of the way we have developed in intellectual and other terms. (It is for this reason that we should think about dating our notes.) Moreover, if we ever need to work on and elaborate a particular theme as part of a wider study, we will certainly profit from being able to reread and reorganize our original notes.

To sum up: in addition to the analysis of the Adorno/Horkheimer text, our study of culture industry will require us to come up with detailed interpretations of cultural products and events. Theoretical study and practical interpretation are activities that run parallel to, and complement each other, as exemplified in the structure of this book. My analysis of cultural phenomena (which appears in this book within the twelve sets of field notes) shows how we may attain a degree of reflexivity towards events approximating that achieved by Critical Theory.[6] It is my hope that the case studies will inspire and encourage readers to engage in their own interpretations – in any case, there is an almost inexhaustible supply of material left to analyse.

Field notes I   Why are you smiling, Leonardo?

On the first day of the Winter Olympics in 1994, Munch's *The Scream* was mysteriously removed from the National Gallery in Oslo. The painting has since been recovered, but in the view of one commentator, Munch's iconic image could not truly be stolen. According to Peter Schjeldahl (then art critic for the New York *Village Voice,* now writing for the *New Yorker*), *The Scream* had long since dispensed with its vulnerable physical form, and now existed only in the insubstantial and trivial mode of kitsch. Schjeldahl takes issue with those for whom the painting had become an object of cynicism and satire, and describes how the sight of the original had changed his life. In Schjeldahl's opinion, the original would still have the power to silence its witty critics: 'As long as *The Scream* hangs somewhere on a wall accessible to the public, humanity will lack one alibi for being stupid about life, art and the human cost of modernity . . .'[7]

   The return of the painting means that it would now be possible to try to verify Schjeldahl's claim, and some people may make the effort to visit the painting in Oslo. Of course, we could just as easily try the experiment on a painting housed in a rather more accessible location – the *Mona Lisa* in Paris would seem an obvious choice. Nonetheless, it seems most unlikely that Schjeldahl's assertion would hold. Indeed, if we were to succeed in pushing our way through the rush hour hordes at the Louvre and into the tightly packed cluster of people gathered in front of the *Mona Lisa*'s glass case, we would still have to fight for a view, our brief glimpses of the painting disturbed by snatches of conversation, smells, jostling from the crowd and other such distractions. Quite apart from all that, we have already seen the image a thousand times, and we would not find anything new or different in the original. In fact, reproductions of the painting have already shown us even the tiniest cracks in its surface. What is more, our view of the original would also be troubled by Duchamp's and Dali's satirical versions of the painting. Flamboyant moustaches would superimpose themselves mercilessly upon the *Mona Lisa*, a painting which, by comparison, appears strangely without meaning. So much for the original – indeed, unbeknown to us, it could long since have been replaced by a copy!

   If we were to compare the original to a reproduction, the original would not provide us with any greater or better reason to change our lives. We would find nothing in the original to suggest that it has any kind of special 'aura'. The renovation work in the Sistine Chapel has taught us all how the venerable appearance of original old masters is often linked to the age of their varnish and to the dust and dirt that cover them. (Of course, it is always possible that a thorough cleaning of the *Mona Lisa* would also help to clarify a few points.) The fact that it is possible to reproduce a work of art will not necessarily detract from its aura (that is, from the quality that makes us experience it in a more intense way than we experience the rest of our world). Indeed, part of an icon's aura may be dependent on our frequent encounters with that icon. This is something that Walter Benjamin failed to realize in his writings on the subject.

It is important to remember that an object's aura does not emanate from its existence as a physical artefact. Instead, the aura is a function of the relationship between subject and object; it is a function of the 'working alliance' that exists between the two parties. In order to examine this, we can turn again to the *Mona Lisa*.

Over time, the reactions to the *Mona Lisa* have been many and varied. Nevertheless, there is one aspect of the painting that people have constantly referred to – its ambiguity or indeterminacy. The smile it portrays has always been considered enigmatic, and there have always been doubts as to the identity of the lady. To some, she appears 'virtuous', but to others she is a 'courtesan'. Equally, the idea that the lady might in fact be a young man cannot be dismissed. In an essay of 1869, Walter Pater went a long way towards shaping our current attitudes towards the *Mona Lisa*. Pater describes the *Mona Lisa* as the archetypal woman; a woman who unites Greek and Roman antiquity, the Middle Ages and the sins of the Borgias; a woman who is at one and the same time Leda, the mother of Helen, and Saint Anne, the mother of Mary.

Such efforts to analyse the *Mona Lisa*'s ambiguity take its suggestiveness too literally and do violence to the painting. What the painting actually shows us is this: a young woman who escapes our every effort to define her. As we look at the painting, we are confronted with a riddle that we are not supposed to be able to solve; a riddle that we could not solve even if we tried. This is all linked to what we know, or rather, what we know that we do not know, about the painting. The painting itself provides us with some clues to this. Quite apart from the *Mona Lisa*'s faint, but renowned smile, there is also and more importantly the way that she looks out of the picture. The *Mona Lisa* does not – to put it in contemporary terms – look straight 'at the camera'. Her look does not follow us and give us the illusion of contact. On the contrary, we have the feeling that the *Mona Lisa* has just looked at us, and that at any moment she might look again. Her smile is what remains from that brief moment of understanding in which her eyes met our own.

This pattern of behaviour is familiar to us. It is the pattern of flirtation. We might be at a tedious talk, or even just walking down a street, when our eyes suddenly meet those of someone else. It occurs to us both that we might find each other interesting, and that we could get to know each other. We know, however, that we will not do so, for it would only end in the tired old routine of mistrust and instrumentalization, of illusory companionship and short-lived happiness (and so on and so forth). All this occurs to us in the brief second in which our eyes meet, and we experience it from its exhilarating beginning to its sorry end. A hint of a smile is all that remains.

A similar play of eyes can also take place between people who are linked in an actual, yet secret relationship. The young lover who finds in his mistress's eyes the *Mona Lisa*'s gaze will be reminded of that dawn moment in which contentment, sleepiness and renewed desire mingle in the first light of day. Their love is secret, and must remain so; yet among a group of unsuspecting others, the woman's eyes seek his. Thus an exclusive bond is forged between the couple, which goes unnoticed by the rest. Such a bond is one of the most intimate forms of relationships, for it is not acknowledged by society and could be broken off at any time. It is this scenario that leads us to believe that the seemingly chaste *Mona Lisa* might in fact be a courtesan.

For us, this bond of exclusivity is fascinating. However, in the case of the painting and of the courtesan (as in the case of every human), the promised exclusivity of the bond is at once ironic: we know that another could easily fill our role and that the promised exclusivity will never be realized.[8] What is true of every human being is particularly true in the case of the courtesan and her painted smile: despite the exclusive relationship that they seem to offer, they do not require a specific partner but could settle for any one of us. This is the absurdity and the charm of their 'deindividualized exclusivity'.

Leonardo's *Mona Lisa* seductively offers us a paradoxical and sham exclusivity. However, this exclusivity has always been one of the key elements of the working alliance in bourgeois art. Thus the individual observer encounters an individual work of art, created by a heroic individual artist. During this encounter, something extraordinary occurs. It is a unique moment, during which we are party to an individual act of creation that permits us to transcend the social order and the structures of domination. Nevertheless, all this occurs in the framework of public institutions – in exhibitions and museums, and at concerts or in the theatre. Furthermore, our behaviour during the encounter is regulated by set rules of conduct, and we are often forced to comply with a dress code. In fact, the encounter is usually a result of our planning, and it does not necessarily arise from any spontaneous desire. It has to be fitted into our social life, and is therefore subject to all the usual aggravations that this entails (time pressures, stress, a shortage of parking-spaces, etc.). Often we have to work hard to secure a ticket or a seat. Sometimes, we only succeed at great financial expense. The individuality of such an encounter is, therefore, of a rather displaced and highly theoretical kind. It is an individuality shored up by money and other such privileges; an individuality that we can only fabricate by these means. In short, it is entirely commensurate with the bourgeois notion of individuality based on competition.

All this explains why the post-bourgeois drive to ironize sham individuality within art took as its target the *Mona Lisa*, that former icon of exclusivity. During the Romantic era, much was made of the *Mona Lisa*, and it eventually became known as the very model of bourgeois art. However, after its theft in August 1911, the *Mona Lisa* became embroiled in the nationalistic disputes that were symptomatic of the decline of bourgeois society. Both the French and the Germans suspected each other of using the burglary to announce – or even to divert attention from – analogous bounty trips in colonial Africa. Even the thief, an Italian artisan, attributed a nationalist motive to his crime, claiming as his goal the return of the Italian painting to its homeland. (Incidentally, this approach to the matter was not without its benefits, for in the end he was only nominally punished by the Italian courts.) As a result of all this, the *Mona Lisa* became the most famous of all paintings. To top it all off, 1919 brought with it the four-hundredth anniversary of Leonardo's death.[9] After earlier attempts by Marinetti and Malevich, it was only logical that Marcel Duchamp should turn to disparaging the *Mona Lisa* in his *L.H.O.O.Q.* (1919) – in the case of the *Mona Lisa*, the paradoxical exclusivity of bourgeois art had developed ad absurdum, to the point at which an artistic response to the situation was inevitable.[10] As reports from the time suggest, a moustache on a 'classic' still had the power to shock. This shows that at that stage the bourgeois working alliance was still relatively intact, for the violation of the alliance was not yet perceived as an artistic act in its own right within a new and reflexive working alliance.

The Dadaists' attempts to provoke their audience led to the emergence and availability of a new working alliance for art (which was represented in a particularly reflexive manner in the person of Marcel Duchamp). According to this working alliance, it was the task of the artists and of their public to develop their own ideas about the institution of art, the roles that each party plays in this institution, and the peculiar norms by which the whole business is governed. The artist and the public would be free to (dis)agree. The crucial factor was that this working alliance would be reflexive in structure. Regardless of its specific form, it would be based on the fundamental belief that the object of art is art itself. Thus this working alliance is directly opposed to that which Dadaism and Surrealism are usually supposed to represent. The reflexive working alliance does not encourage the reintegration of art and life, but leads to an increased autonomy of art.[11] Of course, in a society that is already overflowing with the products of culture industry, this increased autonomy can only be realized in a reflexive manner – by presenting the necessarily unsuccessful attempt to preserve art's autonomous status in the face of the inexorable functionalization of society. There are three main ways of dealing with culture industry's main mechanism, short-lived scandal: (1) by insulting the public; (2) by creating an esoteric distance; and (3) by employing irony. These three methods are not mutually exclusive, and they typically appear in combination. They all incorporate the mechanism of scandal, but they counteract its effect and enable a reflexive attitude towards it.

Many years after *L.H.O.O.Q.*, Marcel Duchamp provided a clear demonstration of the procedures in question: he reversed his original parody of the painting, thereby taking the satire to its limits. In 1965, he acquired for himself a normal and entirely unadulterated reproduction of the *Mona Lisa*, and bestowed upon it the title *raseé L.H.O.O.Q.* This new work was dependent on the fame attained by its predecessor, and it provided a comment on this. The actual subject-matter of the painting was entirely irrelevant – at most, the way in which our notion of 'subject-matter' is satirized could be read as an allusion to our fetishism of fame.

This is a cumulative process. The first satirical work presupposes knowledge of the original painting and is dependent on the effect of its fame. Later works play on our knowledge of a whole series of paintings, each new work revealing its novelty and difference from the rest, or, as was the case with Duchamp's painting, commentating on the fact that the others are so well known. To those of us who do not know about Duchamp's work, and who are familiar only with Leonardo's *Mona Lisa*, *rasée L.H.O.O.Q.* would not mean a thing.

The reflexive and ironic working alliance is closely linked to history, yet it has no respect for it. Ironic and reflexive art depends on its audience's knowledge of history and its uses, particularly those that are currently in operation. Leonardo was much more than an ordinary artisan. (Although, he too, like the medieval artisans before him, was bound by contract to the specific amounts of blue and gold colour that his paintings were to include.) Indeed, Leonardo was not only an artisan, but was also a highly reflexive and ironic individual. As we continue to struggle with the mystery of the *Mona Lisa*, Leonardo continues to smile, waiting for us to realize that his painting is the depiction of a mystery that cannot be solved: the contradiction inherent in bourgeois art.

Autonomy and mass deception – a case of *Dialectic of Enlightenment*

The term 'culture industry' first entered the specialist vocabulary of the social sciences through the title of one of the chapters from Horkheimer and Adorno's *Dialectic of Enlightenment*, which originally appeared as a mimeograph in 1944. There is no denying the provocative nature of that title: 'Culture Industry: Enlightenment as Mass Deception'. However, it is not only this chapter, but in fact the entire book, that takes a rather desperate tone. The book is the work of two academics who were firmly rooted in the European and more specifically, the German cultural tradition, but who had been driven from their German homeland as Marxists and Jews. It was written while they were in exile, their quite convenient, befitting and financially secure Californian lifestyles accompanied by the news of the destruction of humanity through war and by political, administrative and industrial means. The extreme nature of Horkheimer and Adorno's book matches that of their circumstances. Their book describes the reduction of human beings to the state of amphibians and refers to the activity of the ruling class as 'organized criminality' (as the struggle for loot between two 'rackets' that fulfil no reasonable organizational function in relation to the working population). It tells of how humankind is becoming redundant, the latent death threat forming the backdrop to a conformity born of panic. It describes our great Western reason that, due to the structures of domination, now consigns some men to the status of machine operators and others to that of consumers incapable of action.[12] It talks of how Western reason has become a rationality of domination (over the workers, over itself and over nature), revealing how instrumental reason is incapable of objecting to the foundation of societies based on the law of force, or even on murder. It refers to culture industry and explains how anti-Semitism is based on a false projection (whereby the anti-Semite blames the Jews for the evils of capitalist society, hating them for the way in which their image reminds us of the better life that we were promised, yet never granted).

All in all, this book is a radical, angry, deeply pessimistic and thereby realistic text. It is not, however, 'well balanced'. Instead, it thrashes out on all sides, turning the knife in the wound of two intellectuals, for whom reason and enlightenment had been the focus of their work and the elixir of their lives. In social terms, the carpet had now been pulled from under their feet. (In 1944, fascism was the principal, but not the only reason for this.) The book maintains its poise only through its framework of academic style and poetic image, and through the elegance of its complicated shifts in thought, aided by its lofty distance from the subject-matter. Adorno is often considered to be a snob and a cultural elitist. Leaving aside the question of what Adorno actually made of his cultural knowledge, this assessment is accurate in so far as men of culture like him no longer exist today. Nevertheless, this is no reason to dismiss him, or his ideas, or the exemplary elements in his work. As I explain below, snobbism can be understood as a 'working alliance of public aloofness'. In any case, for a man who had seen the world as he knew it fall apart and the talents that he had nurtured within it become redundant, the attitude of snobbism was one of the few ways of retaining composure. This attitude is no longer at our disposal – if we try to adopt it, it turns into a caricature, as for example in the case of today's 'Adornoites'. Nevertheless, there is no doubt that it would permit us to view the emergent (and 'brave') new world clearly and without illusion.

At this juncture, I should like to make it quite clear that we will not be able to learn from Adorno by copying his methods (that is, by imitating his attitudes or his ways of thinking); nor will we learn from him by trawling his work for 'conclusions' that are relevant to our lives today. What we can do, however, is to learn from his texts by 'composing' them anew (Adorno saw this as the most intense way of appreciating music) and by contextualizing them (that is, by reconstructing the social conditions in which the texts were written, as well as the situation of the person who experienced these conditions and who theorized them). From our position of hindsight, it will be easier for us to consider the texts in a distanced and reflexive manner than it was for Adorno. Thus, from time to time, we will have the pleasure of knowing that our attitude towards the texts is more reflexive than that of their author. As our work progresses, we will be in urgent need of this new-found confidence, for we will have to turn our reflexive attitudes towards our own situation, being sure to mark out the differences between our own circumstances and those of Adorno. This is the moment in which we can 'learn from Adorno'. For now, of course, this is an abstract proposition, but in the following chapters I will demonstrate how it can be done.

Let us return to the 'discovery of culture industry'. Adorno was forty years old when he wrote the 'Culture Industry' chapter for *Dialectic of Enlightenment*. Before writing this text, he had studied not only philosophy (Adorno wrote his Ph.D. on Husserl and his Habilitationsschrift on Kierkegaard), but also composition.[13] (Adorno began his studies in Frankfurt under Bernhard Sekles, but in 1925 he moved to Vienna. There he studied under Alban Berg – an experience that was to greatly influence his work.) He also published articles on music criticism and on the philosophy of music. Adorno had set himself the task of writing a philosophical analysis of the achievements of the Vienna School (consisting of Schoenberg and his most famous pupils, Webern and Berg, plus a wider circle of members with varying degrees of involvement). He hoped thereby to explain – and if you like promote – their significance for the history of musical composition, as well as their importance in the history of humanity's struggle for liberation. Alongside his study of musical composition, Adorno perfected his mastery of the piano. (In Vienna, he studied under Eduard Steuermann. Throughout his life, Adorno remained an admirer and devotee of both Steuermann and Berg.) Even during those busy years in the 1960s in Frankfurt, Professor Adorno managed to reserve one hour each day for his piano practice. Adorno identified the phenomenon of culture industry in the 1920s (although he did not use this term to describe it until later on), and he analysed it in terms of 'use-music', 'light music' and 'jazz' (or what was meant by 'jazz' in Europe at that time).[14] He then assimilated this analysis to his understanding of the history of music.

A summary of Adorno's early ideas about culture industry can be found in 'On the Social Situation of Music' (1932), an essay that he wrote for the first edition of the Institute for Social Research's journal. At that time, Adorno was only loosely associated with the Institute through personal connections, not least through his proximity to Max Horkheimer, the Institute's director. In 'On the Social Situation of Music', Adorno writes:

> From a social perspective, present-day musical activity, production and consumption can be divided drastically into that which unconditionally recognizes its commodity character and – refusing any dialectic intervention – orients itself according to the demands of the market and that which in principle does not accept the demands of the market. (p. 131)

It is important to note the clear distinction that Adorno makes here between commodified use-music and light music on the one hand, and art – serious music that demands to be taken seriously – on the other. (For Adorno, this category includes even those pieces of serious music that he feels are of an inferior quality, for instance the music of Hindemith.)[15] There is no mention of 'culture industry' in this essay, but there are several references to the 'industrialization of production' (p. 160). This term is first applied in connection with the Viennese operetta, and then later to describe 'the totally rationalized factories of sound film hits with their capitalistic division of labour' (p. 161) and the 'ready-made jazz industry' (p. 162).

Later on, in the 'Culture Industry' chapter of *Dialectic of Enlightenment*, Adorno was to generalize and extend his discussion of culture industry's products to include radio, film, TV, music-hall, fairgrounds, newspaper astrology columns and so on. In that text, the commodification of culture remains the main criterion used for the analysis.

Before he came to write that text, Adorno composed two other important studies that also deal extensively with culture industry, albeit without mention of that exact term: his essay 'On Jazz' (1936) and central sections of *In Search of Wagner* (which were written at the same time and first published in 1939). He also corresponded with Walter Benjamin about the latter's theory of 'The Work of Art in the Age of Mechanical Reproduction'. All of these pieces were written in Europe, before Adorno had become familiar with the cultural situation of the US. After 1938, Adorno's experience of American culture merely served to reinforce his convictions with regard to culture industry. Adorno's first encounter with American culture was very intense. Upon arrival in the US, he immediately started work on a programme of sociological research into radio listeners. The director of this programme was Paul Lazarsfeld – a Viennese mathematician and psychologist, and the author of the classic study on *Die Arbeitslosen von Marienthal* [The unemployed in Marienthal]. Lazarsfeld had left Austria for New York in 1933. There he conducted empirical social research within a specially designed institute, taking on projects that were financed by industry or through grants. Initially, Lazarsfeld and Adorno enjoyed a good working relationship in their 'Radio Research Project', but finally they became embroiled in serious academic disputes and never succeeded in publishing their report.[16] Adorno's essay 'On Popular Music' (1941) was obviously greatly influenced by these experiences.

Adorno's next project was *Dialectic of Enlightenment*, written in California in collaboration with Max Horkheimer. Adorno used this book to develop and summarize the theory that he had been working on over so many years. He now placed culture industry in a broader context, presenting it as an important example of the 'dialectic of enlightenment', according to which the rational disenchantment of the world reverts to myth: despite, and indeed precisely because of man's liberation from his irrational fear of imposed domination, a new form of domination has emerged. The workings of this complex theory are encapsulated in the subtitle of Adorno's essay: 'Enlightenment as Mass Deception'.

It is important to mention at this stage that Adorno's reference to enlightenment is by no means a reference to the provision of political information. Adorno's focus is not on how we might gain insight into the machinations of political leaders. This form of enlightenment, arrived at with the help of society's fearless intellectuals (or through their modern professional equivalent, the investigative freelance journalist), was at one time liberating, but has now been reduced to the level of inconsequential entertainment.

For Adorno and Horkheimer, enlightenment is something much greater than this: it is our ability to experience the world through working in direct contact with its material and thereby changing it. To get such immediate experience we need to refuse to rely upon pieces of 'information' or 'communication' (whose possible link to domination should in any case arouse our distrust). In Adorno and Horkheimer's view, capitalist domination is characterized by the fact that the structures of domination inhere even within our work (for example, as our labour is governed by machinery, or organized according to a set routine of procedures). As a result, we never experience the material itself, but only the instruction manual for the machinery. Thus, for Adorno, the key to liberation does not lie in citizens having the 'right information' (nor in the existence of some kind of 'undistorted communication'), but in our ability to experience the world through our work within it. Adorno believed that such experience could be attained even in capitalism through the activities of producing and appreciating art, yet he feared for its continuing survival.

Considered in this light, a social institution with the function of distributing information, for example journalism, appears to represent the exclusion of the people from political activity. Thus journalism figures as one of the methods of control that the ruling class deploys to regulate itself, drawing upon the threat that the 'people' could be mobilized against it. The contrasting alternative to such indirect domination – the possibility of freedom – is seen in universal autonomy, that is, in direct participation in public affairs, which would render 'specialist' information redundant.

Adorno/Horkheimer's reference to 'mass deception' can be interpreted in two ways. On the one hand, it indicates deception on a large scale – every single one of us is being deceived. On the other hand, it refers to the deception practised by those who claim that it is possible to 'popularize' art: Adorno and Horkheimer are denouncing the claim that the masses can have instant access to culture simply by circumventing the demands that elitist art makes on our cultural knowledge and experience. We can only engage in the serious enterprise of experiencing the world and society if we are able to recognize and criticize the distortions effected by social domination. It is not possible to gain such experience by immersing ourselves in light-hearted or brash entertainment. If we want to experience the world, it is no good working with cultural products that have been 'dumbed down' to fit someone else's preconceptions about our intelligence. Such attempts to 'dumb down' culture are in fact the very source of the deception: we are treated with a mixture of condescension and flattery, and are allowed to consume only those cultural products that have been stripped of their challenge. However, art must be challenging if it is to merit the efforts of those who participate in it. If a cultural product does not challenge us, it despises us: apparently desperate to comply with our wishes, it secretly scorns us. When culture is commodified – when it promises to instantly gratify our desires – it relies on deceiving its customers.

The use of the term 'mass' also relates to a sociological model. Adorno could have chosen to refer to the 'deception of the people' (although this would have been rather uncharacteristic) or to the 'deception of the working class' (a notion more in keeping with his thought). The counterpoint of the masses is the elite, and the elite dominates, manipulates and keeps the masses happy. The masses are neither structured nor organized, and as such they offer no resistance to their organization from above. (A friend of Adorno's, Siegfried Kracauer, described and analysed this in terms of the 'mass ornament'.)[17] Adorno's and Horkheimer's experience of how the fascists had shaped the Germans into a 'Volk' led them to accept this particular sociological model – a model that also features in other sections of *Dialectic of Enlightenment* and which, for quite different reasons, was also familiar to American sociologists of that time.

According to Horkheimer's analysis, the phase of capitalism that made fascism possible, if not probable, also saw the ruling class degenerate into 'rackets' – into groups of predatory gangsters whose only interest lay in making a quick financial killing. Thus Horkheimer shows how the ruling class renounced its role of safeguarding the necessary conditions for the reproduction of capital and labour power against the specific interests of particular individuals and classes. (This is another way of saying that the capitalist state failed to fulfil its function.) Horkheimer describes how the ruling class turned instead to organizing the masses into a regimented force, on the one hand tempting them with the promise of bread and circuses, and on the other menacing them with the threat of social exclusion. In order to escape this dreadful fate, individuals were forced to participate in the exclusion of others, thereby allowing themselves to be manipulated into obedience. The events of recent history led Horkheimer to the retrospective insight that the bourgeois struggle for liberation had been marked from the very beginning by the deception of the masses. The bourgeoisie had used the masses as an ally in their struggle against the aristocracy, deploying them as a kind of battering ram. The means for their manipulation had remained constant, consisting of demagogy, fanaticism, and the skilful deployment of the mass media – whether through sermons and other such speeches, through mass parades celebrating the anniversary of revolutions (or parliamentary openings, Olympic festivals, etc.), or through virtual mass assemblies convened by way of radio or film. Thus the workings for a political theory of culture industry can already be found in Horkheimer's earlier essay 'Egoism and Freedom Movements' (1936).

This theory was developed further by Adorno, who approached it from a rather different angle. Adorno's approach is grounded in the sphere of art, and in particular of musical composition. The severity of the term 'mass deception' reflects his high opinion of art. The word 'deception' implies that a promise has been made and then broken. This might seem a little strange to us: these days we actually expect the tabloid newspapers and commercial TV channels to provide us with cheap entertainment, and so we are not disappointed when they do so.

In fact, we are usually pleasantly surprised when we do come across a report that is both interesting and informative – a phenomenon that may from time to time occur! Adorno saw all this in a very different light: he believed that art makes a binding promise, which, if broken, constitutes deception. In his view, art promises to provide us with valuable new and authentic experiences that will further the development of our sensibilities and that will permit us to maintain our awareness of alternative possibilities. Culture industry, by contrast, deceives the masses by manipulating and negating their 'sense of the possible'.

The theory of culture industry was further developed in a whole range of other texts written by Adorno. Indeed, at about the same time as he was working on *Dialectic of Enlightenment*, Adorno wrote the section on Schoenberg in his *Philosophy of Modern Music* (1940/1949), which he himself described as a 'an extended appendix' to *Dialectic of Enlightenment* [*Philosophy of Modern Music*, p. xiii]. Moreover, a detailed record of Adorno's views about television can be found in two essays from the first half of the 1950s, 'Prolog zum Fernsehen' (1953) [Prologue to television] and 'How to Look at Television' (1954). Roughly contemporaneous with these essays was 'Perennial Fashion – Jazz' (1953), a text by Adorno that kindled the discussion about his understanding of jazz music in Germany. *Introduction to the Sociology of Music* (1962) contains a chapter on 'Popular Music', and in 1963 Adorno wrote 'Culture Industry Reconsidered'. In his article 'Free Time' of 1969, Adorno used an empirical study conducted by the Frankfurt Institute, to reveal that people do not generally consider the marriage of a princess to be of any importance, although they will eagerly follow the ceremony on TV. Adorno terms this attitude 'split consciousness' (p. 160), regarding it as a chance for consumers to escape from tutelage. This is not so much a revelation as a rediscovery, for even in *Dialectic of Enlightenment* the consumers of culture do not appear entirely constrained by tutelage. (We shall return to this point later on in our study.) Finally, Adorno wrote *Aesthetic Theory* (1970), a text that deals only fleetingly with culture industry, but which provides a definitive analysis of its counterpart, (bourgeois) art.

Field notes II   The President as the bad guy – Clint Eastwood's *Absolute Power*

Films that feature heads of state as bad guys or weaklings are usually Shakespeare adaptations or stories set in faraway places or distant times. We must look to the US for thrillers or comedies that deal with democratically elected presidents from the recent past or from a fictional, yet credible, present.

The reason for this is clear: nowhere but in the US has the distinction between political news and televised entertainment been so entirely eroded. As a consequence, there is a general belief that the real political decisions take place behind the protective screen of entertainment, unbeknown and unbeknowable to the public. This perfect fusion between politics and culture industry creates a fundamentally paranoid atmosphere – an atmosphere well suited to the genre of the political thriller. (Just as the atmosphere of the Cold War was ideally suited to the spy film.) Reagan – the President who had once played the roles of cowboy and gangster – provides us with a striking symbol of this fusion. However, there is no reason to suppose that Reagan was any better at acting than the presidents whose term he preceded or succeeded. (In fact, Reagan was an entirely mediocre actor.)

Another reason for the unusual popularity of President films in the US lies in the fact that certain parts of the American press are obsessed with the sex life of its public figures. Needless to say, this is not due to any frivolous curiosity, but is instead the result of petit-bourgeois prudishness. Mitterrand's erotic double life probably increased his popularity with the French electorate. The German population proved more willing to forgive Willy Brandt his affairs than to condone his remarriage. Even in the case of Austria, President Klestil's ridiculous petit-bourgeois dalliance (which became public when his wife threw him out) had the effect, if anything, of improving his credibility. In the US, however, the discovery that a politician once started – or finished – an ill-fated affair is enough to topple him from power. Nevertheless, ever since Kennedy (if not before), every American President – and in varying degrees, all American politicians – have come under the suspicion of using their power for their own dissipation. Hollywood has lost no time in exploiting this situation.

In the comic variety of the President film, the protagonist dies from a stroke while in bed with his mistress. A doppelgänger then assumes his role, and goes from being a puppet of the men with the real power to becoming a politician with his own (New-Deal-esque) ideas. (See *Dave*, dir. Ivan Reitman, 1992.) In a more serious version of this film, the comedy is replaced by cynicism. In the President film as enacted by Clint Eastwood, the President (Gene Hackman) is engaged in a sadistic sex game when things get out of hand. His bedmate threatens to kill him, and is in turn shot by a Secret Service agent. Clint Eastwood plays the master thief who was forced to hide when the couple entered the room. Unbeknown to them (and on behalf of the voyeuristic audience), Eastwood witnesses the entire scene. His facial expression in this sequence is inimitable. The Secret Service agents arrange the scene to make it look as if the woman had been murdered by a burglar whose activities she had disturbed, but the traces left by the real burglar undermine this story and puzzle the police. Moreover, the real burglar's masterful thefts have gained him such a reputation that the police always interrogate him as a matter of course after a spectacular heist. As the detective and the burglar talk together, it becomes clear that there is a spiritual link between these two 'real men', who otherwise stand on opposite sides of the law. (This is a feature of many detective films, as it is, for example, of the 1990s film *Heat*.) Finally, one of the President's Secret Service agents tries to shoot him and then kill his daughter. The latter is a successful county prosecutor, estranged from her father through his long absence, but in reality most dear to him. Eastwood had originally intended to flee, but now the ageing criminal feels compelled to do battle with the world's most powerful political system. Thus the confrontation begins, and – after a few twists of plot, a number of digressions on the nature of Washington's political machine, some picturesque attempts at murder and a couple of actual murders – the film shows how the little man cleverly exploits the power relations in order to bring about a happy ending. In the cinema on the corner of 11th Street and 3rd Avenue, there was applause for several of Eastwood's scenes, while the audience shared in various outbreaks of collective merriment, finally clapping in satisfaction at the film's conclusion.

Even in his old age, Clint Eastwood still inhabits the corrupt world of well-meaning police officers, cold-blooded Secret Service agents and hyper-conscientious bodyguards. However, he has now stopped trying to tidy up and to impose order. In fact, his sole concern is to avoid being crushed by the political machine. This film is not about political goals, for these are barely mentioned. Instead it focuses on how those in charge retain their power and how they protect it from the potential threat posed on the one hand by their political 'godfathers' and on the other by public scandal. In their attempt to bring both risks under control, they are prepared to embark on all kinds of deception and they do not shrink from permitting 'opportune' deaths among the ordinary – and in their view, expendable – people. Now that Eastwood has all but abandoned the task of imposing order, it becomes unclear as to why our ageing hero should choose to become involved. (As I mentioned above, the film gets round this problem by having him act out of self-defence.) Furthermore, it is equally difficult to determine exactly who these apparent enemies of the ordinary people might be. During the film, it becomes noticeable that the politically powerful are all people who have worked their way up to the top. They are men – plus one woman, the villainous 'Chief of Staff' – who started out with almost nothing, and who are now determined to retain the power they gained. There is no sign of the plutocracy of old and rich families that dominate America's political class. The corrupt and unscrupulous characters are always people who are new to power and to money. The simple moral scheme that makes Westerns and cop films so appealing is no longer available. In Westerns, the bad guys are capitalists, monopolists and their henchmen. In cop films, they are usually police chiefs whose determination to present the 'right' public image makes them inadequate superiors, who insist on preventing our man from doing his job. Now this is no longer the case. The enemies of the ordinary people are the people in power, who – due to their dependency on the political 'godfathers' who 'made them', and as a result of the political vulnerability brought on by their greed and their irregular private lives – are not, in fact, powerful enough. They have just enough power to unleash their henchmen (that is, state power) on to the ordinary people.

Clint Eastwood is still capable of providing us with an effective portrayal of ordinary, hard-working people's discontents. However, he is no longer so keen on the simple solution of violence that otherwise characterizes this genre. (In his earlier films, Eastwood always presented this solution in a kind of fairy-tale manner. Now he gives up on it altogether.) In his old age, our hero has become representative of a very different kind of masculinity. He is still a silent loner, yet he is no longer quite so reticent about his emotions: he visits museums in order to sketch there, and although he is estranged from his daughter, he privately collects photos of her, secretly stocks her fridge, and otherwise protects her as best he can. He no longer relies on his speedy Colt to solve his problems, but uses his cunning and his ability to psychologically manipulate the insecurities and conflicts within the political machine. The relationship between the sexes in Eastwood's films has always been one of distance. Affection, it seems, is only possible between people who have no need for one another. As soon as one person becomes dependent on another, the relationship is swiftly over. In *Absolute Power*, the patriarchal reasoning behind this becomes clear: if in doubt, Eastwood protects women. At least, he would like to be able to do so, and it is an added attraction of this particular film that he succeeds. (As he does in *A Fistful of Dollars* and in *Pale Rider*. In *Bridges of Madison County*, however, he fails.) The ageing lone rider has come to rest and would like his private life to provide him with some moments of happiness. The powerful men of this world should grant him that much by organizing their ridiculous affairs in such a way as to avoid corpses, and especially the corpses of Eastwood's loved ones. In this film, Eastwood exchanges the task of imposing order for the role of the rogue: he becomes an elderly Robin Hood.

P.S. The genre of the President film, of which there are ever more examples, should have warned the American Republicans that although a President's sexual adventures may scandalize the public, they will not necessarily leave a negative impression.

The structure of the 'Culture Industry' essay

Depending on the way the text is laid out, the published version of the 'Culture Industry' chapter comes to a length of around about fifty pages. In addition to this, there are a further thirty-five pages or so of material not published at the time. Traditionally, academics have attributed the 'Culture Industry' chapter of *Dialectic of Enlightenment* to Adorno, and, for the most part, this is indeed entirely fair.[18] However, even if Adorno was the text's main author, we should not underestimate the influence of Horkheimer. The published version of the text began life as a manuscript written by Adorno, which was later subjected to two major sets of revisions by both authors. To the best of our knowledge, the unpublished block of material was never revised. However, both of these texts were in any case written during a period of close collaboration between the two thinkers. Indeed, at that time, Adorno and Horkheimer were working together to develop the common elements of their thought, and to establish them as a basic model of Critical Theory.

If this sort of collaboration is at all possible (as it seems to have been in this case), there is no way that we will ever be able to establish exactly who thought what – and there is, in fact, no call for us to do so. The products of successful intellectual collaboration make a mockery of intellectual property, a concept that otherwise assumes great importance within the academic business. It is not merely a question of deciding whether a title should be entered into both authors' 'list of publications' (a matter that plays no small role in any academic's professional advancement). In fact, it is primarily a case of establishing where a particular piece of work is situated in relation to each thinker's theoretical framework and intellectual development. Even a very lengthy and intensive period of collaboration remains essentially an encounter between two individual thinkers. The resulting product is always the meeting point between two separate intellectual strands: it will not necessarily mean the same thing to each thinker, and it may not be of equal import to the development of their work.

As far as this last point is concerned, it would be fair to say that the 'Culture Industry' essay was of greater significance to Adorno's thought than it was to that of Horkheimer. It had longer lasting and more intensive links to Adorno's preceding and succeeding experiences and essays. Thus, regardless of who contributed the most to the work, it is not unreasonable to associate the text with the thought and intellectual development of Adorno, rather than that of Horkheimer.[19] However, this traditional classification prevents us from pursuing a rather different – but by no means uninteresting – line of interpretation, namely that of the political import of the text. The 'Culture Industry' chapter can be interpreted not only in terms of Adorno's *Aesthetic Theory* and his work on Schoenberg, jazz and Wagner, but also in relation to a trend in Horkheimer's thought. This trend is first evident in 'Egoism and Freedom Movements' and 'The Authoritarian State' (1942), but unfortunately it is not really developed in the texts written after *Dialectic of Enlightenment*. Viewing the 'Culture Industry' essay as the point at which Horkeimer's political theory meets with Adorno's predominately aesthetic theories, we come to notice that the text makes relatively little attempt to deal with the political role of culture industry, while studies of the text devote even less space to this issue.

These days, there is a tendency to discuss culture industry as a problem relating to feel-good art and entertainment, rather than to the destruction of a political public sphere. In one of his important early works, Habermas picked up on the political elements of the 'dialectic of enlightenment', devoting himself to an investigation of the *Structural Transformation of the Public Sphere.*[20] However, even Habermas has now turned his attention towards analysing the moral-philosophical foundations of an intellectual's involvement with politics, rather than examining how culture industry undermines these foundations, however well they may be theoretically justified. Nonetheless, aesthetics and politics belong together. They are different intellectual activities, yet they are both exposed to the same threat of commodification. (This holds true despite the fact that in politics, money is not the only form of currency. Financial income is important, but – fortunately for us – political currency is also calculated in terms of the number of votes that each candidate can be expected to win.) Television has not only transformed the nature of art and entertainment, but – more importantly – it has also turned politics into a form of entertainment. This change has benefited neither politics nor entertainment. The problem posed by culture industry is not limited to opera, film and football. It does not merely affect these activities (whose importance we perhaps tend to exaggerate), for it also influences the way in which states are governed and communities organized. In the chapter 'Culture Industry Politics', I try to go some way towards compensating for the one-sidedness of those interpretations of culture industry that are centred around Adorno's aesthetic theories.

Let us return to the text and to its structure. In the published version of the text, a series of blank lines subdivide the chapter into seven different sections. These sections are untitled, and there is no strict thematic division between them. On the contrary, each new section quite clearly picks up from where the previous section left off. (Incidentally, examining the way in which a text uses its introductions and conclusions can be a useful exercise in interpretation, and it is one that is particularly rewarding where Adorno's work is concerned. Now is not the time to embark on any kind of systematic analysis, but it is possible to summarize the situation by saying that Adorno's introductions do not serve to announce his subsequent arguments, but work instead to provide the text with new starting-points and fresh openings. Furthermore, Adorno's conclusions do not present the reader with any 'result', but tend rather to invert the thrust of his preceding arguments, to open up further questions and to stress the possibilities (of liberation) that nonetheless remain.)

In the light of all this, it would seem reasonable for us to consider the gaps between the sections as a kind of 'breathing space'. The gaps interrupt our reading, allowing us just enough time to absorb what we have read, before we begin again, picking up from where the text had left off. The fact that these gaps do not feature in the unpublished manuscript seems to suggest that they were added in later, in order to mark out the main motifs in this suite of thematic material. It is not difficult to identify the main themes of each section in the published text. However, each theme then appears in a number of variations, as it is approached from different angles and linked to other themes from earlier or later sections. Indeed, throughout the text, the themes are recast in different guises and developed in different directions. With one exception, the sections are of a similar length, each numbering five or six pages. However, the third section is almost twice as long as the others, and has two distinct main themes. The fact that these themes were not treated separately gives us further cause to believe that the sections were not designed as distinct blocks of text to be read as a systematic sequence of subsidiary themes. Rather than viewing the sections as subdivisions of a general theme, it seems that we should consider them as the various facets belonging to an object. Depending on the angle and the light, each facet presents us with a different view. However, if taken together, the facets reveal to us an image of the object as a whole. The essay does not attempt to provide us with an exhaustive account of the object, as analysed in its constituent parts. It does not show the object through the sum of its different perspectives, but offers us an entirely fragmented view, each perspective presenting us with an individual picture of the whole.

The following list is a preliminary overview of the sections' main themes:

Section 1 (pp. 120–4): the industry, and the production of cultural goods.

Section 2 (pp. 124–31): the 'person with leisure' in the grip of culture industry's style.

Section 3 (pp. 131–44): the historic origins of culture industry in liberalism, culture as a means of discipline, and amusement as a form of discipline (p. 135 onwards).

Section 4 (pp. 144–9): the current situation of consumers' forced integration – life (and mere survival) as a matter of blind chance, and the promise of belonging.

Section 5 (pp. 149–54): authoritarian welfare and the abolition of tragedy.
Section 6 (pp. 154–61): the forced integration of the individual, propaganda.
Section 7 (pp. 161–7): culture as advertising.

In the continuation to the manuscript (published as 'The Schema of Mass Culture' (1944/1981)), there is more of a focus on the topic of 'advertising'. This is discussed alongside culture industry's reflexivity (which emerges as a result of the process of self-promotion inherent in advertising) and in relation to the fate of curiosity under these conditions. The topic of 'blind chance' that is dealt with in the fourth section is complemented in the continuation to the manuscript by an analysis of 'sport and gambling' as forms of competition and of the way in which competition is represented. The conclusion of 'The Schema of Mass Culture' focuses on the idea that culture industry is subject to – and itself precipitates – regression.

It is possible to apply to these themes the categories commonly used in modern theories of mass communication. Thus the first section deals with *production*, while *distribution* is discussed in those sections concerning advertising and appropriation (the fourth, sixth and seventh sections, plus the first part of the extension to the manuscript). The question of *reception* is dealt with in the second, third and fifth sections, as well as in the analysis of 'curiosity', 'sport' and 'regression', which appears in the second part of the extension. However, this schematic division of the chapter's themes would have meant nothing to Adorno, who certainly did not think or write in this way. He did not conceive of culture industry in terms of 'communication', involving a sender, a medium of communication and a receiver; nor did he have in mind a stream of production, in which the various stages would appear in a clear and distinct order. Instead, Adorno saw culture industry as a basic characteristic of the modern mode of social integration. Nevertheless, the translation of Adorno's themes into contemporary terminology is useful for two reasons: firstly, in order to emphasize the differences between these two ways of approaching the subject-matter; and secondly to anticipate and dismiss the usual claim that Adorno did not have anything interesting to say about what we today call 'reception', 'reader response' or 'audience' studies. In actual fact, Adorno did not use the term 'reception' because he had arrived at a far more complex model of how each member of society is integrated into culture industry. (This is not to say that he did not rather underestimate the consumers' resistance to culture industry. These days, we are all too familiar with the phenomenon of consumer resistance, but Adorno was writing at a time of hysteria, when listeners were being stirred up into a panic by radio programmes such as 'Invasion from Mars', and, in a different part of the world, incited to hate their neighbours by the propaganda speeches of Hitler and Goebbels. Adorno also underestimated the way in which the media would eventually swamp and satiate the public. This is a point that we will return to later.)

Field notes III   Heartburn and telephone sex

Advertisements are as international as the products they feature. It is for this reason that the European viewer soon comes to feel at home with North American TV. Indeed, even when the adverts are not identical, there remains a very strong resemblance between commercials in America and in Europe. American adverts stand out only by dint of their quantity. In all other respects, there is little about them that the European would find new or different. However, there were two exceptions that struck the uninitiated viewer when flicking through the standard New York cable channels late one evening in 1997. These exceptions were the advertisements for hearburn pills and telephone sex.

'Heartburn' might sound rather romantic to the non-native speaker, yet it is only another name for indigestion. And indigestion went out of fashion in Europe in the 1950s, together with stomach ulcers and athlete's foot. In our age of heart attacks and breast cancer, the simple stomach disorder has been divested of public entertainment value.

Of course, these days, the threat of the heart attack successfully inspires the collective imagination on both sides of the Atlantic. All those who jog or walk their regular laps of the park or town are motivated by the hope that their body's circulation might keep going forever, if only they keep running round in circles. (This hope is also shared by a good proportion of those who belabour themselves in machine-ridden gyms. How apt that we should refer to such self-inflicted torture as 'working out'!) The ever-present promise of 'cholestrol-free' and 'fat-free' products in the supermarket feeds into the same preoccupation. Even fruit is advertised as being 'naturally fat-free'.

Nonetheless, even the ready availability of healthy goods and activities does not seem to protect against the very ordinary complaint of heartburn. The reasons for this become immediately apparent in the course of the adverts. The adverts show us that we need only take the incredibly fast-working and long-lasting heartburn pill, in order to be able to guzzle hamburgers, crisps and chillies with impunity. Without these pills, such a diet would lead to indigestion, a condition that might undermine our success in business negotiations. The adverts attempt to present indigestion as a problem experienced by high-powered managers. However, the incongruous link between business lunches and fast food indicates that this is unlikely to be the case. Instead, the upset tummy is a problem suffered by the overworked small-time entrepreneur who has two different jobs and a mountain of debts, but who has nonetheless remained (or been forced to remain) constant to the American dream of the fast buck and the patriarchal dream of supporting the family. (In the case of the female, the dream is to be a 'superwoman' – a career woman, model mother and desirable lover, all in one.)

The adverts demonstrate that this is what you must expect from life: you have to sweat away to make your living, and you cannot allow yourself a single second of weakness. The wolves are out there to catch you off guard, and those who burp have already been defeated. You have to be able to pack everything in, but also to excrete it out. The pharmaceuticals industry does its best to help you: you only need one pill each day – providing, of course, that it is strong enough and that it represents the latest in medical research. The old pills offered by traditional brands are no longer up-to-date and must therefore be discarded – in our world, there is no place for losers.

Alongside heartburn pills, the second surprising feature of American advertising came in the form of TV commercials for telephone sex. TV ads for telephone sex have only recently reached European cable channels, and so their appearance on the New York cable channels was apt to take the unsuspecting channel hopper by surprise. The novelty and difference of these commercials lies not only in their mere existence, but also in the way that they attempt to sell their product.

Adverts for telephone sex highlight the paradox that lies at the heart of all mass media, namely the mass attempt to address the individual. Indeed, the paradox of the announcer's greeting of 'Good evening ladies and gentlemen' pales in comparison to that of the TV invitation to participate in telephone sex: 'I'm hot for you, call *now*!' In another version of this paradox, the adverts never cease to repeat the promise that everything is 'live', even though the truth of this promise is instantly negated by the medium in which it appears. The promise is also undermined by the regularity with which the same advert is broadcast. (Showing the same advert over and over again is intended to imprint the brand-name on the viewer's mind. This technique may work for washing-powder and cars, but it is unlikely to apply to the telephone number upon which these adverts depend.) As a result of this, the adverts present us with endless repetitions of the same short porn film, showing the same grotesque bodily features and the same supposedly sensuous movement of tongues. They show us the same movement of the arms, as a woman caresses her own body and throws back her hair, along with the same orgasmic invitation for you to pick up the phone and finally call. With each repetition, the whole thing seems to bear ever more resemblance to absurd theatre. Although at times comical, the very form of presentation betrays the alienation and absolute self-instrumentalization inherent in such performances.

The adverts' form of presentation also shows the alienation and self-instrumentalization that we, the viewers, are supposed to engage in. In most of these short porn films, the camera assumes the position of the voyeur, who watches while others do it to themselves, or to each other:

the camera makes of us voyeurs. In some cases, there is the option of adding an acoustic extra – for just two dollars a minute, you can listen to two women having telephone sex with each other. 'You can hear them, but they can't hear you' (although you must, of course, have reached the age of eighteen). A more extreme variety of these adverts places the camera in the position that the viewer is supposed to fantasize about adopting. The camera may thus locate the viewer as the man in a sex act who is looking down at the rhythmic movements of an increasingly aroused woman. The voyeur is transported into the middle of the sexual act.

Another extreme variety of the adverts presents the action with increased reflexivity. We are given instructions as to how we should react to the visual or acoustic pornographic performance. The adverts reassure us that 'It's all right for you to masturbate', or encourage us to 'Snuggle up on the couch with your partner and have a great time watching us'. These are, of course, the two traditional roles of the porn film – the first as an aid to masturbation, and the second as a means for revitalizing relationships. In each instance, the product is presented along with its instruction manual, that is, along with the guidelines for our own self-manipulation.

Another noticeable feature of these adverts is that the protagonists are all white. Asian women are presented as a special variety among the female actors (although 'you don't have to be Asian to call'), but there is never any evidence of any male or female Afro- or Latin Americans. (Perhaps these are available only to those who are really in the know.) The standard cable channels only offer us models in shades of white and yellow, while all dark skin colours – not to mention mixed couples – are excluded.

It could be 'political correctness' that prevents advertising agencies from publicly exposing minorities to the sexual fantasies, to which they are in any case subject. However, even if this were the case, it would only make the ingrained racism of the situation all the more obvious and embarrassing. There is, of course, no right way of dealing with this situation, except by avoiding it. Sexual fantasies directed at persons of a particular skin colour cannot be anything but racist. This is all the more evident in the case of the fantasies of humiliation and domination that are particularly frequent in commercial sex (although they are by no means restricted to this area). On the other hand, this sort of racism might eventually lead to a kind of fraternization. The increased familiarity of the foreign body might lead the voyeur to realize that everyone is more or less the same; that the differences between people are even smaller during sexual encounters; and that if you love somebody, they will always be different and special.

Unfortunately, it is most unlikely that telephone sex would ever permit the customer any such experience of intimacy. Indeed, as with all forms of sex at a distance, the main point of telephone sex is to avoid having to deal with experience at all. Quite apart from this, the adverts' treatment of Asian women is openly racist. The above assumption that the adverts are guided by 'political correctness' is simply too generous. We are dealing here with straightforward racism – with a racist refusal to portray or witness mixed couples. This refusal represents the kind of racism that causes people to invest all their energy into distinguishing themselves from other groups, and that leads them to engage in the fanatical persecution of all those who fail to follow suit. This sort of racism is much more dangerous than the other variant that – for whatever reason – leads people to seek contact with 'the other'. In the case of TV adverts for telephone sex, exclusionist racism is represented by absence.

In heartburn pills and telephone sex we see how double standards of morality are being commercially exploited. You can eat healthily and have conjugal sex or no sex at all. However, if you do want to indulge yourself, both the incentives to do so, and the means to combat the consequences of doing so, are available in commodity form, – in heartburn medicine and in the visual or auditory support for masturbation.

2

On method: look carefully, think thoroughly, and do not let yourself be taken in

Skoteinos, or how to read Adorno

Texts that do not need readers

People who have never really tried to read Adorno tend to believe that his texts are 'difficult'. Indeed, Adorno is seen to be one of the 'obscure thinkers' like Hegel, for whom Adorno himself uses the label 'Skoteinos' (although these days, due to our lack of classical cultural knowledge, this term itself has become rather obscure).[1] The belief that Adorno's work is 'difficult' is usually based on the rather superficial observation that it is helpful to have a dictionary in order to understand it. However, providing that we possess such an article (and it is generally advisable to do so), this should not really pose a problem. We simply become aware that the writer in question was a man of some considerable learning; a man whose range of cultural reference differs greatly from our own. It becomes clear that Adorno had studied both Latin and ancient Greek – an accomplishment that might seem impressive, but that is scarcely remarkable among philosophers. However, it is also apparent that Adorno had acquired a thorough familiarity with Proust's work, a task for which, now, as then, most people lack the patience – even though the paperback editions have helped this monumental piece of literature to find its way into more bookcases than ever before. In any case, Adorno spoke French, learnt English and spent his whole life in the company of books. All in all, these factors make it almost inevitable that Adorno should have had a larger vocabulary than most of his contemporaries. That said, we should not lose sight of the fact that novels such as those of Umberto Eco also demand from the reader a relatively high level of cultural knowledge. (In fact, Eco's texts require an even more specialized knowledge than do those of Adorno.) Eco's novels, however, have gone on to become bestsellers.[2]

Adorno's artistic style of composition presents us with a rather more serious problem. On occasions, it takes some time for us to grasp exactly what it is that his pronouns are referring to. Sometimes we have to rewrite his grammar, reordering each sentence's clauses in order to arrive at the central statement. However, even this does not pose any real difficulty, for we can always read over the passage again, or flick back through the text. (By way of contrast, the fact that Adorno's lectures often resembled his printed texts did indeed constitute a problem for his listeners, who had no means of turning back the pages.) In any case, it is worth remembering that Adorno's texts are at once less difficult and more elegant than those of either Heidegger or Kant (not to mention those of Baudrillard, Flusser and other fashionable philosophers of the moment). It is this elegance that makes the difficulty of Adorno's texts rather easier to bear. Adorno's texts are neither clumsy nor sloppy, and their approach is certainly not arbitrary or eccentric. On the contrary, Adorno's texts are finely crafted final versions.

Adorno (at least in his later work) used to dictate the first version of his texts, and then use the typescript as the basis for numerous revisions. Adorno was never in favour of his lectures being published, for he did not see them as texts for reading, but as oral/aural material. Moreover, he never published any of his work in the kind of academic journals familiar to us today. His texts were never subjected to 'peer review' and returned to him for correction. Thus Adorno was spared a process that is both humiliating and conducive to a certain kind of cautiousness: writers now start work with a pair of mental scissors, cutting out any material that is not entirely ordinary. At the same time, the pressure to publish under these conditions encourages writers to engage in one-upmanship and self-promotion. The end result is the paradoxical situation of a shouting match between town criers, each vying to proclaim the same old news. Adorno, however, was not subjected to such ridiculous pressures. His mode of production allowed him to work in a way that was very different from the contemporary method of electronic text-montage.

In this day and age, we have become accustomed to reading 'diagonally'. This tendency to skim texts is in part a reaction to the conditions of production as described above, yet it is also a problem of volume, as we struggle to cope with the sheer quantity of published material. We want to check in advance that the text has nothing new to tell us, and that we will have no difficulty in categorizing the few crumbs of information that it contains. That way, we can rest assured that there is no need for us to examine it in more detail. We have learnt how to look at the overwhelming quantity of largely identical goods on offer and to pick out precisely those products in which we would like to invest our time. We have also learnt to block out commercial breaks and hidden adverts. These are necessary skills in modern culture: dealing with culture in this way is simply a matter of self-defence. In relation to Adorno's work, however, this approach is just not viable. If we were to try to read Adorno's texts in this manner, we would fail to gain anything from them, and would end up facing a solid wall of words and sentences. We might feel a little ashamed, and we might even respond furiously. 'Who does this man think he is, making his texts so difficult for *me* to read!' . . . 'Why isn't he trying to please *me*, as everybody else claims to be doing?' . . .

This last impatient question brings us back to the substance of the text. As practised surfers of culture industry, we know that the goal is not to please us, but to persuade as many of us as possible to part with our cash. As 'purchasing power', each one of us is entirely replaceable (although, inconveniently for the industry, purchasing power is nonetheless made up of individuals). Adorno's texts, however, are not trying to sell us anything. In fact, they treat the desire to purchase with indifference, if not outright disdain: Adorno's texts are *texts that do not need readers*.

This might seem a rather contradictory statement, but it is not to say that Adorno's texts do not want to be read. (That would be all too easy to arrange!) After all, it was Adorno's decision to publish his texts, and some of his essays even appear in several different editions. Adorno clearly felt that their relevance exceeded the specific circumstances of their genesis – in fact, he saw the essays as part of his ever-evolving, yet coherent 'life's work', and took care to ensure that they were made available to the reading public.[3] Nonetheless, the way in which Adorno's texts present themselves to the public indicates that they have no real need to do so. While the rest of the world is obsessed with the search for new buyers and clients, Adorno's texts appear to the public as self-sufficient entities. This aspect of Adorno's writing can be summarized neatly by the use of the term 'public aloofness'.[4]

The 'public aloofness' of these texts means that we must approach them with both curiosity and patience. We must allow ourselves – and the text – sufficient time for an acquaintanceship to form. We must approach the text slowly, as if it were a stranger that we would like to get to know better, or a musical instrument that we would like to be able to play. It is not a matter of being able to understand and master the material straight away. On the contrary, it is more a question of discovering if – and how – we might be able to get along. This may lead us to develop our own talents. Between ourselves, we might even discover that we have a knack for dancing or for playing the blues. We might find that the process of familiarization is, in fact, quite exciting. It is even possible that our enthusiasm might outlast the threat of boredom. Indeed, our involvement with the text may well continue over time and lead us to discover new aspects to our own character, as well as to that of the text. Of course, all this would require hard work, and we would have to be willing to take the risk. The process would involve a significant investment of effort, but we would be unable to predict the outcome. It might all turn into a nightmare. We may end up trapped in a joyless and antagonistic relationship. Alternatively – and more probably – the experience may at some point seem entirely insignificant. It is always possible that we will return the book to the library, and promptly forget its existence.

It is no coincidence that I have chosen to use the vocabulary and imagery of a relationship between friends or lovers. A modicum of passion is as essential to intellectual life as it is to other social activities. Nevertheless, it would not be possible to describe every text in this way. There are some that slip easily into our possession, allowing themselves to be used. We put them to a purpose and then forget about them – our relationship to them is cold and instrumental. Adorno's texts resist this kind of exploitation. It is this that makes them really 'difficult'.

Authoritarian realism versus reflexive dialectics

Adorno did not write as he did simply in order to make himself look more interesting. He had his reasons, according to which it would have been irresponsible to write in any other way. What Adorno wrote in 'Skoteinos, or How to Read Hegel' in *Hegel: Three Studies* (1963) is also true of Adorno's own thought. (It is for this reason that I chose to adapt the title of this chapter to use as a heading for this section.) Both Hegel and Adorno undertake the treacherous task of trying to do justice to their object of enquiry, while all the time using pre-existing concepts that, due to their abstract nature, do violence to the object described and thus reflect the structures of domination. This is why Adorno tries to write in a way that refuses stable definitions and that resists the attempt to arrive at a constative 'result'. In his writing, Adorno aims to investigate the presence of domination in our conceptual apparatus. He cannot do away with this apparatus (without which we would be unable to think), but he does choose to approach his object by reflecting on it in complex circles and spirals of thought. For Adorno, this object is always the social world, together with its relations of domination and the (im)possibility of its liberation. Writers and thinkers do not stand outside these relations of domination, but are caught up within them. Initially, they will have nothing better to offer in place of the conceptual tools that are already in use within society. Their only option is to use them reflexively, and to interpret them in two different ways at once – firstly, according to what the concepts say about a particular object and how they condition the object, as defined by society; and secondly according to what they reveal about the conditions of domination that are responsible for making the object what it is.

As we read, this process repeats itself within us, leading us to create and engage with our own experiences of the object in question. We cannot use the text to find out what the object is 'really like', but instead must consider the text (and the object it describes) with the same kind of complex distance that the text itself reveals. This will enable us to arrive at a position of renewed reflexivity. For this to occur, the author's function within the text cannot be seen to be that of an authority or of a superior instance of knowledge. Instead, the author must present us with his attempts to investigate domination. It is our task to comprehend these efforts, but at the same time to view them from a position of distance. (Our intellectual distance from the text will increase as our real historical distance from it increases. However, we are already situated at a distance from the text, even before we are separated by time, for the text will almost certainly occupy a social position that is different from – and perhaps even antagonistic to – our own.) There is no need for us to identify with the author, and to do so would not help us in our quest for understanding. Adorno's own texts distance the reader through their occasional moments of 'obscurity'. Indeed, Adorno recommends that the reader maintain a distance in relation to the text, as well as to its concepts, theories and above all its author. 'It is not the worst reader who provides the book with disrespectful notes in the margin' (*Hegel*, p. 145). As we will see, this belief in the value of distance is grounded in a model of truth that runs counter to our usual assumptions about this topic.

In our day-to-day life (as in normal academic life), we have grown accustomed to an 'authoritarian' model of 'truth'. This model states that there is a single and unique truth about the things of this world. Following Popper, we may believe that we can only ever have negative access to this truth. If, as Popper claimed, we are only ever able to prove things to be false, then all that we believe ourselves to understand and to be able to apply is only valid in so far as it has not yet been disproved: our 'knowledge' can always be revised or refuted by scientific progress. Nevertheless, the 'authoritarian' model of truth still implies that, somewhere out there at the end of history and science, there is a true truth – it is just that we cannot see it yet. Consequently, even now there can be only one true representation of truth. Only one of the competing schools of theory can be right, while the others must all have got it wrong – their supporters were evidently poor thinkers, or just the victims of ideology. Naturally, we will always count ourselves among those who are right. As for the others, we must treat them as our rivals and fight, despise and fear them, using all possible means to assure ourselves of their defeat. This is often the ways things work in intellectual, and above all, in university life. Needless to say, it serves neither thought, nor the thinker.

Reflexive dialectics, as masterfully practised by Adorno, starts out with a rather different model of truth. In this era of photos and film, it seems sensible to describe this model with reference to an object that has been photographed and filmed from a variety of different angles. Let us take a building as our example. Each photo or video taken of the building would contribute to a picture made up of different perspectives. With each new shot, the overall picture would gain a new dimension. Although each contribution would be different from the rest, none would be either right or wrong. We would not be able to identify the 'true' image by a process of elimination. In fact, every image would be incomplete in itself, its perspective always slightly distorted. The real task would be to compare the different perspectives present in the images, and to fit them together. In order to do this, we would have to reconstruct the camera angle, as well as finding out about the specific features of the equipment and how it was used. We would not be able to get the 'whole picture' by distilling its true nature from the collection of images. Instead this picture is to be found in the whole constellation of possible perspectives represented by the different photographers. (And obviously, these photographers would not be there for fun. They would each have a particular purpose, as well as a particular attitude, whether of conflict or cooperation, towards the other photographers.)

All this should lead us to realize that we cannot find the right perspective by eliminating all the false (or 'falsified') ones: there is, in fact, no 'right' perspective. Instead, it is a matter of describing in as much detail as possible the constellation that is formed by the building and the cameras. Authoritarian realism attempts to discern the true nature of an object by dismissing all the other possible perspectives as 'errors'. Reflexive dialectics, on the other hand, attempts to describe the entire constellation and to identify the social conflicts and relations of domination that form the backdrop to each different perspective, including that of the person conducting the analysis.

Seen in this light, our angle of enquiry can be said to be appropriate if:

- we manage to avoid the trap of 'authoritarian realism' by actually trying to analyse the constellation of descriptions and its backdrop in the social relations of domination;
- we are able to draw on an in-depth knowledge of what – to go back to our example – could be described as the features of the camera, the camera's different settings, the possible camera angles, and the methods of editing, superimposing and retouching an image; that is, if we can reconstruct fairly precisely the circumstances in which the picture came to be taken;
- we can retain this detailed information, yet at the same time take a step back and consider a greater number of possible images and perspectives (temporal distance, therefore, is always an advantage);
- we are able to use the position from which we are conducting our analysis to gain further knowledge, while at the same time taking account of it within the analysis itself: that is, if we can succeed in working reflexively, both by revealing our own position within the constellation, and by treating this position as a particularly useful sample perspective that – due to our familiarity with it – can be of great help in investigating the structures of social domination that lie behind all such perspectives;
- we are able to draw on all of this information in order to reconstruct the 'working alliance' that binds together the entire constellation. This will enable us to examine the key social elements that determine all of the above conditions.

This approach to social knowledge and science means that we do not have to get involved in the debates about explanation versus interpretation, or quantitative versus qualitative methodology, or those over the different types of hermeneutics. It is an approach that refuses to invest any scientific method with privileged access to 'truth'. In fact, it suggests that we should analyse each method in order to discover which particular perspective it embodies.[5] Adorno and Horkheimer's critique of 'positivism' was not an attack on empirical research. (Indeed, Adorno and Horkheimer figured among the pioneers of this type of research in Germany.) What Adorno and Horkheimer were actually denouncing was our blind faith in facts. In their view, data have the same doubling effect that Adorno attributes to 'realist' film and entertainment: they allow us to experience – and become accustomed to – the oppression that we have to experience all day long, whether at work, or on the dole. Data must always be examined and analysed, no matter how they have been arrived at (whether quantitative or qualitative, general statistics or a single observation). There are no mere 'facts' that would not require interpretation.

The dialectical process of understanding does not provide us with any kind of 'method'. It is not a secret formula that will lead us to the discovery of extraordinary and profound insights, nor does it function as a reliable algorithm that we need only to follow if we want to arrive at the truth. As far as Adorno's texts are concerned, there is little danger that they will be taken for algorithms, for this kind of misunderstanding is more common in relation to highly systematized methodologies. With such methodologies, we can easily get carried away by the excitement of mastering a complicated mathematical system or a difficult computer program, and thus fail to examine how the data were actually collected or which assumptions were used in order to tabulate and interpret the results. In the case of Adorno's work, we are much more likely to fall into the trap of reading it as a secret formula that will allow us to derive privileged insights. (This is particularly true of those 'Adornoites' who claim to have arrived at a method of interpretation derived from Adorno's own thought.) We might be attracted to the idea that we could 'penetrate the superficial content of the text in a methodical and controlled manner in order to arrive at a more profound (or, in other words, 'latent' or 'hidden') layer of meaning'.[6] This is the old motif of 'gnosis', based on the idea that the message (of God) lies within the text, either beneath or between its lines. The message is invisible to the ordinary reader; yet, if we were to succeed in reading it, we would be numbered among the privileged few selected to inherit a higher knowledge. As such, we would always know better than everybody else, and our superiority would be beyond dispute.

Adorno's texts, if studied properly, do not lend themselves to such misuse.

Field notes IV   Woody Allen, or the film critics' blindness to irony

Film critics – at least in Germany – thoroughly misunderstood Woody Allen's film, *Hannah and her Sisters*. This misunderstanding was a result of the critics' faulty perception of much of the film, as well as of their failure to spot Allen's use of irony, the scope of which – as ever – includes both the director (Allen) and his audience (ourselves).

To begin with, there is the general consensus among the critics that *Hannah and her Sisters* has a 'happy ending'. This assessment of the film is based on two observations: first, that the three sisters in question all end up married to the man who – at that point in time – is able to return their

love; and second, that the film ends with the words: 'Mickey? . . . I'm pregnant'.[7] However, with this triple bill of marital contentment, the film seems
so stereotypically 'happy' that it can only make us laugh. As for the film's
final line, Mickey reacts to it by embracing Holly and kissing her 'passion-
ately' (screenplay, p. 181). However, all this has nothing to do with Mickey
'feeling . . . good for the first time in his neurotic life', nor does it represent a 'moment in which his panicked existence is finally conquered', as
one critic would have us believe.[8] It would be rather rash to see the film
as an 'uncustomary . . . glorification of family life', or to view it as evidence
of Allen's 'newly awakened and rather conservative family feeling'
(although Siegfried Schober of *Die Zeit* does just this).[9] The film does not
even have the temporary happy ending that some of the less sentimental
critics have seen in it. 'In Mickey, Hannah's hyperactive ex-husband (as
played by Woody Allen), she [Holly] has found a suitable partner who is
able to match her own neuroses . . . until the next Thanksgiving dinner,
that is,' claims Heike Kühn.[10] 'This is the customary happy ending to an
ordinary romance. Or is it? In actual fact, what we have seen is only the
grouping of characters during one particular sequence of the dance – this
sequence may last a little longer, but sadly not forever,' writes Hellmuth
Karasek.[11] None of this, however, has anything to do with the film's final
line.

Those of us with rather more effective memories will recall that the
entire 'dance' first commenced with Hannah and Mickey and with the
breakdown of their marriage, due to the diagnosis of Mickey's infertility.
Hannah is desperate to give birth and arranges for herself to be artificially
inseminated – with sperm donated by Mickey's business partner, Norman.
The scene in which Norman is first approached about this is grotesque and
particularly painful to watch. It is also painful to watch Mickey's doctor as
he talks to the couple, trying to break the news gently that Mickey is infer-
tile. In fact, it is painful to watch each and every one of the doctors that
feature in this film. These doctors busy themselves confronting the
hypochondriac, Mickey, with the mortal threat of brain cancer – or else
relieving him of his fears. (Until he realizes that a medical 'all-clear' only
means that he will not die right now, unless of course he gets hit by a bus!)
If we cast our minds back over the film, it soon becomes clear that the final
line, 'Mickey? . . . I'm pregnant', is there to show us that the entire plot –
which began with the news of Mickey's infertility – hinged, in fact, on a
mistake: a faulty diagnosis was responsible for starting the whole 'dance'.

'Woody Allen's genius lies in the fact that he is able to move from his
characteristic and unpoetic mode of realism to the quest for metaphysical
meaning,' opines Seidel (*Frankfurter Allgemeine Zeitung*, 2 Oct. 1986, p.
25). However, this judgement overlooks the fact that Allen treats both the
'quest for metaphysical meaning' and the people who worship it or profit
from it (the two things seem to go together, especially in the case of Allen's
priests, psychotherapists and 'sophisticated' intellectuals) with irony, derision and scorn. Quite apart from this, it also fails to acknowledge the by
now familiar link between metaphysical problems and the condition of

being happily, unhappily or not at all in love. This link is thematized in *Hannah and her Sisters*, as it was in Allen's earlier work (see in particular *Love and Death* and *Annie Hall*). The quest for meaning is ironized twice over: first of all, as it is reduced to the question of being (temporarily) out of love, and then again, as the whole chain of action is led back to a mistake made by one of the administrators of meaning. None of this was picked up on by the critics, who wrote instead about the satisfactory (although perhaps only temporary) resolution to the problem. The reasons for these misreadings must lie elsewhere, beyond the specifics of the film.

It would be fair to say that this film does not actually present the family as an institution in which people drive each other to suicide, despair or murder. However, it does show the family to be a highly problematical arrangement, which, although relatively easy to leave, is an unstable entity that never fails to claim its victims. It may allow us some moments of happiness and periods of contentment, yet it is equally likely to bring with it bitterness and strife, as well as other more subtle forms of mutual hurt. The case of Hannah and her second husband Elliot (who has an affair with Hannah's sister, Lee) demonstrates that stability is in fact the result of ignorance, misunderstanding and self-absorption. According to Seidel, Allen's film uses the family to show 'what it is that poisons their reality – the lack of communication in their actions'. However, even if this were true, it must also be clear that this family's utter collapse has only been averted by precisely this 'poisonous' lack of communication. The fact that Hannah and Elliot do remain together is never presented as a positive outcome, but appears instead as the result of laziness and coincidence. If Hannah had found out about the affair, if the couple had 'had it out' with one another, things would not have worked out any better and the dance would still have continued – with other sequences and other combinations. It is possible that the change might have brought with it the abrupt exclusion of yet another character from the film. Frederick, Lee's cynical boyfriend disappears in this manner and, once he has been ditched by Lee, we do not hear another thing about him. Of course, it is easy for us to guess the pattern: he stays single, or finds someone else, or dies. In fact, he probably does all three things and in exactly this order. The film treats marriage and the family in an extremely ironic manner – in *Hannah and her Sisters*, marriages and families always need a little outside help if they are to survive. Even then, they sometimes work out and they sometimes do not – just as in all other arrangements of this kind. In the end, it does not really matter.

This attitude towards marriage and the family contrasts greatly with the film's severe treatment of those responsible for administrating life's 'meaning'. In *Hannah and her Sisters*, these people are not only doctors (a professional group that is relatively new to this position), but also priests (the traditional administrators of meaning). The attack on the Catholic Church is particularly harsh, although this aspect of the film is always toned down or – more often than not – entirely ignored by its reviewers.[12]

It seems to me that both the scene with the picture of Christ whose eyes are 'especially designed to blink' (screenplay, p. 133) and the scene with Mickey and his newly purchased religious goods could hardly be clearer. Nevertheless, in reviews of the film, these scenes are described in a very imprecise manner. Seidel recounts the story of Mickey and his religious goods:

> The son of an American Jewish couple, Mickey believes only in 'death and sex', and yet he allows his shopping bags to be stuffed with Catholicism purchased from a religious store. After the shopping trip, the religious goods are left lying in a pile alongside doughnuts and hamburgers. They are the unappetizing centre of a commodified world, and the only effect that they have on Mickey is to revive his sense of aesthetics. (*Frankfurter Allgemeine Zeitung*, 2 Oct. 1986, p. 25)

This scene in the religious store exists solely within the critic's imagination, for in the film you only see Mickey unpacking the religious goods. There are no doughnuts or burgers in evidence, and I could not find any indication in the film that Mickey's sense of aesthetics is at any point revived. In fact, there is no sign of it ever lapsing, or of it being at all important to the film. All this is a figment of Seidel's imagination. The scene is rendered rather more accurately by another critic, Hellmuth Karasek: 'He [Mickey] takes home with him a small crucifix, a picture of a saint and a hymn book, all packed into a brown paper bag' (*Der Spiegel*, 6 Oct. 1986, p. 231). In the film, however, Mickey does not carry a hymn book, but a copy of the New Testament (see screenplay, p. 134). In fact, Karasek even gets the order wrong: the book comes before the picture. In spite of all this, Karasek's version is at least a little more accurate. By way of contrast, the scene is not even mentioned by the critic in *Die Zeit*, while the review in the *Frankfurter Allgemeine Zeitung* merely refers abstractly to the 'purchasing of devotional goods'.

In order to make things perfectly clear – there is no scene in the film in which religious goods are *bought*, but only one in which they are *unpacked*. Commodified religion is not ridiculed by any reference to a large quantity of random goods (such as 'shopping bags stuffed with Catholicism'), but rather by the way in which the goods are laid out on the table. The crucifix is placed down flat, rather than being propped up, as one might expect. The book is balanced unsteadily over it, followed by the picture. However, the joke of it all (which the German critics missed) lies in the fact that to top it all off, a loaf of 'Wonder Bread' is then placed over the picture, while a jar of Hellmann's mayonnaise is stood next to the precarious construction. We have become so familiar with these brand-names that we would not think to associate 'Wonder Bread' with miracles and by extension with Catholicism. Nor would it occur to us to link 'Hellmann's' to damnation and the devil. The film presents contemporary religion (and in particular the dominant Christian variety) as a hopeless and lost cause. It does this by returning references that were once religious (and that we no longer perceive as such) back to their original context. We find the scene funny because the 'wonders' or 'miracles' to which advertising has accustomed us suddenly demand to be viewed as such and to be worshipped on bended knee or admired with open mouth. On the other hand, we see how cult objects like the crucifix are purchased, unpacked and laid aside as commodities. The film presents us with a comic picture of how religion is being irreversibly profaned: it demonstrates how the secrets of religion have been absorbed into the language of our everyday affairs and above all into the jargon of advertising. It shows how the administrators of meaning have been absorbed into the business world and have adapted themselves to the dominant commercial practice.

The target of the film, therefore, is not the frailty and absurdity of human life. Woody Allen's use of irony is always far more reflexive than this. Allen's irony focuses on current attempts to deal with the absurd in a 'profound' and psychologized framework. Such attempts form part of the flourishing industry in psychotherapy, and they are used by intellectuals as a topic of conversation for after-dinner chat. However, this way of dealing with the absurd trivializes and stylizes the irony of life. In the light of the increased popularity enjoyed by psychoanalysis and existentialism, and in the wake of Kierkegaard, Strindberg and Camus, there is no longer any scope for ironists to make their name by exposing the absurdity of life and the black depths of the soul. In our current condition of 'enlightenment', there is nothing for it but for irony to apply itself to the psychoanalytic and existentialist trends themselves, as well as to the more or less trivial products of the literature and film industries in which these trends are now ensconced. It is precisely this type of irony that features in Woody Allen's films. Allen's films always deal with culture industry and with us – the spectators who are unable to distinguish between actor and character, who watch the films inattentively, who overlook the details and who are far less able than the director to use the film to reflect on their own position.

In this way, what we read in the critics' reviews unwittingly illustrates the film's purpose. The fact that the critics misunderstood the film is part of the objective irony of culture industry, and it is this that provides Allen with his theme.

Countertransference and analysing the working alliance

Since its beginnings over a hundred years ago, psychoanalysis has spawned countless different schools, some very different from the original, and some more successful than others, but each with its own particular guru and its own culture industry brand of trivialization. Nevertheless, when assessing the psychoanalytic phenomenon, it is still fair to say that all those many years ago Sigmund Freud was responsible for discovering and describing one of the fundamental principles of human interaction: transference and countertransference. Interaction occurs in the play between two different sets of expectations. Each of the parties involved mobilizes a particular set of expectations in accordance with their understanding of the situation, that is, they interpret the situation in analogy to previous experiences that were of decisive psychological importance to them.[13] Normally, we would try to get the other party to enter into our own understanding of the situation and to respond to it with emotions that are complementary to our own. This process of countertransference is also influenced by the particular analogies that we use to understand the situation. Countertransference can be a useful way of increasing our understanding of things: once we become aware of it, we begin to see through the strategies that other people use.

In order to understand a situation, we must understand the rules that govern it. The situation is the result of the process of transference and countertransference between participants, as it occurs, triggered by social norms and signals from the physical surroundings. Thus the situation's rules are set up and negotiated in accordance with the organizational, institutional and social context of the interaction in question and as a result of the expectations of the parties involved. These rules can be described as the 'working alliance'. Hence, in order to understand, we must reconstruct the 'working alliance' within which the phenomenon 'makes sense'. This applies to our understanding of texts, as well as to that of artefacts and events. It is a general principle that covers all methods of understanding. Such methods may be ordered into those that are based on countertransference and – at the opposite end of the scale – those that are blind to countertransference. This is just another way of separating those methods that work reflexively (and that distinguish themselves from the everyday mode of understanding) from those that do not.

The everyday and the reflexive approach to texts

In everyday encounters with written or spoken communication we usually react in the manner previously described as 'authoritarian realism' (see pp. 42–4 above). We view the information as if it were a reflection of reality, reading it as we would a police statement or a report on an expedition. We go through it, wanting to find out about the places that we have not yet seen and the events that we did not witness. The narrator saw it all, and we need to know exactly how it happened. We are keen to find out about all these things that we have never experienced. It is up to the narrator to describe to us as precisely as possible this reality that is as yet unknown. In fact, we will even oblige the narrator to do so, enquiring: 'But is it really true Mrs X?'

The situation is a bit more complex in the case of stories that are clearly fictional but that we nevertheless enjoy listening to. Even here we talk of 'realism'. We expect fictional accounts to be 'accurate' in their particulars, and 'credible' as a whole. We feel that we have been cheated if the plot of an otherwise realistic murder mystery turns on the fact that the killer can fly and was thus able to escape without trace from the scene of the crime. This type of plot belongs to the genre of the fantasy story – a genre that we know, accept and perhaps even love. However, the realism of this genre, like that of poetry, is of a rather different kind: fantasy stories are 'realistic' in that they evoke emotional states (dreams, desires, fears and so on) that lie outside our everyday experience yet within the bounds of comprehension. We expect a fictional story to be a valid and credible expression of a psychological reality. We can accept that this reality may be a little out of the ordinary, but we nevertheless expect it to appear relevant and coherent.

If we take the stance of 'authoritarian realism', there are two ways of interpreting such stories: we can read them with reference to the author, viewing the texts as an expression of his or her obsessions, neuroses or dirty mind; or, we can see them as evidence taken from a cultural pool – as symptoms of collective emotions and as an expression of society's traumas. (We find the latter explanation particularly convincing if the story in question has been very successful and sold well, or if it reveals motifs that repeatedly occur elsewhere.)[14] In the case of the first explanation, we respond to the story by posing the familiar and ridiculous question: 'What is the author trying to tell us?' In the case of the second, we aim to show our skill in deducing hidden information about the nature of society and the way in which it functions.

This psychological or sociological interest in cultural artefacts can be seen first and foremost as an interest that comes into play in situations that may (irrespective of whether the participants are aware of it or not) be understood and conceptualized as situations of communication. These include the desires and interests of all those directly involved in the situation, not least the desires and interests of the person conducting the analysis – regardless of whether it is a question of getting to grips with an everyday situation, or of evaluating and interpreting cultural products as a professional activity. Professional critics and interpreters take account of the process of countertransference and thus of their own role in the interpretation: professionals take themselves as the starting-point for the interpretation, and so proceed reflexively. Ordinary people, by contrast, will adopt the attitude of 'authoritarian realism': they will disregard their own position and try to discover an objective truth. Yet it is precisely this attempt to exclude oneself from the equation that ensures that the quest will fail. Indeed, given the plurality of social perspectives, objectivity is something that can only be had reflexively.

We can start off, then, by examining these desires and interests as they occur in a situation involving an encounter with a written or spoken text. People who use the everyday approach to interpretation will want to find out something about the world, and in particular its strange and novel aspects. They will want to know all about the place described, so that they will know their way around when they finally get there. They will want to feed their desire for travel and adventure, as well as their longing for the unknown and the new – and perhaps even for a better world. It is possible, however, that they will only want to hear about a better world so as to be able to settle down all the more comfortably in their familiar and secure environment. This environment does not confront them with any of the demands associated with the other world. (That is not to say that the familiar world does not make its own demands – it does; it is just that they do not enter into this particular equation.) An ordinary person engaged in interpretation will be torn, therefore, between fascination, boredom and the pleasure derived from both conditions – from the new and unfamiliar, as well as from repetition and familiarity.[15]

In its relatively pure form, this wish for realism leads us to read texts as travel guides or instruction manuals. What we really want from them are precise instructions as to how to achieve particular practical goals. Many academic or theoretical texts can also be (mis)read in this way.[16] The self-help book was the result of applying this instrumental approach to our own lives. Earlier manuals had drawn on spiritual notions of a hygiene of the soul, as well as on the idea of puritanical self-examination and self-discipline, but court and bourgeois life required a new type of self-help advice that would show how to keep competition within socially acceptable bounds. These days, self-help books tend to provide us with tips that are designed to help us instrumentalize ourselves purely in order to achieve career goals.

In most cases, however, we are also looking to be entertained. We want to hear stories about love or rivalry, or about success against the odds. We like tales that have miraculous twists, or tragic complications and conclusions. It may be that we take pleasure in an orator's skill, in the sound of their voice, in the accompanying music or dance, in the objects or pictures on display, in the speaker's wit, in the irony or power of the performance, and in the feeling of awe that it inspires in us. During all this, we want to relax a bit with our friends. We want to be scared or shocked, and we want to be aroused. Being entertained clearly also means being addressed as a man or as a woman. It means stories of masculinity and femininity – of heroism and endurance, loyalty and betrayal, belonging and exclusion, attractiveness, achievement and independence. In short, it means stories about the relationship between the sexes and its variants, all told within the framework of dominant patriarchy and its faulty and breakdown forms.

The narrator (and let us think of the errant Odysseus as an example) also has his own desires and interests. He will want to impress us with his extraordinary experiences and insights, not to mention, of course, with his narrative skill. As a stranger, he will buy his entry into society by telling interesting stories about the place from which he comes. He can then be accepted into our midst – or left in such a position that, the next day, when the magic has been replaced by early morning gloom and when nothing is left of his tale but an insipid aftertaste, he has already moved on, to live beyond the range of our disappointment, a slippery yet fascinating fellow. In the academic world, narrators are akin to ethnologists – they are the only people qualified to tell of strange and exciting tribes, since they alone have won their trust. They are melancholic people who also tend towards cynicism. They have already seen all there is to see, suffered all there is to suffer. They no longer experience excitement or enthusiasm, but acknowledge events with a bored nod of the head. Above all, they are know-alls who defeat us with their facts and who are able to talk us down with their masterful and detailed arguments.

It is constellations such as these that emerge when we encounter a text, whether it is a nonsense rhyme or an academic work. Our first task is to find out what kind of constellation we are dealing with. This is the first and most important frame that gives the text its meaning, and it is the most immediate, and therefore the most significant part of the working alliance within which the interaction between the text and its interpreter takes place.

Analysing the working alliance

Conducting a sociological interpretation of events is more demanding and more complex than we might like to think. It is not a question of selecting the 'right' interpretation from among all those in circulation, but of gathering the interpretations together, and using the differences between them to determine the position of the object in question within the field of forces and conflicts. It is within this whole constellation – of which the person conducting the analysis is one element – that we must look for the meaning. Thus the first step in the process of interpretation is to identify and collect all the possible ways of interpreting the object. This is rarely, if ever, accomplished. Engaging in group, rather than in individual work is a step in the right direction, but most groups are far too homogeneous in their composition. Most interpretation groups consist of social scientists who differ from one another only in their personal backgrounds. This means that there is never any really serious attempt to gather together ways of reading and interpretation that are truly diverse. For this, it would be necessary to find people with radically different horizons of experience who could contribute their interpretations. Precisely those types of people who would not want to become involved would have to be included.[17]

The differences that would become apparent between the various interpretations are all equally interesting, but they only provide us with the source material that will allow us to continue our investigation. The next step is to examine the premises that make each particular interpretation appear plausible. If different people describe the same stone as 'strangely fissured', 'solid and heavy' and 'too big', there would be little point in trying to find out which of these descriptions 'really' fits the stone. In actual fact, the stone 'really' is all this, and indeed more – all depending on the particular perspective. Our real task would be to uncover the perspective that the interpreting subject has taken for granted and left unspoken. This is the perspective from which the description will 'make sense'. It is possible, for instance, that each of the three individuals was comparing the stone to a different model – the first to the shiny stones polished by the current, the second to the stones used for catapults and the third to the type of stone used for bricks. The stone's social significance lies in the different contexts within which it might be considered. As interpreting subjects, our task is to reconstruct these possible contexts and so to voice the unspoken. The significance of a social object is to be found within the tacit assumptions that lie behind the ways in which it is interpreted.

The range of possible assumptions that may influence the way in which an object is interpreted is never quite so abstractly open as in the above example. In fact, this range is limited quite drastically by the social institution within which the object is being considered. If the stone is to be interpreted within the framework of 'art', then the assumption that it might be used as a brick will not figure so strongly. However, if the stone is to be interpreted in a practical context, then the first interpretation (based on the notion that a stone might be 'beautiful') will seem somewhat irrelevant. Social institutions lay down rules and norms that serve to limit the range of possible interpretations for the objects that appear within them. These rules and norms constitute the 'working alliance' for each institution. They also supply the framework for the more specific working alliances within each institution's various establishments (for example, for the 'museum' or for the 'concert' within the general institution of art).

What gets taken for granted in an interpretation is not simply a result of the subject's personal experience. Indeed, for integrated members of society, the unspoken perspective is strongly socially determined. Nevertheless, every now and then a personal element may well come into play. This could, for example, take the form of a tendency (established in childhood experience) to interpret situations in analogy to a rivalry with an overpowering father or for the attention of a dismissive mother. Whatever the reasons for this tendency, it might lead the subject to perceive events in a childish manner and to behave accordingly – either unreasonably aggressively, or in a way that betrays a desperate desire to be loved. The subject might even behave in both ways at once, with expressions of rivalry as unchecked as the shows of affection. Clearly, such tendencies are not so much individual as typical of the way in which a particular society organizes its family relations, and of the problems that these then face. This means that even the 'additional' psychological aspects are liable to sociological interpretation.

In view of all this, different layers within the working alliance can be discerned. Thus we have the *personal* working alliance (that comes into play in certain situations as a result of the subject's individual experience), the *organizational* working alliance (that comes into force within a particular type of establishment); the *institutional* working alliance (that determines a whole area of social behaviour); and the *social* working alliance (that proscribes the basic mechanisms for a particular mode of production).

When interpreting an object, it is useful to make these kinds of distinctions (although we need not be too strict about them), for they will help to remind us of the various levels that remain to be analysed. For each level of interpretation, our task is to investigate the working alliance by identifying the information and norms that have been taken for granted and that are needed for the phenomenon to 'make sense' (within the framework of a given institution). What information has been left unspoken but is nevertheless necessary for the event to take place within society, and to be understood as it is being categorized? And what is the structural distribution of the information and norms that have been taken for granted?

How to conduct a thorough and skilful interpretation

Whatever any of our 'great interpreters' may claim, there is no fail-safe method of interpretation. Hermeneutic approaches are by no means social theories – they are just tricks of the trade that enable us to make the business of interpretation that little bit more difficult and so distinguish academic study from the everyday manner of rapidly assessing events.

There are three main prerequisites behind most methods of interpretation. If we want to interpret an event, we must:

(1) Look carefully   The everyday manner of rapidly assessing events often requires us to pass over many of the details. In order to be able to act confidently, we need only identify the relevant generic term – the finer distinctions are of no concern to us. In a restaurant, it suffices to successfully identify the waiter if we wish to avoid the embarrassment of mistaking fellow diners for staff. We do not need to know anything about the waiter's attitude to his job: it is not necessary to know if he goes about his work grumpily or with enjoyment, and we certainly do not need to find out about how he gets paid etc. We are not interested in ascertaining whether his legs hurt, or if he hates the diners. Once we have identified the waiter, we know that this is the person whom we should approach if we want to stand any chance of getting our food. However, if we want to achieve a better insight into the social structure of a restaurant, we must be prepared to take an interest that goes beyond our immediate needs.

But how can we force ourselves to pay more attention to such details? The most direct way of dealing with this problem is to create a set of rules for describing objects. This might mean starting the description by commenting on 'the material on which the text appears' or by describing the context of the conversation that is being held. It might mean beginning with 'the very top left-hand corner of the page'. (So, in the case of a letter, we would have to start with the address of the writer or with the opening greeting, while in the case of a newspaper, we would begin with the header. Either way, before embarking on the 'actual text', we would always start by examining the contextual details.) These kinds of rules can be combined with other tips such as 'first of all, note down anything unusual or irritating about the object.' It is indeed necessary to register and record our immediate reactions right away, for the more time we spend reading the text, the more likely we are to forget about the passages that struck us as unusual or that made us stumble or get stuck. We are also likely to lose hold of the emotions that we initially experienced. All this would entail the loss of valuable information. It is possible to combine these two types of rules since it will always be necessary to run through the interpretation several times (and if possible in different ways).

(2) Think thoroughly   Thinking thoroughly about the object is what really distinguishes a proper interpretation of events from everyday understanding. It is an essential part of the process and we must do our best to create the right conditions for it (for instance, by ensuring that those conducting the analysis are not too busy and involved to reflect properly, and by documenting the event so that the evidence is preserved and may be viewed repeatedly). The type of thinking that we are dealing with here is of a particular kind: it involves trying out the different perspectives that might be adopted by all of the people that could conceivably be involved. This type of thinking seeks and finds comparisons that are as 'far-fetched' as possible, and draws on all the available sociological theories that could prove helpful. This is when it becomes especially clear that the task of interpretation cannot really be carried out by a single person alone. It would evidently be better to work with a group, and in ideal circumstances we would be able to look actively for co-workers who have radically different per-spectives. The first sets of results would be used mainly to discern which additional perspectives would be possible but are still missing from the interpretation.

(3) Do not let yourself be taken in   This is actually quite tricky and primarily involves treating with the utmost distrust the social assump-tions that are already present within the concepts at hand and within the way questions are formulated for us. The best way of doing this is to begin by reflecting on our preformed beliefs and their emotional investment. This is where the 'irritation' mentioned above comes into play. The fact that we are irritated by something alerts us not so much to personal 'prejudice' as to the norms of society. These norms are expe-rienced in the form of fear, embarrassment and surprise, etc., and as such they become subject to analysis. It is possible to analyse such emotions in order to discern the social norms from which they were generated. To put this more technically: countertransference is not a 'mistake' that needs to be corrected – it is a means of understanding that will enable us to analyse and critique concepts, questions and statements claiming to be 'fact' or 'reality'. All this involves examining the material several times over, for the results obtained at each indi-vidual stage will act as correctives to each other and so force us to go back through our interpretation. Once we have analysed the ideology inherent in a concept, an explanation or a theory, we need to go back to the original observations and descriptions and re-examine them. Sometimes this will not happen as fully as we would like. It is always possible to take shortcuts, and on some occasions this might even be desirable. The scope of intellectual enquiry is infinite, but not every question is important enough to merit unlimited attention. In any case, the lifespan of the thinker is certainly not infinite, and the tasks we face are many and varied.

When summing up an interpretation, a general formula needs to be found. This means finding a balance between precision of detail and broad meaning, a compromise that can only be justified by the usefulness of the results. This summary of the main interpretative result characterizes the 'working alliance' in which the object of interpretation 'makes sense'. Using the term 'working alliance' makes it clear that concepts of this kind always describe a relationship – they express the basic structure of the link between the object or event and the persons engaged in interpreting it.

Before we move on, we should run through a few ways in which the above information should be qualified.

In many cases, it is simply not possible to conduct the time-consuming research that would be necessary in order to investigate the many different interpretations that might exist within a given society. Sometimes, we will only have our own interpretation to refer to. That is not to say that we should simply give up. Provisional results can be found if we reflexively analyse the interpretation in relation to our social position. In addition to this, other possible interpretations can be deduced and interpolated by mobilizing our knowledge about others (and about other subcultures), by examining written documents (in the case of media products, they might be reviews); by investigating various statements from the audience that we overhear; and by analysing discussions and conversations that we initiate. The complete analysis, as described above, should be seen as a kind of ideal model of interpretation – it is very rare that anybody is ever able to fulfil all of its requirements. Nevertheless, once we have grasped the basic principle of the thing, we will at least know how close we have come to it in our own efforts and how cautiously we should treat our results.

Understanding this principle will also enable us to criticize other interpretations, even if we cannot conduct an alternative investigation right away. We will be able to relativize dogmatic claims and to insist that the necessary preliminary research is undertaken. We will also be able to argue that things are not quite as simple as either authoritarian realism or academic rivalry (intellectuals vying for the position of the 'great interpreter') may make them seem. Most importantly, we will be able to make clear that it is always a question of the *interaction* between an object and an interpreting subject, and that, socially speaking, the opinion of the 'educated classes' (not to mention that of academics) is by no means the measure of all things cultural.

Field notes V   Talk Radio – insulting the audience

Talk Radio (dir. Oliver Stone, 1988) is based on a play by Eric Bogosian. Bogosian starred in the play, and he also stars in Stone's film, playing Barry Champlain, the 'host' of what was then a relatively new type of radio show – a show in which listeners call in and express their views. Bogosian's 'host' (a term that seems a little inappropriate in this case) stands out due to the fact that he voices his liberal views about society, the world and his Jewishness just as aggressively as he does his arrogant contempt for his listeners. The latter he confronts, revealing their dubious motives for calling in a most embarrassing way. As a result, he attracts a large number of listeners, as well as many callers with far-right or Christian fundamentalist tendencies. These callers voice their opinions just as aggressively – although for the most part, not as masterfully – as Champlain himself. Champlain also receives a substantial number of spoken and written death threats. One of these threats eventually leads to murder. This is a reference to a real event, for in 1984 a talk-show host was murdered by a neo-Nazi. For the most – and more exciting – part, the film consists of conversations between Champlain and his listeners. The film, however, is also the story of a life and a career, for it features a lengthy and detailed flashback into Champlain's earlier life, as well as showing the reappearance of his wife (who separated from him long ago) and telling the success story of the show. (A big radio station is planning to buy the show and to broadcast it nationwide. The episode in which Champlain's wife takes part in the show is the nerve-racking sample programme intended to decide the fate of this deal.) The film's futile and tragic ending makes it seem as if it might be either (a) a story about the success and ultimate failure of a thoroughly outspoken guy who finally says just a little too much; or (b) the more sophisticated scenario of an honest man who decides to tell the world the truth about culture industry and about our role within it, and who then discovers that this approach is the perfect recipe for success (spoilt only when a madman he insulted finally brings him down).

Film critics in Germany saw in *Talk Radio* this second, more sophisticated, story.[18] For them, it was the drama of the last remaining representative of honesty in a culture industry fast approaching madness; the drama of an upright man who, in order to stay that way, has no choice but to trample over others; the drama of the critic who is universally hated for his work. Quite clearly, the German critics saw the film as the story of their lives – they too would like to be as quick-witted, outspoken, ruthless and, of course, successful as Champlain. They too are as heroically honest – even if in their case their honesty goes unnoticed.

This interpretation does not account for the strong emotional power of the film, which is liable to engulf us if we do not consciously distance ourselves from the plot. This power is the result of the rather interesting working alliance offered by the film. This working alliance turns the film into a reflection on what it means to be part of the audience, and on the nature of the 'reality' that we experience in this way.

For the most part, the film focuses on the studio and on the actions of the relatively small group of people within it. The callers all remain faceless, apart from Kent, a crazy adolescent who is invited into the studio and who goes on air with Champlain. The other callers are just voices coming from somewhere 'out there' – like a media version of the anonymous 'citizens' that desperate politicians appeal to in times of need. The callers lie out of our range – indeed, when one man rings up and announces that he is about to rape a woman, the call cannot even be traced. The voices are vain, self-important, foolish, evil, mean and disgusting. In every instance, however, they are there only to provide the cues and to make the callers seem ridiculous. At the press of a button, Champlain can make them disappear. At the end of the film, the voices become autonomous – against the background of a night-time cityscape, they commentate on the murder, a succession of chattering voices now utterly disembodied in the ether. It would appear that the drama takes place in the claustrophobic space of a goldfish bowl, from which the outside world may be seen, but never understood. This sense of isolation is heightened by the constant movement of the camera, as it repeatedly and unmistakeably goes round in circles.

After a while, however, even those among us who are least prone to self-reflection cannot fail to notice that we too are *spectators*: we are in the process of despising an audience to which we ourselves belong. By the time we get to Champlain's closing speech, we ourselves, the spectators, have become a target of his abuse. Champlain poses the question as to what it is that drives his callers to ring in. Why don't they leave him in peace and keep their perversions (political or otherwise) to themselves? Why don't they just turn off their radios? And all the time we sit there in the dark and watch unmoved as a man wears himself out, tortured by despair and self-loathing. Is it really OK to be entertained by this kind of thing? Of course, the man is not really suffering – he is an actor and he is currently engaged in earning his living by acting out the reality of an actor. He does this so convincingly that we forget our own reality. In this reality, we are sitting in a cinema, going along with this performance of a performance. As such, we are doing precisely that which the play is mocking. We are the people who are being insulted in this scene that takes place for our entertainment. We are these bigoted and grotesque people. At the same time, the fact that we get to see the performance makes us cleverer than these people and cleverer than Champlain, about whom we get to know more than he knows about himself. Indeed, a film's spectators are always cleverer than its producers, for the latter cannot do anything to stop us from doing as we like with their film.

Several of the scenes from the flashbacks are repeated in the main action. In these scenes, we see how the outside world infiltrates the show, as well as the subsequent attempts that are made to ward it off. One such scene features the weirdo, Kent. Champlain's career had started up when he was invited on to a talk show and then 'discovered'. As Champlain had done before him, Kent goes on the show and interrupts a conversation between a caller and the host. In Kent's case, the result is a tired parody. Champlain is speechless and has Kent thrown out. This piece of reality is just as grotesque as the disembodied voices of the callers. Kent comes up with the cliché that lets us know that it cannot in fact be real: 'It's just a show!'

The second repeated scene is rather more complex. Earlier on in Champlain's career, his wife, Ellen, had phoned in and insulted him. He countered her criticisms by demanding that she put down the phone: if he gets on her nerves so much, then why doesn't she just hang up? The fact that she continues the call, reiterating her hatred for him, is seen by Champlain as a proof of her love. The scene works very well, masterfully balancing performance and reality. When Ellen calls in for a second time, it is to confess her love for Champlain. She does this in proper talk-show fashion, by pretending to speak about another man. Champlain also reacts in talk-show fashion, telling her that she is being sentimental and that she is probably mistaken – in all likelihood, the man is just not interested any more. This time the balance between performance and reality tips against the reality of the potential lovers. The performance has wounded Champlain in his life outside the show.

The reality constructed by the media is always the reality of the viewers and listeners, who treat the information as fiction and put it to their own purpose. Sometimes this means incorporating it into their lives and so they start to play a part in it. Some branches of the media actively encourage this kind of behaviour and they use the public's participation for their own ends. The result can be quite hurtful for all concerned. Every single one of us imagines that it is the 'others' who are stupid, and that we ourselves are able to see through it all. We behave like travellers who despise the other tourists. It is precisely through this type of behaviour that the media get a hold on us – and we cannot even admit that we have been insulted or hurt. And that is what entertains us: 'It's just a show!'

3

The production of cultural commodities

Problems involved in producing cultural commodities

In the first instance, producing 'culture' does not really require much effort. It does not cost much to equip ourselves with paint and brushes, a trumpet can always be borrowed, and a pen and a beer-mat would suffice to jot down a haiku. Indeed, a certain amount of cultural production has always taken place in this relatively straightforward manner – adolescents write poems and try their hands at novels; some clear out their utility rooms and have a go at pottery; while others are engaged in short-lived attempts to learn a musical instrument. A small proportion of these efforts then feed into the official business of culture. Only very few of the people who are 'producing' culture ever come to think of themselves as 'artists'. Artists are defined by having made art their profession, and they have long since become distinct social figures. After the artisan, the monastic 'master craftsman', the court musician (or painter/poet) and the aristocratic (and then bourgeois) dilettante came the professional artist. The demand for culture came first from the church, then from political leaders and later from prosperous bourgeois 'private individuals'. Most recently, it has been coming from banks and multinationals. (Incidentally, although large corporations are keen to sponsor cultural production, art still has no place in the factory.) As the demand for culture has changed, new systems have emerged for organizing its production: from guilds to commercial publishing houses, from state-maintained radio stations to the profession of the artist. In the course of all this, the means of production for culture have become ever more costly and ever more fraught.

As the link between artist and audience becomes ever more anonymous, so the artist's means of production must come to include the process of securing access to the public. If artists want to make a living from their art, the art must involve gaining and guaranteeing an income. When competition and superior achievement become a part of art, elaborate and expensive training becomes a part of the artist's means of production. This is all the more true when the call goes out for artistic 'progress' – when it is no longer enough for artists to perfect their use of the existing techniques and they are required instead to produce something 'new'.[1]

The demands placed on artists by their means of production vary in accordance with the nature of each different cultural product. As Ernst Krenek remarked:

> It is all right if you're a painter. When your picture is finished, you just hang it on the wall, and anybody who wants to is free to take a look. However, if you are a composer, you will need musicians – and they will never be as good as you would like. What is more, you might even need the huge apparatus of an opera stage. You will only be happy when you are actually composing. After that, it is downhill all the way.[2]

This means that artists always have to compete with one another in order to gain access to the costly means of production. The 'apparatus' becomes autonomous: a cultural 'establishment' forms with the power to prevent new artists (as well as those who do not conform) from accessing the means of production. The cultural entrepreneur then comes into being – for the most part, as an independent and distinct social figure, although sometimes as a part played by the artist. Cultural entrepreneurs deal in cultural products, yet they are as fundamentally indifferent to them as are factory owners to the sweets or toys they manufacture. In some cases, the cultural producer will come into contact with several such entrepreneurs, each of whom will control a different section of the means of production. Thus artists might deal with a publishing house, a concert promoter and the agent for an orchestra. Given the importance of having a large audience, they will also have to concern themselves with the critics, as well as with all the other people who are involved in organizing the public's interest. In the past, artists were dependant on their powerful patron's favour and 'appreciation' of art. Now they are at the mercy of a rather opaque and terribly complex apparatus, within which a multitude of different interests coalesce or compete.[3] Art places high demands on artists, yet the way in which their products are received rarely has anything to do with their quality. This discrepancy has been an important theme in literary texts, and nowadays we are well aware of the extent of the problem. In the current situation, you would have to be totally naïve – or else blinded by vanity – to interpret public success as proof that your work is important. We all know that public success is really commercial success (of which only a small part will ever be enjoyed by the cultural producer) and that this type of success is engineered. This can make us quite distrustful – even to the point of extreme described by Schoenberg:

> But as soon as the war was over, there came another wave which procured for me popularity unsurpassed since. *My works were played everywhere and acclaimed in such a manner that I started to doubt the value of my music.* This may seem like a joke, but, of course, there is some truth in it. If previously my music had been difficult to understand on account of the peculiarities of my ideas and the way in which I expressed them, how could it happen that now, all of a sudden, everybody could follow my ideas and like them? Either the music or the audience was worthless.
> While the music proved to be lasting, these audiences were unstable.[4]

We must also consider the part played in all this by both the state and local authorities. These were quick to step into the role previously played by aristocratic and bourgeois patronage. (This occurred not only in relation to the arts, but also in the case of science.) State and local authorities now finance and organize crucial sections of the cultural infrastructure – the opera houses, radio, TV, orchestras, theatres (most of which could not survive without such funding), museums, large-scale exhibitions, literary awards, bursaries and libraries, plus the numerous courses and the jobs associated with them that allow people to produce cultural goods, whether professionally or as a sideline. This means that cultural producers not only have to fight their way through an economic jungle, but that they also have to struggle through a spoils system that is often obstructive and full of cliques, as well as being subject to political interference. And all the time they are carrying the burden of their 'art', which – in order for artists to maintain some degree of autonomy and self-respect – must be of a significance existing independently of the conditions of production and evaluation, a significance that they will have to assert against the odds. 'Art' is a game between numerous instances of power – the public is only one, fairly insignificant such instance.

At the turn of the twentieth century, the cultural scene in Vienna (and indeed elsewhere) was characterized by the startling frequency with which artists tried once more to free themselves from the evolving cultural apparatus and from their public (albeit in a manner that was necessarily ambivalent). These attempts fall into two very different categories. Firstly, there was the attempt to improve the collective market position and power of the artists by joining together in trade unions or professional organizations. It was hoped that this might lead to the artists being able to instrumentalize the state (through laws protecting copyright etc). This was in line with general developments. The other approach to the problem was more interesting and more radical, consisting of the attempt to gain control of the means of production, with the aim of solving the problem of competition and gaining independence from the public. The Secessions in Vienna and elsewhere are the best known – although not necessarily the most radical – example of this. More radical was the attempt to retreat into elite and lofty heights, as for example in Stefan George's or Schoenberg's circle, or in Karl Kraus's absolute autarky. The irony of such attempts lies in the fact that it was precisely the elitist effort to distance themselves from the general public that survived through time and that ensured their popularity (at least within certain circles) – as indeed it was intended to.

These successful attempts at achieving autonomy for art are part of a historical tradition, and they represent the last effort to wrench art free from a culture industry that was already well developed. As far as music is concerned, the most important stages within a long tradition of trying to achieve emancipation were marked by the advent of domestic music-making, the secular concert and the festival. Then, at the dawn of the twentieth century, came the idea of self-organization. This signalled a shift in the notion of what one had to emancipate oneself from. This shift was characteristic of the development of bourgeois society in general, and it saw artists moving from a struggle against feudal domination, to a struggle against the laws of the market, that is, bourgeois domination.[5]

We can begin our examination of this historical development with Mozart – a composer who lived and worked around the time that bourgeois society was beginning to emerge. Mozart's father, Leopold, was still firmly in the service of the Prince-Archbishop of Salzburg, and it was only due to his two child prodigies that he managed to escape this dependency – albeit only temporarily. He took leave (some of which was unpaid) in order to introduce his gifted children (focusing of course on his son rather than his daughter) to the big wide world of music. They went to Vienna, Mannheim, London and Venice. All the same, the child wonder Wolfgang Amadeus still ended up in the service of the Prince-Archbishop. The earlier successes of the

young Vice-Kapellmeister had spoilt him for such a role. He dared
to aspire to finding new and 'better' patrons. He was even prepared
to try making his way 'freelance' in the new concert and opera
business that was emerging independent of church or court control. He
went to Paris (where his mother died) and then finally to Vienna.
Of course, he also aspired to finding a position at the court and he
sought after aristocratic patrons, yet his symphonies and concerts
also stood a chance as public performances. Operas were still better
suited to court and state theatres, but the *Magic Flute* was written for
the Theater an der Wien – i.e. with the intention of making it a
popular success. Mozart had started to liberate himself and his
music from feudal dependency – firstly, by moving in international
circles, and secondly by using the 'wider public' as an alternative
to the narrowness of his feudal sponsors and patrons. In this way,
the music that he wrote did not depend on the approval of only *one*
master.

At that time, another opportunity was emerging that would give
composers the chance to get their music heard, as well as allowing
them to earn a small amount of money. Publishing houses were beginning to print and sell sheet music for use by domestic music-making
ensembles. These popularized the 'quartet' and then later the piano
score. This was a welcome development, yet it also placed a clear
restriction on composers. Just as in the case of the part music written
for amateur musicians at the court, these pieces had to be easy enough
to play so that their appeal was not limited to highly trained virtuosos.
On the other hand, the fact that 'chamber music' was played by a small
number of people in an intimate setting meant that the composers
could do away with pompous effects. Instead, they had the chance to
write delicate and intricate passages that were masterfully interwoven
into the development of the piece (whereby the danger arose that they
would more or less pass the listener by). As such, chamber music was
surely at least partially responsible for the bourgeois ideal of music
appreciation as an activity requiring knowledge and an ear for the
subtlety of the composer's technique.

While Mozart lived at a time when the bourgeois relationship
between the composer and the public was just beginning to emerge,
Haydn was still firmly in the clasp of feudal dependency. It took a fair
amount of time before the transition was completed, and most bourgeois composers still remained at least partially dependent on aristocratic patrons. It is a well-known fact that this was true of Beethoven,
and it was evidently the case for Wagner, whose economic situation
Adorno described as follows:

It is not for nothing that the period of his rise to fame coincided with that economically precarious age in which opera had ceased to enjoy the security of courtly patronage but had not yet acquired the protection of civil law and regular royalties. (*In Search of Wagner*, p. 15)

For quite some time, bourgeois composers had no longer been in a position of direct feudal dependency, yet they still had to rely on the aristocracy and thus practically beg for their living. (Adorno makes a case of this for Wagner, while Mozart's begging letters have been much discussed.) In connection with all this, it is perhaps useful to remember that the lifestyles of Mozart and Wagner were strikingly aristocratic. This plunged both composers into a lifetime of debt but did not stop either of them from keeping up their extravagant habits.

Although stuck in this unsatisfactory transitional phase, Wagner took a huge step towards the bourgeois condition by inventing the musical 'festival'. To some extent, this invention was born of necessity: Wagner would have preferred to have had a royal patron to pay for everything, including his own concert-hall. However, he could not find anyone prepared to go to such lengths for him – at least not as a permanent arrangement. Eventually, he had to take on the responsibility (financial and otherwise) for his plan to free himself from the shortcomings of the court and state theatres. In a way that was typical of early bourgeois society, Wagner's method consisted of dividing up his patronage – he distributed 'patronage notes' at 300 talers apiece. This form of financial support turned out to be impracticable, and without the intervention of a royal patron the whole enterprise would never have got off the ground. Nonetheless, Wagner did succeed in winning for himself a greater independence, even though this first festival at Bayreuth ran up debts that he was still trying to pay off until the day he died. The loss made by the 1876 festival delayed the next festival for a further six years, but this second festival was a financial success. Hans Mayer writes of the 'trivial pragmatics of the enterprise. Of course, Richard Wagner and his followers saw this enterprise as an act of cultural-political renewal, yet it was also . . . a financial enterprise and an organizational scheme of an entirely new kind, as well as an exercise in marketing and propaganda.'[6]

It was only with the likes of Jacques Offenbach that composers started to finance their art form in a truly bourgeois manner. Of course, as a result of this, Offenbach also had to face the bourgeois fate of bankruptcy, but this in turn meant that he could permit himself to express a little of his contempt and scorn for the aristocracy. However, composers such as Offenbach were the exception. In most cases, the state stepped into the role formerly occupied by the aristocracy.

At the tail end of this historical development, we have the attitude exemplified by Schoenberg, who tried to make his music and its performance independent from financial backers and the paying public. The classic bourgeois way of realizing this goal was, of course, to form a society – by drawing together the regular customers from a particular venue, or by establishing a reading group or a bourgeois 'secret' society. (To come back to the case of Mozart, even at that time the Freemasons played an important role, not least in financing his work.) From this it is clear that the idea of combating the dominant elite by forming one's own elite group is one that had been tried and tested. Moreover, forming an elite group is also a means of enabling the bourgeois patrons to take on bigger and more long-term projects, as well as a way of limiting the financial burden on the individual sponsors.

The case of the Viennese Secession had shown that stylizing yourself as an outsider in the culture business is by no means an untried method of achieving success. Schoenberg, however, never experienced this kind of success with his own societies. The first society lasted for only one season, and the second survived until 1921, when it had to be dissolved because of financial difficulties. Nevertheless, in a period of three years, it managed to put on 117 concerts.

The Society for Private Music Performances was founded in 1918. Journalists were banned from its performances, and clapping was forbidden. (Naturally, any expression of disapproval was also utterly outlawed!) The programme for these concerts was never announced beforehand, thereby preventing the audience from selecting which concerts they would prefer to attend. In the case of this society, it was clearly no longer a question of attracting, but rather of excluding the public. Only a small circle of connoisseurs and enthusiasts were admitted, and these in turn took over the financial patronage of the concerts. It was only when the society was in dire financial straits that it put on a public concert with arrangements of Strauss's waltzes. At this concert, clapping was permitted. After the concert, the original copies of the arrangements for chamber orchestra written by Berg, Schoenberg and Webern were auctioned off.[7] With the exception of this event, there were never any real 'concerts', but rather rehearsals with listeners. This way, it was no longer necessary to put on an actual 'performance'. Performing music was seen as an inadequate expression of music's true nature, and instead, music was presented as an invitation for thought. Every effort was made to impede its 'appreciation'. The society did without the 'public at large'.

It was precisely in its relationship to the public that the Society for Private Musical Performances differed from the Secession. The Secession aimed to reach the public without having recourse to the cultural establishment. Schoenberg wanted to be able to choose his own audience – to be more precise, he wanted to bring into being his own notion of how the relationship between composer and public should function. In an article written at about the same time as the society was founded, Schoenberg describes this relationship clearly and succinctly: 'One or more people make music, recite, sing; others anxious to share this experience are permitted to listen.'[8] As such, the composer should not be in any way dependent on his listeners, least of all as far as the finances behind his means of production are concerned.

All in all, Schoenberg's model of the composer in absolute control of his own means of production is very similar to that developed by Stefan George in relation to the writer. However, it is considerably easier to put this model into practice for literature than it is for music: you can found a journal, publish your own material and organize private readings. If you are not intent on building up a huge business, then it is far easier to finance the means of production for literature than it is for music. We need only imagine the difficulties that we would have in putting on an opera using nothing but our own resources. As far as the goal of autonomy is concerned, it would have been logical for composers in the European tradition to do away with performances altogether and to produce 'music for reading'. Schoenberg did not take that step.

Thus the project of autonomy, as pursued by Schoenberg and Stefan George, is inherently contradictory. Indeed, the continued use of publication and performance makes it a project of demonstrative autonomy, a form of *'public* aloofness' – a turn away from the public that is performed for all to see. Fundamentally, it is a display of elitism, which either invites you to join the lofty heights of the privileged, or informs you that, as a 'mere mortal', you can have nothing to do with the enterprise. Either way, artists gain their freedom at the expense of those others who are not permitted to share in it. The project of autonomy involves stylizing both 'art' and the 'artist' to such a degree that it sets them quite apart from the ordinary people. At the same time, it demands that these people acknowledge the artist's freedom as something 'special' and 'valuable'. It is a kind of 'credo quia absurdum' – 'I respect, since I can't understand.' It is really quite a cheek.

Adorno was closely linked to the Vienna School of composition and in particular to Alban Berg, under whom he had studied composition in Vienna for six months in 1925. (Adorno had also developed a personal friendship with Berg, although his relationship with Schoenberg was always highly ambivalent.) Consequently, Adorno was quite ready to accept the model of 'public aloofness'. What is more he saw it as the only possible model for the responsible production of art and intellectual enquiry. This meant that he had little understanding for some of the cultural developments that emerged as the century progressed and culture industry developed. (He had no time, for instance, for Dadaism, Surrealism or jazz.) It even led him to diagnose the 'end of art'. The model of public aloofness was not suitable for general use and in any case it was soon appropriated by the rapidly developing culture industry in its 'Fordist' transformation of the capitalist mode of production.

Adorno's theory of culture industry has two starting-points: firstly, the 'public aloofness' model of art that Adorno uses to provide the contrast against which the contemporary reality of culture is measured; and secondly, the belief that this reality is determined by the conditions of the age of 'Fordist' production.

It is now time to take a closer look at the opening pages of Adorno's 'Culture Industry' chapter and to illuminate the link between his theory and the mode of production.

Fordist standardization: 'Uniform as a whole and in every part'

False identity

The 'Culture Industry' chapter begins with a list of examples that at first sight seem rather peculiar. It starts off with 'Films, radio and magazines' (p. 120), that is, with the kind of mass-sale and high-frequency media that we might expect to find under the rubric of 'culture industry'. These characteristics, in conformity with the principles of Fordist mass commodity production, make for a schematic and repetitive form. However, on this first page of the chapter, the only example dealt with in detail has been taken from the field of architecture. Adorno writes of exhibition centres, the headquarters of multinational companies and housing estates, seeing in these buildings both homogeneity (a sameness that exists in 'authoritarian countries and elsewhere') and a well-organized force of order: 'the false identity of the general and the particular' (p. 121).

What connects these examples is that they presuppose and produce 'identity'. 'Identity' is always the result of classifying an object in abstract terms by linking it to a concept. The concept, however, will never be able to do justice to the object – precisely because of its abstractness. Thus, even if I am right in identifying myself – or letting myself be identified – as being 'Austrian', the term may describe my passport, but it does not describe my individual character. Being 'Austrian' does not mean that I display all – or indeed any – of the characteristics typically associated with 'Austrians'. There are certain situations and specific circumstances when I may allow myself to be identified as 'an Austrian'. On some occasions, I might even encourage this identification, for it might bring me certain advantages. However, there are many other situations in which I find it thoroughly unpleasant to be identified as 'Austrian'. As a description of my individuality, the classification 'Austrian' is very wide of the mark. Identifications are abstract descriptions and categorizations that are used in the service of both large- and small-scale politics. They describe only one aspect of the individual and thus inevitably fail to account for the unique difference of that person.

Identificatory thinking cannot escape this pattern, and so it always does violence to the individual object in question. The only way that the problem can be overcome is through the shifts in thought achieved by dialectical and reflexive thinking. In dialectical and reflexive thinking, objects are never fully identified with concepts, for the process of classification is kept in flux. Indeed, the social nature of the process is itself an object of enquiry. The Hegelian and Marxian theory behind this is the insight that concepts always describe a social *relationship*: to see them as representing either one of the two poles would be inaccurate. Stabilized in the form of language, concepts are put to a social purpose. In our various forms of abstract interaction (whether we are trying to organize others on a grand scale or communicate on a one-to-one level), we call upon and use concepts, thereby modifying and redefining them. It all depends on who is using the concept and whom or what they are trying to define, for it is this that creates the framework within which that person or thing will be dealt with. In this way, concepts are part of the structure of society, and in particular of domination.

However, if concepts are implicated in the relations of domination, it follows that they are also a part of the dialectic of liberation. Of course, the dialectic of liberation does not consist of changing the concepts that we use, but rather in dealing with them in a reflexive manner – in analysing their implication in domination. It is precisely because concepts have been shaped by domination that we can use them in order to find out something about domination. We can do this by examining the objects that these concepts serve to dominate. If approached reflexively, identificatory thinking can be used in order to analyse the role of domination in shaping the object. Domination is reflected within the concept and can be recognized as an aspect of the object. Of course, it would be misguided to believe that we could ever liberate thought from the relations of domination. Some people are convinced that we can push aside the relations of domination simply by banning some words and replacing them with terms that are 'correct'. However, this type of 'political correctness' merely seeks to impose a new set of rules (which for the most part are in any case confined to university life) on how we talk and write. If we want to be serious about tackling domination, then we will have to start dealing with its material conditions. Nonetheless, concepts can – and should – be used to analyse domination. In fact, this is a precondition of tackling domination and so should not be dismissed as being 'impractical'.

Adorno's claim that 'under monopoly capitalism all mass culture is identical' (p. 121) should be read in the light of these complex episte-mological arguments. Adorno is not just saying that 'everything is all the same anyway' and that there is no variation at all. What he is really getting at is that the process of abstraction (or the purely instrumental treatment of humans according to a 'ticket mentality', as Adorno and Horkheimer term it elsewhere) has resulted in culture becoming bound up with domination. The implication of this is that culture need not necessarily be linked to domination, but that it could instead provide us with a pocket of resistance, permitting us to deal with the world and with each other in a different way. Perhaps culture could even validate the claim to individuality. This cannot be achieved in identificatory thinking, for the logic of the latter is inextricably linked to abstract concepts. We can only use identificatory thinking for the purpose of criticism and self-criticism. As soon as it is used to make a positive claim, it gets caught up in an act of domination. This is the 'dialectic of enlightenment'.

Instrumental reason is characterized by the way in which abstract notions that are conceived according to external purposes are then used to plan and administrate and also to reduce human beings to the 'work-force', 'consumers', 'competitors', 'the unemployed', 'legal claimants' and even 'trouble-makers'. In extreme cases, they are presented as a burden to the state or the *Volksgemeinschaft* [racial community], and are thus liable to exclusion or even elimination. Sometimes we can even begin to understand ourselves in relation to these categories. It is not unknown for people to instrumentalize themselves, seeing themselves as the holders of a particular qualification or skill (as 'computer experts', 'tireless workers' or 'experienced managers') or as people with a particular set of preferences in terms of product consumption. (This last phenomenon is particularly important in youth cultures, but, as sociologists, who are no longer interested in social classes, have diligently shown, it is by no means limited to this group.)

Reality doubled

Adorno's next step (top of p. 121) is to describe how culture industry makes a show of revealing how culture has become involved in domination via instrumental reason. For Adorno, this is another instrument of domination: 'The truth that they [movies and radio, i.e. culture industry] are just business is made into an ideology in order to justify the rubbish that they deliberately produce' (p. 121). Through statements such as this, it is shown that there is nothing more to be revealed and that we already know all there is to know about the role of commerce in culture. Culture industry tells us this and turns the 'revelation' into propaganda.[9]

The above citation demonstrates that ideology is not necessarily the opposite of truth. It also shows that truth can even be used as ideology. The self-conscious proclamation that art is nothing but business becomes ideological as soon as it is used to prevent art from developing in any other direction. Ideology does not just consist in misrepresenting what is real, but also in repressing what is possible. Presenting empirical reality as if it were the only possible form of reality can prevent us from even conceiving that there might be other possible ways of life and other possible paths for the development of society – whether in the past or in the future. This is what Adorno was criticizing about 'positivism' and its fixation with empirical reality – he takes issue with the way in which it tries to prevent us from exploring (or at least fails itself to explore) other possible forms of reality.

This is particularly true due to the influence of domination on reality: dominant reality is the reality of the dominant. We adapt to it by deeming it inevitable. However, the reality that we are currently inhabiting (our own interim era of history) is just one of the many realities that would have been historically possible. Nevertheless, it is the reality that was chosen by domination and that is now held in place by it. It is inevitable only in so far as the current form of domination is invincible. Horkheimer and Adorno put a damper on the relative optimism of Marx's dialectic of liberation, which looks to the development of the forces of production. They noted a parallel development in the means of domination – the conditions necessary for liberation were improving, but at the same time the means of repression were being strengthened: domination was becoming more sophisticated and indeed more invincible. For Adorno and Horkheimer, the rise of Nazism and the defeat of the labour movement were sobering examples of this. However, to allow real domination and the domination of reality to triumph over the possibilities of our *thought* is self-imposed tutelage – or ideology.

This is the significance and place of culture industry – culture industry is an instrument of domination, for it takes away the resistance once represented by bourgeois art. The domination exercised in culture industry does not have to disguise itself. On the contrary, it gains in power by self-consciously revealing itself: 'They call themselves industries; and when their directors' incomes are published, any doubt about the social utility of the finished products is removed' (p. 121).

Fordist cultural commodities

In the next, quite lengthy paragraph, Adorno takes issue with those who explain culture industry in terms of the standardized processes of mass production and mass consumption. What he is criticizing here is clearly the 'Fordist' model of capitalism: he does not actually refer to 'Fordism' by name, but prefers simply to denounce the claim that culture industry is the result of consumer demand and technological development. In Fordist capitalism, the increased production of consumer goods, together with the expansion of the internal and external markets for them, becomes the leading economic interest. The idea of producing consumer goods on a mass scale could not come into being were it not for the technological capacity to manufacture them, which was developed as Taylor introduced the minute subdivision of labour and its reassembly on the production line. The mass production of consumer goods also relies on a system of remuneration according to which those workers employed to execute single repetitive tasks (unskilled work that is designed to fit around the requirements of the machinery) are paid sufficiently well for them to be able to purchase the same kind of mass-produced goods as the ones they are engaged in manufacturing.

It is at this point that culture industry took on interesting new dimensions and started playing a significant role: through the adverts that were necessary to promote the goods, the influential cultural sector of 'applied art' emerged. Cultural products were turned into mass-produced consumer goods. This development was dependent at various points in time on the invention of the media that would enable the technological reproduction and the mass trade in cultural goods (newspapers and paperbacks, radio and records, art prints and film, television and video, and finally multimedia PCs and the net). Adorno does not further elaborate on his claim that: 'This is the result not of a law of movement in technology as such, but of its function in today's economy' (p. 121). Nonetheless, there is no doubt that he is right, in so far as the need for a system for mass distribution (and hence the need for new ways of producing cultural goods as mass-market commodities) would not have arisen were it not for the Fordist variety of capitalism. Without the latter, the above-mentioned media would never have been invented (and if they had, they would have remained mere technical experiments – nothing more than curiosities).

It is clear, therefore, that culture industry is bound up in a very particular way with the decisive changes that occurred in capitalism at the beginning of the twentieth century. Culture industry took on a range of specific functions after the advent of mass consumption and the related notion of 'free time', together with the instrumental approach to work (work is to be carried out in exchange for as much money as possible so that we can spend it in our free time, which constitutes our actual purpose and our 'real' life). The 'Fordist' system required an instrumental attitude to work and so in turn was responsible for producing it. It is difficult to grasp just how dramatic these changes really were. Previously, the idea was to make the workers labour for as long as possible and to pay them as little as possible. Subsistence work and housework then played a crucial role in helping the workers reach subsistence level. However, later on, the radical changes in capitalism meant that the workers were asked to perform routine tasks in exchange for a salary that would permit them to purchase consumer goods. The time taken up by subsistence work was replaced as far as possible by free time, which the workers could spend pursuing the range of consumer products on offer. This meant that the rate of reproduction was indeed raised, while the consumption of large quantities of commodities became the criterion for assessing our standard of living. Culture industry and entertainment were linked together through the rise of commodified entertainment, and as entertainment became a characteristic of all commodities. Commodities should not just (or even necessarily) be useful, for they should (also) be fun. Better still, the act of purchasing them should be fun – it should constitute a 'consumer experience', quite independent of the commodity's use-value. It is in this context that culture industry developed.

Organized markets – organized production

When Adorno talks about organized markets and organized production (pp. 121–2), his primary target is the old ideology of the market in which it is claimed that what organization is doing is merely (and moreover masterfully) linking the range of goods for sale to the needs of the consumer. If goods are not bought up, they will no longer be made available for sale. Adorno takes issue with this view, presenting his own counterthesis: 'The attitude of the public, which ostensibly and actually favors the system of the culture industry, is a part of the system and not an excuse for it' (p. 122). Adorno illustrates his argument with a string of examples: in contrast to the telephone, the radio organizes a one-way system of communication, delivering exactly the same content to every listener. Even those 'amateurs' who are helplessly engaged in trying to make their own radio programmes are organized from above by the official broadcasting institution and are hunted down by 'talent scouts' searching for the next generation of presenters. Moreover, the message that is being conveyed through genres and media that are widely divergent is in essence exactly the same: social problems should be seen as technical difficulties and must be overcome as adroitly as possible. (As examples of this, Adorno lists soap operas and jam sessions in jazz, as well as popular adaptations of classical music and world literature; see p. 182.) The 'spontaneous wishes' of the public are never allowed expression – they are organized by the industry and influenced by the continual repetition of the same set of maxims that are intended to guide the public through life under capitalism.

The content presented in the media is indeed determined by the 'economic mechanism of selection' (p. 122), which is put into force and strictly controlled by the 'technical and personal apparatus' (p. 122) and by colluding, or at least like-minded, 'executive authorities' (p. 122). This claim may seem to smack of conspiracy theory, yet it is swiftly followed by an ironic statement that serves to undermine it: have things really got so bad that the World Spirit [*Weltgeist*] is now represented in the 'hidden subjective purposes of company directors' (p. 122) and not, as Hegel had it, in Napoleon 'on horseback'!

Once again, the interested parties are shown to operate within a strict hierarchy: the 'executive authorities' censor the material in accordance with their own ideas about themselves and about the consumers (who have in any case already been evaluated and tabulated according to their income groups). However, the 'executive authorities' are in turn dependent on 'the most powerful sectors of industry – steel, petroleum, electricity and chemicals' (p. 122) and they must guard themselves against 'purges' (p. 123). It is not clear exactly what Adorno and Horkheimer meant by this, but evidently they were not referring to 'expropriation', for sometime between 1944 and 1947 they rejected this expression, as corrections to the manuscript reveal. In any case, when Adorno and Horkheimer wrote of the 'dependence of the most powerful broadcasting company on the electrical industry, or of the motion picture on the banks' (p. 123), they were referring to the structure of big corporations of the kind that we are familiar with today. The fact that certain companies are under the same ownership does not have anything to do with the type of commodities they produce. From this we can conclude that the way in which production is controlled has become so abstract that the same management would be equally capable of producing a whole range of different commodities.

The reference to the 'extreme concentration of mental forces' (p. 123) reflects somewhat the old notion of the progress of the forces of production, yet it is shown to result in the nature of the product becoming increasingly insignificant, in so far as this progress allows 'demarcation lines between different firms and technical branches to be ignored' (p. 123). Ever since the demise of manual production, it has no longer been necessary for capitalists to know anything about the goods in which they have invested, but now this has become particularly obvious. At one time, art was traditionally produced in the manner used by artisans – technically speaking, in a 'petit bourgeois' manner – with each piece of art treated as a unique product. The use of the production line stands in stark contrast to this.

At this point in the text, Adorno/Horkheimer slip in a sentence that immediately grabs our attention: 'The ruthless unity in the culture industry is evidence of what will happen in politics.' They use this analogy between culture industry and politics to round off their observations about the structure of big corporations and begin again with a different theme. The unity of politics that is alluded to can only consist of the neutralization of conflicting interests, as individuals are required to devote themselves to the 'common good'. (At the time that *Dialectic of Enlightenment* was being written, this meant devoting yourself to the *Volksgemeinschaft* of the fascists and Nazis, to the 'revolutionary' formation of the Soviet Union, or even to the anti-communist exclusion of 'un-American' elements in the United States.) Once again, it is a question of domination – of the false identity between the general and the particular. Individuals are compelled to subordinate themselves to the state, rather than being allowed to achieve autonomy. Adorno and Horkheimer's claim is rather vague – they are talking about 'what will happen' in politics, and culture industry is seen as a sign of what is to come. They leave it up to us to figure out exactly how politics and culture industry are related.

Whatever else we may conclude from it, the claim is a reminder of the fact that during their time in the US, Adorno carried out empirical research on the 'authoritarian personality', through which he hoped not least to explain the phenomenon of National Socialism in Germany. The claim bears witness to Adorno's belief that the social and personal preconditions for the rise of dictatorship were present in the US, just as they were in Europe. Even though Adorno does not refer to this directly, it is clear that culture industry and the way in which we are appropriated by it (first noticed by Adorno in Europe and then examined in more detail in the United States) represents a real political danger. The dismal condition of culture is only one manifestation of the general state of society and politics.

The remainder of the essay's first section deals in detail with the differentiations (in intellectual level etc.) made between the different groups of consumers that are served by the culture industry. The claim that Adorno failed to recognize the differences between consumers is therefore totally unfounded. In fact, the organization of the public into different categories that must be treated in different ways is one of the key characteristics of the culture industry's way of supplying its customers: 'Consumers appear as statistics on research organization charts, and are divided by income groups into red, green, and blue areas; the technique is that used for any type of propaganda' (p. 123). Just as with any other commodity, market research is undertaken, and the product is put on offer in a range of plain or luxurious varieties. Special offers are advertised for different groups. Adorno sums all this up in one decisive sentence: 'The varying budgets in the culture industry do not bear the slightest relation to factual values, to the meaning of the products themselves' (p. 124).

These differences are purely superficial – they are imposed by sales consultants, who have spent their time planning them, with the help of academic research. They all conform to the same criterion – that of 'conspicuous production': 'The universal criterion of merit is the amount of "conspicuous production", of blatant cash investment' (p. 124). The phrase 'conspicuous production' is a witty and well-targeted play on Thorstein Veblen's notion of 'conspicuous consumption'. In both cases, the main aim is demonstrative wastage: goods need to be expensive and eye-catching, no matter how uncomfortable, impractical and generally pointless they are. The product is made attractive by the fact that the management spared 'no effort or expense' in bringing it to us. (This was once the cry of the ringmaster at the circus, but there is certainly no lack of more up-to-date examples. Indeed, there is a certain type of Hollywood blockbuster that is promoted solely on the basis of the multi-million dollar sums that are swallowed up (or even poured away) in the course of its production.) We can link all this to the work of Bourdieu. Bourdieu analyses the way in which we consume culture in order to achieve social 'distinctions'. This type of cultural consumption is characteristic of culture industry. Although Bourdieu does not refer to it in these terms, his theory can be seen to describe the way in which culture industry society deals with the differentiations that are made within the range of goods on offer – differentiations that are built into the production process and of which the consumers are clearly aware. (By concentrating exclusively on the

social distinctions that we hope to achieve through the acquisition of
cultural artefacts, Bourdieu's theory fails to tell us anything about the
actual content of the goods on offer.)

Adorno's theory probes beyond the appearance of manufactured
variety to investigate the unifying principle of social integration that
lies behind it. At the end of the section, Adorno refers to this principle
as the self-glorifying 'triumph of invested capital' (p. 124). He describes
how each and every one of us is made to face the importance and
absoluteness of this triumph – as he rather melodramatically puts it,
the triumph of invested capital is 'etched deep into [our] hearts' (p.
124). If we read back through the section, we will notice that Adorno
has interpreted the culture industry in economic terms – his analysis
may not be particularly detailed, but the main contours of the argument are clearly visible. Nonetheless, Adorno refrains from investing
the economic factors with undue importance. The state of the economy
is also that of society. The latter is committed to preserving the order
imposed by wage labour and to maintaining the corresponding form
of political domination. This is not without consequence for our lives
as individuals (and so we see that these areas are all interconnected):
it is not our shared or individual needs, wishes, desires and interests
that form the criteria for social production. On the contrary, we are
compelled (on pain of social exclusion) to devote ourselves to the
'common good'.

It is clear then that it is not simply a case of culture industry manipulating us into a state of subordination. In fact, it is really a matter
of the whole of society being constructed in such a way that the
standardization of commodities (and in particular the commodity of
'labour power') is always already controlling us. While bourgeois
culture initially offered us a contradiction and a glimmer of resistance
(indeed, this resistance is inherent in the idea of bourgeois culture
and in particular art), culture industry *conforms* to the pattern of
domination.

Developments in the mode of production

Adorno's description of the capitalist mode of production is very
basic and only accounts for two different stages: the liberal phase
(autonomous small-time producers compete on a self-regulating
market), and the phase of monopoly capitalism (production is controlled centrally and the market is in practice non-existent). It is
amazing how much can be analysed just by using this quite coarse and
general description of the production of cultural commodities. These

days we have more precise tools at our disposal for describing the economic conditions of capitalist production and its variant forms.

The concept of monopoly capitalism soon came to trouble even Horkheimer and Adorno (as we can see from the revisions they made to the text). These days it is not monopoly capitalism, but rather the move to 'Fordism' that we tend to consider as the decisive change in capitalism (and in the production of cultural commodities).[10] The advent of mass production and mass consumption in capitalism led to the unexpected development of the culture industry, with the latter then becoming an essential component of the mode of production. Nowadays we work on the assumption that Fordism is being replaced by a different mode of production that is creating divisions within society and that is concentrating intensive consumption within one rich and stable economic segment. However, this is not true of our main medium, TV, and it only applies to certain elements of culture industry, that is, those requiring high levels of expertise and financial input. (The internet is perhaps one example of this.) Nonetheless, the theory of Fordism and our experience of it still provide us with a good basis from which to analyse the culture industry.

Another adjustment that we can make to Adorno's description of the capitalist mode of production is to distinguish more precisely between the different economic phases of the culture industry.[11] The transition to increasingly globalized 'oligopolies' that are no longer strongly associated with one particular medium has allowed TV to emerge as the main medium, around which the other media are grouped. It has also encouraged the development of new genres such as melodramatic soap operas and 'infotainment', as well as the emergence of 'special effects' films. Behind all this lie new strategies for organizing consumption, such as the 'invention of the teenager' and all that this involved (for example, for the music industry). There is also the continual struggle to achieve autonomy in production, undertaken by actors, writers and directors such as Charlie Chaplin, Woody Allen, Jim Jarmusch and even Clint Eastwood. This struggle has by no means been unsuccessful, and it has had – and still has – an impact on film production and on films themselves. Even though, or indeed precisely because the economy has been concentrated and globalized, spaces have been opened up (or at least left free) that can be used to achieve some form of autonomy.

Conducting a detailed analysis of the developments in the mainstream modes of production is important – not only in order to understand mainstream products, but also in order to comprehend the phenomena that try to distance themselves from the mainstream and put it to their own purpose, attempting to add their own touch to it.

Details in the forms of production for each medium can also affect the people directly involved in the production of that medium, for such details determine the conditions they will encounter in their struggle to win control over the means of production and to secure autonomy for themselves and their products. The economic details of production show that although culture has been appropriated, it is still in various ways a disputed territory between production and reception. Looking at the 'cultural' details of production (although not neglecting the underlying economic structures) allows us to seek out the contradictory elements of culture industry. Continuing the analysis of culture industry in this way is not a betrayal of Adorno's intentions. Instead, making the analysis more specific helps support Adorno's theory and helps us to work towards reflexivity.

Field notes VI   Exoticism and music

The term 'exoticism' describes our enjoyment of colonial commodities – it refers to a form of domination that we actually take pleasure in exercising. In the case of music, exoticism takes the form of terribly banal 'steps across the border'. In practice, this means that colourful drops of folk-music from countries around the world are built into the computer-generated stream of continual noise that is the basis of music in culture industry.

Rather than proceeding to define 'exoticism', I am going to provide a few examples. These examples were all taken from the mass media, and they are of the kind that you might come across any evening while watching TV or reading the paper. The first example of 'exoticism' comes from an article published in the *Frankfurter Rundschau*.[12] The article deals with the Rödelheim Hartreim Projekt [the Rödelheim Hard-Rhyming Project], a Frankfurt hip-hop duo, whose exoticism functions in two directions at once, utilizing both the foreign and the familiar. They have the appeal of the 'foreign', for they give themselves over to the myth that casts hip-hop as the music of black American kids from the ghetto. In promoting this story of origin (which is probably only partly true even in America), the German duo are appropriating a foreign biography – a tale of disadvantage that is not their own. However, the duo's exoticism also draws on the familiar, for the singers stress their local roots (Rödelheim is the name of a district in Frankfurt, Germany), and so cash in on their native homeland. The article in the *Frankfurter Rundschau* describes how the duo – and thus the district of Rödelheim – are becoming increasingly well known. It also recommends the duo's latest CD. In an earlier article that appeared in *Der Spiegel*, one of the duo, Thomas H., was confronted with the reproach that German rap does not spring from the ghetto, but from the middle classes. Thomas H. responded very well: 'The middle classes? That's just not true. In fact, the two of us are distinctly upper class.'[13]

In the magazine *Die Zeit* I found an interview with the singer Aziza Mustafa Zadeh.[14] The piece was entitled 'Mystik' [Mysticism], and it concluded with the details (including the price) of Zadeh's latest CD, *Seventh Truth*, which readers were then supposed to go out and buy. In the interview, Zadeh asks the reporter to make sure he writes something 'original' about her. She describes *Seventh Truth* as the 'path to God'. The reporter tells us: 'A mix of jazz, Bach, and Muslim folklore, it features wonderfully drawn out notes that rise and fall and that the singer has taken from the Islamic call to prayer. Or perhaps the Muslims borrowed it from her?' The reporter then goes on to tell us about Zadeh: 'Just like a real mystic, Zadeh laughs at every possible opportunity. She claims that the sick have been healed just by attending her concerts . . .' And so the article continues, till it ends abruptly in its commercial conclusion.

'Exoticism' is even being used by so-called exotic women as a way of making money.

If we are looking for extreme cases of 'exoticizing' the familiar, then we need search no further than the Bavarian folk musicians, yodellers and other country musicians that appear in duos, trios, sibling groups and child combos. The groups' names testify to their local, countrified flavour, and their music meets with commercial success. Such music also sells well when combined with electronic instruments and a rock beat. It would not occur to anyone to associate this kind of music (or the forms of it that appear on TV) with real folk-music. That is why the chosen category used to describe it is 'country' music.

However, we will also find evidence of exoticism if we examine the example of jazz. Once considered as purely subcultural music, jazz became the only truly international form of music. In the 1930s, it was the dominant idiom of dance music. It is forever being recast as the music of dissent, and it is always being reclaimed from the lofty heights of respectable academia to be used in the everyday attitudes of 'rhythm and blues', 'funk' and 'soul'. One feature of jazz that is particularly conducive to exoticism is the legend of the (racially) shunned genius who draws on the discrimination, pain and depression that he or she has been forced to suffer in order to create this wonderfully melancholy and/or angry music.

It suits exotic elements to figure as colourful flecks in the otherwise homogeneous internationalized music business. The fact that these elements are then immediately appropriated by the business comes as no surprise. It is common knowledge now that 'outsider' status can be a successful sales ploy in culture industry – there are no new and shocking revelations to be made on this count. The real question is whether it is at all possible to escape forced integration into the business.

Two examples: Broadlahn and Charlie Parker The example set by the Austrian group *Broadlahn* in their two pieces 'Gastarbeiterroute' [Guest worker road] and 'Abdullah Ibrahim in der Steiermark' [Abdullah Ibrahim in Styria, Austria] (from the CD *Broadlahn*, The Fab Records, 1990) indicates a way out of the problem: the meeting between different cultures can itself be taken up as a theme, and what is familiar can be made to seem foreign. This is what happens in both of these songs. Melodies that are strongly reminiscent of Alpine folk music are developed in exotic directions – sometimes sounding Turkish or Oriental and at other times more African or jazzy. What is more, this combination proves to be most enjoyable. The foreign music seems more energetic and is rhythmically and melodically more exciting. The local music seems melancholic and very exotic. Both songs are accompanied by a commentary:

Guest Worker Road
It was at the services off the guest workers' road in the 1960s that for the first time folk musicians from Styria came face to face with folk musicians (the so-called 'guest workers') from Turkey, Greece and Persia. Without prompt- ing, they started to play, their melodies combining and competing.

Abdullah Ibrahim in Styria
Abdullah Ibrahim, formerly known as Dollar Brand, hailed far and wide as the best musician in Africa, was passing through Styria when he encountered for the very first time a group of local farmers. The farmers were sitting at the edge of the woods, dressed in nothing but their traditional leather trousers, and were . . . yodelling. 'The sight of the primitive people sitting naked in their natural environment is an unforgettable experience,' thought Abdullah Ibrahim. He yodelled back and they began to make music together.[15]

The familiar becomes exotic, while the foreign appears familiar. The meeting between familiar and foreign is presented with great insight, but this is something that not even this group always succeeds in doing. In fact, *Broadlahn* usually presents the local environment in a thoroughly sentimental manner, even if the group does include regular hints as to the underlying everyday nature of its 'exoticized' home- land.

At this point, I would like to examine the phenomenon anew, this time with reference to Charlie Parker's 'Lover Man', as recorded on 29 July 1946. I arrived at the following interpretation of the piece with the help of a group of students, none of whom was previously familiar with the record- ing. We found that the most noticeable feature of the piece was the way in which the saxophonist is utterly absorbed in himself and his music. Parker shuts the listeners out, giving us the impression that we are eaves- dropping on a moment of intimacy and making us feel almost ashamed for doing so. As a group, we found Parker's music to be 'caustic' and 'aggressive' and we talked of it in terms of 'ironicized kitsch'. As a matter of fact, it is true that this piece does stand out for the way it unpicks the hackneyed melody with minimal effort, as well as for the repeatedly delayed entries,[16] the sharp tone and for the only occasional transitions into short and intensive runs. It is also noticeable how the pianist takes care to prepare the entries and how, towards the end, the trumpet ensures that the piece holds together and that it is rounded off – it is a secondary element in the music, but it provides the foundations that support what is in fact an extremely self-absorbed solo.

As jazz fans will know, Parker was suffering from withdrawal symptoms at the time of the recording. He had been addicted to heroin since his youth, and was using alcohol to help stifle the cravings. He had not wanted the recording to be released. It is only thanks to the routine he had established, as well as to his talent and to the support of his co-musicians that he was able to play, and play so well. In spite of everything, this recording is much better than several of Parker's other renditions of 'Lover Man'. It is better than recordings such as that of 8 August 1951 (with Red Rodney, John Lewis, Ray Brown and Kenny Clarke), during which John Lewis intrudes into the foreground with playful flourishes, while Parker plays almost entirely on the beat. This recording is almost regimentally in key, and the tone is noticeably softer, becoming rougher in only two of the entries (including the first one). Parker is a virtuoso, but this time the improvisation is entirely typical of his style. The piece's conclusion seems artificial and childish in its frivolity. All in all, it creates the kind of atmosphere that you would find in a concert-hall. What we are listening to is a sleek and entirely conventional artistic performance. We remain at a distance from the music.

Knowing the circumstances surrounding the recording of 'Lover Man' on 29 July 1946 has a curious effect on us as listeners – an effect that we can examine by analysing the corresponding scene in Clint Eastwood's film about Parker, *Bird* (1988). The impression of drug-induced misery begins to overshadow the quality of the music and the talent of the musicians. All of a sudden, we know exactly what it was that we were listening in on – it was the private pain of a man who is ill. Admittedly, this is not something that we can pick up on from the music itself. Once we know about Parker's addiction, what we hear is no longer an interesting moment of withdrawn self-interrogation carried out between the player and his instrument, but a moment of impairment and agony. What we have done is exactly what is encouraged by *Bird* and by the whole Parker legend (as well as by the Billie Holiday legend, the Chet Baker legend, the Art Pepper legend, the Janis Joplin legend and the Jimi Hendrix legend, etc.) – we have done the music and the musician an injustice by reducing good music to human suffering. What is more, we have already made a correlation between the two things, reaching a conclusion that Parker for one always strenuously rejected; without drugs, he would have played even better.

The drugs legend surrounding jazz musicians, blues singers and rock stars (in particular black jazz musicians, blues singers and rock stars) is the touristy kind of exoticism that is encouraged by culture industry. However, we can escape the voyeurism that is being imposed on us by trying to separate the music from the legend and by listening to it on its own terms, analysing it in relation to our own situation as listeners. Presenting the musicians in the context of their musical ability is something that a non-touristy jazz film should aim to do.[17]

The jazz legend is still alive in the experiences of discrimination frequently recounted by white musicians: white musicians still have to defend themselves against the assumption that only black musicians can play jazz. However, the relation of well-educated, urban Afro-American musicians of today to their rural slave forefathers is no less complicated than is that of contemporary well-educated, urban whites to their peasant or working-class ancestors. The myth of the black jazz player has little to do with the historical reality of the African slaves, and the ability to play good jazz has similarly little to do with current instances of discrimination. I have never heard the problem (or indeed its solution) addressed so frankly as by the blues singer Doug MacLeod. In the liner notes to his CD *Come to Find* (Audioquest Music, 1994), he describes a conversation that he had once had with a black blues musician:

> I told him, man, I don't know anything about picking cotton or anything like that, but I really like this music. What should I do? And I'll never forget what he told me. He said, 'write about what you know. Write the truth, and don't ever play a note you don't believe.' He said, 'Doug, haven't you ever been lonely? Ever been scared? Ever been broke? Well, write about that!' And ever since that time I've tried to sing about things I really knew about, and to be more selective in my choice of material.

Doug MacLeod succeeds in avoiding exoticism by concerning himself with his own story of oppression and by refusing to adopt somebody else's. We take Parker seriously because we take his musical achievements seriously. In jazz that always means that we take seriously the achievements of the situation – achievements that cannot be ascribed to one person but only to a collaboration. This means that we look beyond the one person of genius. If we want to take Parker seriously, we must avoid seeing him in culture industry terms as a figure of genius who was discriminated against and who despaired of the way his talent went unrecognized. We must refrain from making him a figure of fake heroism or false pity, and instead engage with 'Lover Man' as the evidence of a felicitous coincidence of tone, phrasing, improvisation and cooperation. If we have to see it as an expression of distress, then we should see it as the expression of a distress that has been overcome in music – we should admire it as evidence of human ability, and not pity it as the product of destructive social forces.

We can situate what is foreign in a kind of false proximity to us, asserting our right to care for and protect it. We can also relegate what is foreign into a falsely distant sphere, declaring that it has nothing in common with us at all. We can even lend a false proximity to our place of origin, refusing to acknowledge its strangeness.

However, what we can do is to create a degree of strangeness towards others that will allow us to avoid and criticize both intrusive appropriation *and* rejection based on the refusal to empathize. This is the political task that we face, and not just in relation to music.

Working alliances in the cultural history of the twentieth century: bourgeois, modern, avant-garde and reflexive

In Vienna in the early twentieth century, Schoenberg was trying to achieve autonomy for his art and control over his audience, in line with the model of 'public aloofness'. At roughly the same time in Zurich, the Cabaret Voltaire was taking shape. Founded in 1916 at no. 1 Spiegelgasse, the Cabaret aimed to dupe, irritate and shock the public through its performances and recitations. It was made up of young emigrants who had arrived in Switzerland before World War I – and who had 'abused' the country's hospitality, as the authorities of the time were wont to claim. (Of course, these days the authorities' attitude towards foreigners is so much more enlightened and humane – not just in Switzerland, but also elsewhere!) These young emigrants had realized what a ridiculous part art and culture were playing in the war. In 1914 even the educated classes had been gripped by war fever. Elderly existentialists such as Richard Dehmel were prompted to march into battle, and enlightened aesthetes and reflective sociologists such as Georg Simmel took to making patriotic speeches. (On the other hand, one outraged observer, Sigmund Freud, was catalysed into discovering the death drive.) All this led the artists of the Cabaret to conclude that, if high culture (and in particular German high culture) could not save its best minds from such madness, its end was surely nigh. (World War II and the Shoah provided further, more radical and more brutal proof of this: high culture is clearly not the opposite of barbarism and it certainly offers no protection against it.)[18] The artists' sense of outrage at the debased situation of the intelligentsia, as well as at the destructive work of the propaganda machine (which was intent on mowing down everything in its path, silencing all rational protest) led to a new relationship emerging between the artists on the one hand, and art and its public on the other. To the artists, there seemed no reason why either art or its public should still be taken seriously. Why shouldn't artists lash out at the public? How could they possibly attract attention to themselves, other than by breaking taboos, offending people's sense of decency and mocking respectable opinion? Why shouldn't they confront the public with the unreasonable nature of its demands and expectations of 'art', when 'art' has in any case long since been debased? Why shouldn't they rub the public's face in the hypocrisy and pretentiousness of 'learnedness' and respectable society? Why shouldn't they confront it with their rage?

Out of this combination of arrogance, scorn, anger and the desire to provoke was born a new attitude towards the public sphere, the public and art itself. Indeed, art was no longer to be understood in terms of individual 'works' of art. It is no coincidence that this attitude was developed through the performance of scenes and recitations, that is, in the context of 'art as an event' that came to replace the framework of 'art as individual artworks'. Art now meant confronting the public with situations that would allow it to find out something about itself and about its expectations of what art should do. Art also meant placing artists in experimental situations and seeing how they extracted themselves from the affair. This type of art does not lead to the production of permanent artefacts – what is produced is at most the trace of an event and it only interests us in the context of that event. Consequently, even the act of painting can become an event.

At this point, we should add that this understanding of art could hardly have been more different from Adorno's own. Although it is perfectly possible to understand music as an audio event, Adorno always gave the score priority. (While if we understand music as an audio event, the score is nothing more than the means to enable the reproduction of this event.) In Adorno's view, when we listen to music, we experience its composition – the piece is 'composed anew' [*nachkomponiert*]. As such, Adorno's aesthetics are clearly an aesthetics of the artwork. Artistic developments in the latter part of the twentieth century (as well as those in the earlier decades that Adorno either failed to acknowledge or chose to reject) cannot be understood in these terms. What we need today is an 'aesthetics of interaction' that does justice to each and every party involved in the event. From the current vantage point, it is clear that the 'work of art' was a unique development that was predominant in bourgeois art alone. Before the bourgeois era, there was no question of an abstracted work of art that might be transferred out of the church or marketplace and into a location designed especially for viewing art (now known as the 'museum'). By the time Dadaism appeared on the scene, the era in which the work of art had dominated was definitely over, and the event had taken centre stage.[19]

Now that we have gone some way towards contextualizing the situation, we can proceed to compile a historically informed typology of working alliances. These will express the fundamental contradiction within art, namely 'autonomy versus commodification' or 'truth in the experience of art versus culture industry'. This contradiction is a product of society, and it issues from the conflict between intellectual and material production within the context of commodification. It is the conflict between the 'educated classes' and the 'owners of the means of production' within the bourgeois class – between the professions (motivated by politics) and the business people and managers (motivated by economics). In sum, it is the conflict between the educated and the wealthy sections of the bourgeoisie. The historical types of artistic and other intellectual working alliances consist of the different attempts to work out this conflict. They express the various possible degrees of this tension, and they may be combined together or modified, never appearing in pure form.

(1) Let us start with the *'representative'* or *'classic bourgeois'* working alliance. Under its regime, the work of art is created autonomously by the artist as an expression of his or her individuality. There is a 'truth' to the work of art, in that it represents an external or internal reality, as created by an artist who has mastered the medium to perfection. The artist (or 'genius') and his or her extraordinary creation are kept strictly separate, as are the artist and the public, who in the best-case scenario will be receptive to the artist's work. In order to glimpse something of the divine spirit that animates the work of art, the public has to approach it respectfully and with devotion and patience, using its cultural knowledge to engage with it. The work of art is autonomous with regard to space and time – in the form of a painting, it can, for example, be transported from one place or era to the next, without any change in its meaning. In fact, its ability to 'stand the test of time' is seen as proof of its importance. The institution of the museum is the main place for presenting art, and art can only be viewed properly under the conditions that it offers, such as neutral surroundings, calm and individual displays.

(2) The *avant-garde* working alliance: the avant-garde attitude to art and the public is concerned with instruction in the broadest possible sense. It makes use of the familiar paradox that the teacher is working in the interest of the pupil, albeit independent from the latter's wishes and often even against them. The teacher knows best about what is good for the pupil. In art, this translates as instructing the public in (and about) its 'best interests'. Sometimes this leads to what is in many ways a very enlightened relationship between parties that are actually very unequal in terms of experience. At other times, it results in the public being manipulated into a situation in which it is only allowed to think and do 'what's right'.

When considering all this, we should bear in mind the original meaning of 'avant-garde', for it is a political term that has nothing to do with the current usage that equates 'avant-garde' with the 'latest trend' or a 'fairly radical stance'. Historically speaking, after the bourgeois revolution, the cultural avant-garde was made up of engineers and other kinds of technological experts who were responsible for enlightened progress and the progress of Enlightenment. The second important historical meaning of 'avant-garde' lies in Lenin's understanding of the party as the avant-garde of proletarian emancipation – if need be, the avant-garde would form a small circle of conspirators who would precipitate revolution and would lead the masses in the necessary uprisings and battles. Avant-garde intellectuals are those who work unselfishly in the service of progress and in the service of those who will benefit from progress (and who, if they had not been blinded by oppression and false consciousness, would be fighting for it themselves). Such beneficence is by no means harmless.[20]

This avant-garde working alliance takes on various forms in art. In some cases, it can take the form of a fairly loose association of (likeminded) producers and their audiences. In others, it can appear as an utterly manipulative form of power play in which the public is 'stirred up' and 'mobilized' in a populist fashion. (The most obvious examples of this are political speeches addressed to the masses and other such forms of political propaganda.) The avant-garde working alliance is embodied by people such as party intellectuals who openly combine power and didacticism, but also by those who have 'betrayed their class' and who use the knowledge they have gained about domination through their membership of the ruling class in order to promote liberation. In cultural terms, this working alliance often appears in combination with other working alliances, for example as 'avant-garde public aloofness' (as in the case of Hanns Eisler) or as 'avant-garde reflexivity' (of which Brecht's theatre and poetry provide the most striking examples). Examples from the realm of the fine arts include Constructivism and Suprematism, with artists such as Malevich, Tatlin, Rodchenko, and Stepanova, who tried to use abstraction in order to promote revolution. This meant using design as the expression of a new society and deploying it for the purpose of achieving a better life. It meant working towards the revolutionary struggle with artistic means, and it was eventually halted in Russia by the emergence of 'Stalinist realism'.

(3) With the continued development of culture industry in the nineteenth century, the notion of 'high art' lost all credibility. The *modern* working alliance of 'public aloofness' (discussed above with reference to Schoenberg) can be seen as an extreme case of the 'representative' (or 'classic bourgeois') working alliance, arrived at via an increased emphasis on 'art for art's sake'. It was an attempt (analogous to the social figure of the dandy) to withdraw from culture industry and from a public that pursued 'cheap pleasures'. Its aim was to maintain the

importance of art by propelling it into ever more esoteric heights. This working alliance is characterized by the artist's withdrawal from the general public and by the turn towards small groups of disciples, experts and aficionados who were happy to conform to the demands that were made of them. There are still some manifestations of this today, for instance in withdrawn literary sages such as Peter Handke. On occasions, Miles Davis actually played out this working alliance by performing with his back to the audience. Nonetheless, the 'modern' working alliance is certainly not the dominant form of working alliance.

(4) In fact, the 'modern' attempt to gain autonomy from culture industry was soon superseded by the *reflexive* working alliance: the conditions of artistic production and reception became the subject-matter for art. In the reflexive working alliance, the artist does not attempt to avoid culture industry and the public (and in particular the public's culture industry mode of reception), but tries rather to make these things more visible. It is important to remember that the necessary precondition for this was the shift from art as the individual 'artwork' to art as an event. This is clear in relation to the Dadaists' performances and to the Surrealists' attempts to shock the public. It also appears rather more subtly in Duchamp's displays, such as his 'ready-mades' that take art and the public's interest in art as their subject-matter. It is evident in the 'happening', and in the work of the Viennese actionists, such as Mühl, Brus, Nitsch and Schwarzkogler. It is even clearer in Joseph Beuys's 'social sculptures' and in the 'wrapping' initiatives of Christo and Jeanne-Claude where the artistic event includes the whole process: from the initial idea, through the bureaucratic and technical hitches, right up to the temporary realization of the project and its final dismantling, including the reaction it meets with among all those involved.

In all of these examples, there's no longer any kind of artefact that could be hung on a gallery wall or purchased by a collector. At most, the artistic event leaves a 'trace' – a mere memory of what occurred during a particular period of time between an artist and other participants, and in some cases some kind of medium. The public become participants in the event – they are drawn in and they are worked upon. Usually, the events will lead them to think about what art and the institution of art really mean – what it means to exhibit or spectate, and what the audience desires and where these desires originate from. There is another element to this working alliance that is rather more uncomfortable for the spectators. For the first time in the history of art, negative emotions (such as aggression, hatred, anger, scorn and envy, etc.) are played out openly between the different parties. In many cases, these emotions then become the subject-matter of art, which may mean that we can allow ourselves to be amused by them. On other occasions (as in TV shows that involve the audience) the negative emotions are lived out by the participants. The audience is supposed to laugh at itself in a more or less good-natured fashion, while it is being shown to be voyeuristic and cruel, insatiable in its thirst for scandal, and devoid of any concern for the dignity (and even the safety and life) of the artist. Sometimes the audience is made to seem stupid and far too easy to entertain, appreciative of material that is really quite silly. The audience is condemned and attacked. There is no right way of reacting to such insults.

The development of reflexivity in the twentieth century

The 'reflexive' working alliance and art as an 'event' developed in Dadaism and Surrealism out of the problems surrounding the struggle to attract attention within a loud, crowded and hardened public sphere. (At the time of Dada in Zurich, the focus was on the war fever surrounding World War I and on the widespread indifference to the possible death of a whole generation of young men. It was due to these developments that the members of the Cabaret first emigrated.) Scandals were now the only way of attracting attention – the public had to be shocked into seeing the truth. This was the reason for the introduction of forms of performance, of events, of situations and of happenings that were designed to act directly on the audience. A working alliance of 'participation and reflection' emerged. In the context of a cultural market that demanded artefacts (and more specifically 'high-class commodities': artefacts that were one-off, high quality and valuable, as well as being difficult to produce and to comprehend), this was already an act of subversion.

Surrealist art took seriously the idea that artists express the unconscious (both that of the artist and of society) in their work – what made art remarkable was its power to reach beyond the conscious mind and the control exercised by it. In Surrealism, artists tried to organize events in such a way as to ensure that the unexpected could occur – the material should be allowed to express things that were neither intended nor planned. The artist and the audience are exposed to experimental situations. One extreme version of this is the type of experiment in which the artist risks or incurs injury. (Chris Burden allowed himself to be shot at, while Gina Pane and Marina Abramovic invited the audience to watch while they inflicted wounds on themselves.) Such experiments are a form of self-discovery and also an attempt to find out just what can occur in the context of 'art' before the spectators change the rules and start trying to prevent the artists from hurting themselves.

At the same time as all this, Marcel Duchamp was working on his own unique projects. It was he who pursued the dimension of reflexivity most consistently. Duchamp focused on art as a way of imparting insight into the process through which something is defined as 'art'. He saw art as a way of drawing attention to the norms of 'art appreciation' and to the expectations and wishes that are mobilized when we approach something that we have identified as 'art'. His first projects of this kind were the 'ready-mades' – a variant form of the 'objet trouvé'. Contrary to what many people think and indeed thought at the time, his famous *Fountain* does not demonstrate the beauty of industrially produced objects (such as the urinal he exhibited as *Fountain*), but demonstrates instead how anything can be turned into 'art' just by placing it in an 'artistic' context (that is, by displaying it at an exhibition). *Fountain* is the archetypal exercise in reflexivity.

In fact, Duchamp had already done this in his early Cubist paintings, or at least in one of them, entitled *Nude Descending a Staircase*. Other paintings of this ilk, such as *Sad Young Man on a Train* (a painting that many identify as a self-portrait) did not attract much attention, yet *Nude Descending a Staircase* caused a real scandal at the Armory Show in New York in 1913. In fact, what these paintings are doing is nothing more exciting than trying to solve the problem of painting motion by using a particular technique, namely that of multiple images – a method used by various painters of the time. However, *Nude Descending a Staircase* provoked a scandal because it frustrates our expectations of 'nudes'. It is scandalous because it makes us aware of the erotic pleasure that we gain from watching – it draws our attention to the eye as an organ of sexual pleasure. Duchamp played with this theme in many of his products, and it is dealt with in an extreme way in his last work, the installation *Étant donnés* (1966). This installation forces the spectators to become voyeurs. In some art books, the photos of this installation only show what the spectators can see inside – they show a nude female form, but without the old wooden door and the two holes you have to look through, and without the crack that you are forced to wedge your nose into. Such photos completely miss the point of the installation. In fact, trying to reproduce the installation on paper is in any case impossible, since a photo of the installation cannot reproduce the situation of shame that the spectator is placed in. Indeed, Duane Hanson's life-size sculptures are similarly impossible to reproduce on paper, for the point of the sculptures is the sense of insecurity that overcomes us when we move around among them, uncertain at times whether we are looking at another visitor or just at a sculpture, and not knowing if we will be mistaken for a statue if we stay in one place for too long.

The new working alliance of the twentieth century is one of participation and reflexivity – 'I will put you in a situation in which you will be presented with material that will allow you to reflect on the meaning of art and its consumption.' This working alliance of reflexivity also links art to culture industry in an entirely new way. It is no longer a case of trying to avoid culture industry by escaping into 'loftier heights' (an approach that is in any case doomed to failure), but rather a matter of taking an interest in what happens in culture industry and of actively adopting culture industry media, forms and content. Artists no longer stand on the stage with their backs to the audience – the audience is drawn in and made to participate. It is subjected to aggressive attacks, it is exposed, it is confronted and it is duped. It is shown ugly, revolting and taboo material that is guaranteed to shock it, and it is presented with puzzles that will make it lose its confidence. It is encouraged to participate in the irony and the derision, and it is asked to join in the bitter laughter about the media, art, society and itself.

After World War II, the dominant form of art was a type of abstract art that clearly aligned itself with the 'modern' working alliance. (Take Kandinsky or Mondrian, for example.) The 'reflexive' working alliance played only a secondary role. (This is not to say that it disappeared entirely – in fact, it continued in the work of artists such as Max Ernst, Magritte and Duchamp, whose fame and reputation were rising.) In the 1960s, 'reflexive' art increased in importance, especially in the neo-Dada movement, including Yves Klein and Piero Manzoni and the music of John Cage. Gradually, it regained its status as the dominant form of art, with Joseph Beuys in Europe, 'happenings' in Europe and the States, and Pop Art, first in the United States and then elsewhere. It is certainly fair to say that Warhol was working within the framework of an artistic tradition, namely that of the 'reflexive' working alliance. It is only if he is seen in terms of the 'modern' working alliance, that is, in comparison to Pollock, de Kooning, Rothko or LeWitt, artists with whom he had little in common, that he appears to be radically new and different.[21]

The art movement of the 1960s is sometimes described in terms of a 'return of the avant-garde' (and of the political dimension associated with the avant-garde). However, if by 'avant-garde' we mean something more than 'the latest trend' (that is, if we distinguish between the different types of working alliance, as outlined above), we will find little evidence to support this comparison. Even in the politically orientated student movement, the anti-authoritarian fraction was clearly aligned with the reflexive working alliance. (In France and Germany, it was also directly linked to Situationism as a surviving form of surrealism, as well as to the format of the happening.) It was only in the dogmatic groups that formed after the breakdown of the anti-authoritarian movement that avant-garde attitudes emerged. (These dogmatic groups reproduced the struggles and the methods of the labour movement in the form of farce, but with regrettable consequences and sometimes at a terribly high price.)

Since then, it has become even clearer that what was 'new and different' about the cultural history of the last century was the emergence of forms of reflexivity, both within culture industry and in reaction to it. It was this that marked the twentieth century, right up to and including the work of contemporary artists such as Koons. (Jeff Koons's art embraces the world with a postmodern lack of selectivity and once again takes as its object art's self-proclaimed commercial basis.) Nonetheless, there is no reason to see this as a definitive break with 'modernity'. On the contrary, these different approaches exist alongside one another, even appearing in combination. Of course, this is only true if by 'modernity' we mean a distinct form of intellectual working alliance and not a temporal movement. (In most discussions about 'modernity' and 'postmodernity', 'modernity' is described in chronological terms as a movement that began at the beginning of the twentieth century and that had its origins in the era of Enlightenment. This type of temporal definition makes no attempt to describe the nature of the 'modern'.) In conclusion: if we, first, distinguish between the 'modern' working alliance of 'public aloofness' and the separate working alliances of 'reflexivity' and the avant-garde, and second, focus in on the relationship between art and culture industry, we will be able to arrive at the following overview:

* The main element in intellectual and artistic development is the dialectic of autonomy and culture industry.
* We can distinguish between the different phases and styles within art and culture by identifying which form of the attempt to gain autonomy was dominant in each one.
* In every type of 'working alliance', there are manifestations of 'selling out'. 'Public aloofness' can lead to elitism and to 'exclusivity' and 'high performance' – two characteristics that are frequently used to market commodities. Using shock methods and breaking taboos in order to achieve 'reflexivity' can lead to art becoming sensationalized. On the other hand, it is clear from this that the forms of autonomy originate in and develop from certain features of the

commodity. It is evident, therefore, that there is no strict separation from culture industry, but rather a dialectical relationship.

• In a certain sense, the various announcements about the 'end of art' or about the start of an entirely new phase of intellectual development are themselves a culture industry manoeuvre. This aside, we can use them to find out whether they are symptomatic of a change that is taking place in the dominant working alliance.

Field notes VII   The obsolescence of high culture's critique of society: the case of Carolee Schneemann

Carolee Schneemann was once a prominent happening-artist renowned for her scandalous creations. These days, she has become much quieter. In her late fifties and made up to look pale, she sits on the panel at a discussion forum on the women of Dada. All around her are bronzed, younger people and female academics. The latter are well practised in the art of mobilizing the political gains of the women's movement and then using them to their advantage. On this particular occasion, they are busy analysing the macho attitude of Duchamp and Man Ray. They are merciless in their determination to reveal how the women in the New York Dada group were oppressed. This oppression consisted in everyone being mad on Duchamp, and Duchamp being mad on Rrose Sévaly. Carolee Schneemann describes what a woman from within this tradition could do in the 1960s and in the following years. She tells of how 'sexy' the men in the group were – men whom she first met when they were already advancing in years.

Downtown in the New Museum the centrepiece attraction is a retrospective Schneemann installation *Up to and including her limits*. One corner of the room is covered with white paper that reaches along the walls and floor in all three directions. The paper is covered in what seem at first to be fairly 'meaningless' coloured lines. In the middle, there is a rope hanging down with two loops. To the right and to the left there is a stack of monitors that are showing snippets of the happening taken at different moments in time. The traces of the happening are evident in the coloured lines. On the screens, you see a young woman hanging naked on a swinging and twisting rope, her feet in the two loops and crayons in her hands. As she swings through the air, she draws lines with the crayons. In order to reach up higher, she has to stretch out and launch her body towards the walls – gravity is not exactly helping. What you cannot see and what you have to have been told is the sheer duration of the happening that took place in 1973 and in which Carolee Schneemann pushed herself to the point of exhaustion.

As far as the content is concerned, the happening fits into the category of the kind of artistic self-representation where the artist shows himself or herself to be vulnerable and exposed – it is art as torture and obsession. The installation now shows the traces – uneven yet almost delicate, wild and yet determined – of an action that at the time must have been extremely embarrassing to watch, given the presence of a naked (and probably sweating and groaning) woman who was torturing herself and gradually becoming weaker and weaker. The temptation to look or walk away in order to put an end to it all must have been great, yet the beautiful naked body will also have exercised its fascination. Thus the spectators' voyeurism and the violence and cruelty of their position will have been made unmistakably evident. The images on the screens allow us to imagine all this, but without the presence of the woman the installation is now calm, sublimated and almost sterile. Only the rope serves to remind us of the chamber of horrors. The refined traces of the crayon show no correlation to the violence that was involved in their production. Yet the pictures of the artist's exhaustion and the traces are presented together, and we experience them through this discrepancy.

The installation reveals the same contradiction that can be sensed during Schneemann's lecture, for Schneemann, as everyone is bound to have commented, is still a 'very beautiful woman'. It is not easy to forget about the exhibitionist masochistic female form when listening to the considered explanation of the woman. The installation is as pale as Schneemann's current make-up and it seems to deny all knowledge of the sado-masochistic obscenity and the harsh nature of the work that went into its production. The monitors, on the other hand, bear witness to all this. In both cases, the observers are allowed to aestheticize the situation, but as soon as they have done so, they are forced to feel ashamed of it.

The similarity with Duchamp's *Étant donnés* of 1966 is difficult to miss (despite the fact that Duchamp's installation was begun some twenty years earlier). There is no other installation in which the observer is transformed more shamefully into a voyeur than in *Étant donnés*. The spectator peeks through two holes in an old door, sticking his or her nose into a convenient crack in the door and catching sight of a supine female form; the head and the face are not visible, but a crack between the legs can be seen that is anatomically impossible and that seems to bear more resemblance to the shadowy area in the same place on Man Ray's photo of Baroness von Freytag-Loringhoven 'after she had shaved off her pubic hair'. In the Philadelphia museum, visitors (both male and female) usually look over their shoulders as they walk away, trying to find out if anybody else has seen what they have done. It is a case of pure voyeurism – with our noses pressed into a crack in the door, we become intensely aware of the pleasure (a 'masculine' pleasure, but one that is not entirely alien to women) that we derive from viewing subordinated, alienated and naked females. This pleasure becomes a disgrace to us. We can usually aestheticize and thus banish the embarrassment that art causes us. Now this embarrassment becomes coarse and all-encompassing.

Schneemann adds another dimension to all this – she presents artistic work as a painful struggle and shows the work of art to be the result of tremendous effort, suffering and violence. This is clearly a fundamental weakness of high culture and its manual mode of production: its critique of the violent conditions of production (that elsewhere have long since become more abstract) is already obsolete. An analogous installation showing the shabby elegance of a mass-produced plastic bathtub along-side screened pictures of the violence involved in its production would not reveal sweating heroes of labour, but equally elegant robots who complete the process with efficiency. We do not have to feel ashamed about late-industrial production – or in any case it would be almost impossible to illus-trate the reasons as to why we should do so.

There is not even any possibility of salvaging high culture's critique of production by considering it in relation to housework. The analogy would be as flawed as is the notion that the housewife is 'exploited' by her wage-earning husband. (In Marxian terms, 'exploitation' is designed to describe a structure and not a personal relationship. Only the law (or in any case the Austrian law) is careless enough to refer to 'exploitation' in connec-tion with pimping.)

The petit-bourgeois mode of production used in art means that high art is incapable of producing any kind of valid critique of the relations of production in other areas, such as those in industry. (Of course, it would be possible to claim that this petit-bourgeois mode of production is the least alienated and therefore the most desirable mode of production. This would not be entirely erroneous, but historically – and also more recently in what was called 'alternative economy' – this mode has always failed as a generalized form.) Art is more successful as a critique of relations of pro-duction when it limits itself to presenting its own working alliance of exhi-bitionism and voyeurism in such a way as to allow observers to see and reflect on it. That alone is no small task.

4

What is wrong with consensual entertainment?

Amusement – 'released from every restraint' or the 'prolongation of work'?

Visitors to New York soon notice that this is a place in which the goals of contentment, job satisfaction and 'fully functional' relationships appear imminently attainable. This optimism is evident in everything from people's daily conversations to the television commercials: New Yorkers never go so far as to claim that they have actually attained real happiness, but they do talk a lot about 'managing' themselves and about dealing with emotional issues in a way that is reasonable, open-minded and considered. They are forever exchanging tips and advice on how this can be accomplished. The key to success involves ensuring that you always get your required amount of entertainment and amusement. Leading your life in a disciplined fashion means apportioning the right dose of undisciplined time wasting. Of course, this would not have met with the approval of the American heroes of bourgeois self-discipline from the time of the Pilgrim Fathers onwards: for them, going to church and taking part in the life of the community were the only activities that should be allowed to interrupt an honest day's work. Entertainment was usually seen as a waste of time, if not the work of the devil.

This attitude to leisure no longer prevails – it was changed over time by bursts of frivolity, organized relaxation and demonstrative silliness. (Of course, this only applies to certain social classes.) One such moment of change took place in the nineteenth century during the reign of Louis Bonaparte in France. This was an era of casino capitalism, of world

exhibitions, of tourist trips to Paris and of Offenbach's ironic spectacu-
lars. At times, this kind of frivolity was almost serene, at others it was
frenetic; either way, it was responsible for turning Paris into the 'capital
of the nineteenth century'. Walter Benjamin and Siegfried Kracauer,
both of whom were close friends of Adorno, were fascinated by
nineteenth-century Paris, and they both wrote on the topic.[1]

Another moment of change in our attitude towards entertainment took place during the 1920s in Germany (or more specifically, in
Berlin) and elsewhere. It was the era of the 'white-collar workers',
another phenomenon that was analysed by Kracauer. Adorno was
rather less enthusiastic about this period, viewing it as a time of 'sta-
bilization' and 'reaction'. For Adorno, the 1920s saw the end of the
revolutionary promise held by the immediate postwar period, and
he describes how the decade eventually paved the way to fascism.
'Musical reaction' and expanding culture industry were both a part
and a symptom of this phenomenon. This also manifested itself in the
feverish cheerfulness and insincere optimism that served to divert
attention away from the imminent or existing catastrophe of international economic crisis and fascism, as well as from the usual miseries
of capitalism.[2]

It is clear from the 'Culture Industry' text that Adorno's critique does
not target the attempt at distraction, but rather its failure. In Adorno's
view, entertainment encourages just the kind of attitude that we want
to be distracted into forgetting: it encourages a state of exhaustion and
resignation. Adorno illustrates this argument by referring to a cartoon.
It is easy for us to imagine the scenario from the short description that
he provides (see p. 142). Adorno writes of resignation and of our flight
from the possibility of resisting everyday drudgery. Entertainment in
culture industry does not distract our attention from the dominant
forms of life, but instead repeats and affirms them:

> The escape from everyday drudgery which the whole culture industry
> promises may be compared to the daughter's abduction in the cartoon:
> the father is holding the ladder in the dark. . . . Pleasure promotes the
> resignation which it ought to help to forget. (p. 142)

According to Adorno, it would be possible for us to be distracted into
forgetting resignation, and this would even do us good. It would allow
us the time to step out of the bustle of preformed life and temporarily
to inhabit another world. However, culture industry products only lead
us back into everyday life. This is summarized by Adorno in his reference to the experience of the cinema-goer and in his reconstruction of
one of culture industry's maxims:

The old experience of the movie goer, who sees the world outside as an extension of the film he has just left (because the latter is intent upon reproducing the world of everyday perceptions), is now the producer's guideline. . . . Real life is becoming indistinguishable from the movies. (p. 126)

While outlining this situation, Adorno does not neglect the possibility that culture industry products can also be used in a way that does not conform to these maxims. In the examples he gives, the fact that the spectators put the cinema experience to their own purpose means that the content of what is on offer is neglected. What is being put to use is the situation: it permits us to watch films idly and without purpose. It even allows us to participate sentimentally or sadistically in the stories that we can put together out of, for example, the central features of a street scene. The situation of watching a film at the cinema permits us to sit back and relax in a comfortable chair with the light dimmed and the temperature regulated. The fact that there is a film flickering away in the foreground need not disturb us:

In spite of the films which are intended to complete her integration, the housewife finds in the darkness of the movie theatre a place of refuge where she can sit for a few hours with nobody watching, just as she used to look out of the window when there were still homes and rest in the evening. The unemployed in the great cities find coolness in summer and warmth in winter in these temperature-controlled locations. (p. 139)

Disregarding the content of the product on offer is one of the principles of analysing culture industry artefacts. It alerts us to the working alliance: the media create a situation for the audience, and it is this situation that is more important than anything else – including the by and large ideological content that each medium is transmitting. This is what Enzensberger meant when he described TV as a 'zero medium'. What counts with TV is not the content it transmits, but the situation it creates.[3] In the case of TV, this situation is the sovereign situation of the viewer who at any given time has the choice between twenty or fifty (and soon probably as many as 500) different programmes. These programmes can be divided up into a small number of well-known genres, but in all other respects they are practically the same. There are car chases and punch-ups (sometimes disguised as 'sport'); talking heads; pop programmes with excitable presenters; clowns and idiots that are willing to make fools of themselves; disasters and scenes of horror; scantily clad women; and relationship dramas (although given its literary origins, this kind of programme is probably on its way out). With these categories, you can deal with almost anything. Any variations within the categories are negligible, and can in any case be reduced to changes in setting and costume of the kind found in holiday brochures.

The situation of TV is that of the supermarket: there is an overwhelming but insignificant variety of products on offer. (Moreover, in the case of TV, there are not even any 'bargain buys' or 'special offers' to help you make your choice.) This means that once we have worked our way through the range of products and experienced the temporary – and with hindsight rather embarrassing – enthusiasm that they inspire in us, we are left to contend with the eternal return of the Same. Being able to recognize products is certainly gratifying, and it eliminates the element of surprise. What is more, it all takes place without pressure in a relaxed situation where nothing is at stake and where we are served products such as car chases and punch-ups, etc., etc.

Enzensberger does not go quite far enough in his analysis of TV as a 'zero medium'. The 'Buddhistic machine' sends us not so much into 'transcendental meditation' as into a rather less exotic deep sleep. I am not aware of any published research on this topic, but, having taken to observing the behaviour of myself and others, I would hazard a guess that late at night the wide-screen TV tends to beam its perfect picture to an audience of closed eyes.[4] TV is a zero medium purely because the situation of reading has taught us to focus on the content and ignore the situation. (We also tend to ignore the situation of attending a theatre or a concert performance by assuming that the audience is there primarily or solely because of the content of what is being performed. We need only consider this a little bit longer in order to see that it is just not true.) Even in the case of reading, the situation in which we 'consume' a book (whether 'cosy', nocturnal or 'secret', etc.) is important. We need to remember that the situation also has its own content and rules.

When Adorno writes about 'amusement', he is referring to the situation and not to the content of what is being presented:

> Amusement under late capitalism is the prolongation of work. . . . The ostensible content is merely a faded foreground; what sinks in is the automatic succession of standardized operations. What happens at work, in the factory, or in the office can only be escaped from by approximation to it in one's leisure time. All amusement suffers from this incurable malady. (p. 137)

Adorno takes as his example the cartoon film, which 'accustom[s] the senses to the new tempo' and which 'hammer[s] into every brain the old lesson that continuous friction . . . is the condition of life in this society' (p. 138). Cartoons turn distraction into 'exertion' and commit 'violence against the spectator':

> Nothing that the experts have designed as a stimulant must escape the weary eye; no stupidity is allowed in the face of all the trickery; one has to follow everything and even display the smart responses shown and recommended in the film. (p. 139)

Culture industry deals with sexual desire in an analogous fashion to this. Sexual desire becomes 'unsublimated forepleasure' (p. 140) as culture industry repeatedly exposes 'the objects of desire, breasts in a clinging sweater or the naked torso of an athletic hero' (p. 140). However, 'the promise, which is actually all the spectacle consists of, is illusory' (p. 139):

> In the culture industry, jovial denial takes the place of the pain found in ecstasy and in asceticism. . . . In every product of the culture industry, the permanent denial imposed by civilization is once again unmistakably demonstrated and inflicted on its victims. To offer and to deprive them of something is one and the same. This is what happens in erotic films. (p. 141)

Again it is a case of the performative contradiction that inheres within paper or electronic pseudo-eroticism. These forms of eroticism arouse us, make promises to us and show us a quite particular type of sexuality. The 'deception' that Adorno refers to here (p. 142) and in the subtitle of the essay – Enlightenment as Mass Deception – does not consist in the fact that satisfaction is not attained, for how could it be? No, the 'deception' lies in the original promise that was given. According to Adorno, amusement consists in laughing about this deception and in identifying with the dominating force, as we do in dirty jokes. Culture industry is by no means puritanical: 'What is decisive today is no longer puritanism . . . but the necessity inherent in the system not to leave the customer alone, not for a moment to allow him any suspicion that resistance is possible' (p. 141).

If you look at this statement in relation to the earlier remark – 'Works of art are ascetic and unashamed; the culture industry is pornographic and prudish' (p. 140) – it is evident that some clarification is needed. Should we understand 'puritanism' to be 'ascetic' or 'prudish'? Is pornography the flipside of puritanism? Where could the resistance lie? Could it be found in 'the gravity of the lover who with foreboding commits his life to the fleeting moment' (p. 141)?

To be frank, I more or less lost faith in Adorno's views on sexuality after I studied his work on the sexual significance of jazz music.[5]

Nonetheless, Adorno is certainly right in saying that culture industry emphasizes genital intercourse as the only goal of sexuality, even though the situation it presents is one of voyeurism. In performative terms, it is a matter of masturbation and of the pleasure that we derive from watching. In the case of music (and in particular of music that we dance to), it is also a question of autoeroticism. In spite of this, the content of what is being presented all points to hetero-sexual intercourse, which outside porn films is usually only ever hinted at – although in an increasingly detailed and suggestive way. In terms of the material available to Adorno, one kiss was already enough.

The peculiar features of the sexualized film include the 'mass production of the sexual' (p. 140) through the standardization of women's faces (see p. 140), the 'erotic activity' (p. 141) and 'sex to the accompaniment of resounding laughter' (p. 141). From this, Adorno concludes that it is not a matter of voyeuristic satisfaction, but rather a question of typifying what constitutes sexual attractiveness and of setting down the rules for the marriage market. Sexual promises are used as a kind of cover for all this.

Amusement is spoilt by the fact that it is overdetermined by moral instructions about work and sex. It loses its power and is turned into 'elevated pleasure' (p. 143): 'Amusement, if released from every restraint, would not only be the antithesis of art but its extreme role. . . . Pure amusement in its consequence, relaxed self-surrender to all kinds of associations and happy nonsense, is cut short by the amusement on the market' (p. 168). The 'self-justifying and nonsensical skill of riders, acrobats and clowns' and the 'mindless artistry which represents what is human as opposed to the social mechanism are being relentlessly hunted down by a schematic reason which compels everything to prove its significance and effect. The consequence is that the nonsensical at the bottom disappears as utterly as the sense in works of art at the top' (p. 143). Culture industry does not permit amusement since it has to combine it with ideology by 'cultivating' it.

Field notes VIII   Clowns, performers and shows – the not quite so respectable arts

'Art' in the – albeit increasingly anachronistic – sense that we understand it today is a comparatively recent invention.[6] In literature, 'high art' refers to the kind of fiction that targets the needs of a demanding public. This kind of fiction is supposed to tackle serious issues in a profound way, and to have true poetic and aesthetic value. 'High art' is something that is appreciated by those with good taste, who experience the need to engage with the 'serious questions of life'. It is fairly obvious who these people might be – they are the educated middle classes, whose understanding of art sets them apart from the 'uncultured and 'uneducated'.[7]

Such people have need of a particular kind of artist. This kind of artist is the exalted genius, a figure that is best represented in the literary genre that focused on the fate of the heroic, suffering and struggling writer or painter. (This figure was propagated in a large number of novels and plays, etc.) The suffering genius writes in order to:

> express the pain that he must experience in life due to his own creativity. This provides the dramatic conflict, which lies in the tension between subjectivity and the soaring imagination of the genius on the one hand, and the inartistic, philistine nature of his environment on the other; between passionate exuberance and the moderating force of reason. It is an inner conflict in which the gift of creativity is cast variously as curse or blessing.[8]

This type of artistic genius who lives and produces under the sign of his own uniqueness came to life at a very specific point in history, namely in the last decades of the eighteenth century, during the period of 'Sturm und Drang'.[9] The 'artist as genius' stands in opposition to his predecessors, the artist/artisan and the learned artist. In spite of the numerous crises and attempts at reform, the figure of the 'original genius' still exists in art today – although these days we all know that the 'original genius' is now used by PR experts in order to market the 'image' of their latest 'stars' and to secure for them an artistic life span (which in most cases turns out to be extremely short). In fact, this is equally true of those 'stars' who are exalted within the various academic disciplines.

While 'art' or 'high culture' has only been in existence for some 200 years, popular culture has been around for time immemorial. 'Popular culture' does not have the same profundity as 'art'; it is not as demanding, and it is employed for our entertainment and distraction. It is used to accompany or brighten up other events and occasions, for example as a musical backdrop to the banquets that were once held at court. Of course, this kind of music has little to do with 'the people', but it is clearly a form of use-music. This pre-bourgeois example demonstrates with no further ado how the 'high' in 'high culture' is linked to the 'upper' of the 'upper class' that created (and could afford to create) this kind of 'art'. Good orchestras that played 'demanding' music were only to be found at court. However, court culture was not necessarily the same as 'learned culture', and the latter was usually cultivated by the church and in the monasteries.

'Learnedness' only really became a determining characteristic of culture after the rise of the bourgeoisie, whose educated members did not have anything but learning with which to back their claim to status. (They could not, for instance, claim to have a special relationship with God – something to which learnedness had previously been subordinate.) Prior to the bourgeois distinction between 'art' and 'popular culture', the arts weren't necessarily associated with a learned class. This meant that the arts (as practised by specialists rather than by lay people) did not shy away from being noisy or showy. The public had to be drawn in by the sight of something unusual or remarkable, and it was necessary to entertain it in such a way that it would stay to the end and contribute to the collection. This was true even of the 'nobler' public. The spectators wanted to be mystified and entertained; they wanted to be astonished and amused by the performance, before they would pay for it. Actors and entertainers invented themselves and their shows for the marketplace and the court. They were often associated with the 'itinerant people', and they were usually viewed with a similar kind of suspicion.

In the light of this, it is clear that the people responsible for the performances were always already 'outsiders' – it is not surprising that this ambivalence of their position was also reflected in their products. The performers were willing to adapt themselves to the wishes of their audience; they wanted the audience's approval, but at the same time they despised, hated and feared it. They were prepared to entertain it, but they were equally glad of any opportunity to poke fun at it and mock it (or at least certain social figures within it – the farmers were particularly popular targets).

In this sense, the performances were always tinged with an element of subversion. The joker and performer astound and entertain the audience, but at the same time they show the spectators things that the latter are not capable of doing. In the Commedia dell'Arte, the servants provide the comedy and are far superior to their masters. And even in the case of the freak show, the different varieties of humanity on display will astonish and shock the audience (assuming that they are not totally narrow-minded) into losing at least some of their self-assurance. The fools reveal the truth to their rulers. Musicians who encourage their listeners to dance are amused by those who dance to their tune. They try to draw them into their music in the hope that the dancers will forget themselves and behave in a way that they will regret the next day – when the musicians have already moved on. Entertainers and actors are strangers who use their outsider status and their curious artistic accomplishments to make themselves appear attractive and seductive. They entertain the audience and make them laugh – it is only when they are gone that the audience realizes that it is the entertainers who have had the last laugh – they are the ones who have set the audience up.

Entertainers, performers and actors have their own form of critical distance from society – a form of distance that is different from that of the bourgeois artist. Bourgeois artists demand to be recognized as special and different. The entertainer is simply an outsider or a marginal figure. In the bourgeois era, artists had to become respectable and to construct their distance from society as elite superiority. This meant disassociating themselves from the role of the entertainer and speaking in disparaging terms of 'mere entertainment'.

The dichotomy of high art and 'common' entertainment was designed in order to enable the bourgeoisie to distinguish themselves from the 'uncultured masses', as well as for the 'educated elite' to set themselves apart from the wealthy and entrepreneurial bourgeoisie. The struggle for status against the 'nouveau riche' – the uncultured property-owning classes who were industrious and successful, but lacking in refinement (just as the decadent aristocracy had been before them) – was deemed more important than the status battle with the proletariat. (In fact, the cultured bourgeoisie actually sympathized with the proletariat, for the capitalist was a common foe.)

It was in this context that culture was required to become more 'demanding'. Art was made autonomous and became incomprehensible to the outsider. The scornful talk of 'mere entertainment' allowed the bourgeoisie to belittle the 'uncultured'. At the same time, the position of the outsider (that is, of those unable to promote themselves to the elite) was devalued: we now view it as a position in which the pressure to conform is extreme. Outsiders are expected to be eager to adapt themselves to the norm, and we no longer acknowledge the possibility that their position may allow a certain critical distance. However, it is clear that a position of need, instability and questionable respectability can easily lead to an attitude of ambivalence and anger, as well as to the ability to see through some of the deception. This does not mean that we should go to the opposite extreme and declare all marginal groups to be 'revolutionary subjects'. Nonetheless, we should not foreclose the question as to which position might offer the best chance of establishing an art without illusion that could be 'true' in its portrayal of society – is it that of the outsider or that of the bourgeois artist? One thing that is certainly clear is that the art forms we are dealing with (that is, the performing arts) are far less respectable in origin than we might imagine.

The performing arts started out in the marketplace and in the individual acts that were promoted and performed there. Entertainers would master and perform a single trick, or would display a physical abnormality that they had inherited or cultivated. The spectators would follow the performers' procession or walk around the marketplace and watch the different acts – it was for them to put these 'acts' together and to arrive at a 'performance'. This principle is still active in the circus or at variety shows. It is also part of the spectacle, where each individual act is a sensation – something truly remarkable in itself. Such performances are often thrilling, yet the real atmosphere is still one of comedy. We may feel a certain sense of foreboding at the sound of the drum roll, as it announces the next death-defying act, yet the decisive moment comes when this tension is broken by laughter. What is really important is the transition to comedy as the clown starts to parody the performer.

It was the combination of this comic atmosphere with a very specific way of organizing the acts that led to the birth of modern European theatre in the Commedia dell'Arte. The Commedia dell'Arte was organized through the use of stock characters. The most important of these were the ignorant and clumsy (yet crafty and conniving) figures of Harlequin and Brighella, along with their female counterpart Columbine; the crafty

Pulcinella (who later evolved into 'Mr Punch' of 'Punch and Judy' fame); the elderly men (especially Pantaloon); the boastful and ridiculous soldiers; the Doctor whose apparent learning is mocked as mere pretension; and finally, the lovers. These characters would appear in different variations and guises. Yet from this repertoire of stock types, it is already obvious what kinds of themes are privileged in these plays. The plot of the Commedia dell'Arte always revolves around the relationship between the master and his servant, whereby the servant invariably reveals himself to be the cleverer, the more cunning and the more able of the two. The plays deal with the struggle between the old and the young – they pitch patriarchal rule and the power of reason (as derived from property ownership) against vitality and love. The sword, property and learning do battle with shrewdness and the kind of common sense that refuses to allow itself to be silenced by the pretentiousness of others.

It is clear from the characters and the plot that the Commedia dell'Arte is not particularly respectful of the social order. However, on the other hand, it is not especially seditious either. The plays do not target the monarch or the church, but simply enact the conditions of domination, as they appear in everyday life. It is a fairly coarse type of drama and it is often melodramatic or lewd. In those days, the boundaries between what could be passed off as comedy and what would provoke revulsion (or disgust and pity, etc.) were drawn rather differently.

The description 'dell'Arte' ['of art'] was designed to indicate the 'professional' nature of the theatre troupes in question. In most cases, each actor would take on the role of one of the stock characters and would keep that role, even into old age. The actors would also be expected to acquire the necessary physical skills, some of which required a degree of acrobatic mastery. They also had to be able to improvise and to interact with the other characters. They needed to be familiar with their own character's signature 'Lazzi' – a set gag or self-contained comic piece such as the pantomime of the 'invisible' fly that is caught and eaten, and that continues to buzz around in the character's tummy. In short, the actors had to be able to put on interludes in order to bridge gaps and raise an extra laugh.

Traditionally, the plays were put on by travelling theatres, but these groups would often stay for quite considerable periods in the big towns and cities. Their appeal was not limited to the coarse taste of the people, for the plays also found favour at court. This led to the performances developing in the direction of 'high culture' – a change that is sometimes seen as the beginning of the end of the Commedia dell'Arte. The performances became rather more 'refined', and the use of stock types gave way to psychological characterization of the kind later used by Molière.

The Commedia dell'Arte finally met its end in the bourgeois theatre business, as 'worthy' themes and characters came to the fore. In bourgeois theatre, the playwright, and not the actors, determines the performance. In northern Germany, the transition to bourgeois theatre was enforced most rigorously in the eighteenth century, as theorists collaborated with troupes of actors (most famously with that of Caroline Neuber) and banned the German clown 'Hanswurst' from the stage.[10] The reasons behind this reform are to be found in the changing way that the 'cultivated' classes viewed the theatre. They now saw the theatre as an instrument of propaganda or a 'moral institution', and they began to create an ideology around it. They wanted the theatre to be a place for bourgeois communication and self-representation, and this meant ensuring that both the upper and the lower classes were excluded. At the same time, the aim was to form a German *national* theatre in competition with and in imitation of the French theatre and the dramas of Corneille and Racine. (This was in keeping with bourgeois ideals at that time. In the eighteenth century, the German nation was an emerging cultural concept. It did not exist as either a political or an economic reality.) The clown Hanswurst was driven underground, although with much less success in the southern regions. In fact, the Viennese Volkstheater [People's Theatre] survived, and with the advent of Raimund and Nestroy, it found its way back into 'high culture'. [11]

Caroline Neuber and her theatre troupe did not do particularly well out of their attempt to bring about a renaissance of drama. Neuber died poor and forgotten in 1760. Nonetheless, some of the actors from her ensemble carried on the attempted reforms in their own troupes. In any case, the decisive change had occurred: theatrical performances were now to be divided into 'high culture' and 'mere entertainment' of the masses – with the occasional inclusion of the middle classes. Every now and then the middle classes were permitted to 'let themselves go' in a cultural sense and revel in an Offenbach extravaganza. (Compare this to the way in which the institution of bourgeois monogamy did not bring an end to the institution of prostitution, and could even be said to have made it all the more necessary.)

Bourgeois hegemony in the world of theatre meant that the reign of the actor had come to an end. From that point onwards, the theatre was determined by the script and the dramatist. The whole apparatus of the theatre was turned into a machine designed to carry out the intentions of writers – to put on *their* plays. Naturally, this change was by no means uncontroversial, and the transition period between the two theatrical models was marked by conflict.

The change of focus can be seen even more clearly if we examine the history of music. In bourgeois terms, a concert performance was no longer a matter of making music, but of delivering a composition to an audience. Adorno had rather extreme views on this, and held that the performance of a composition was already a reproduction and had no independent value – for Adorno, music should be read and not heard.

With the advent of 'high culture', art became a serious matter. Humour was still just about acceptable, but there was no longer any place for proper jokes or pranks. The bourgeois struggle was simply not a laughing matter.

At this juncture, I propose to interrupt our historical analysis of the dichotomy of high culture and 'mere entertainment' and to turn instead to an analysis of the comic element of the performing arts – to an examination of what 'entertainment' really is. If we start looking for instances of irony (the awareness that all is in vain) and comedy (the insight that even those in power are vulnerable), it soon becomes apparent that there is a lot more to some genres of 'entertainment' than straightforward 'distraction' and 'escapism'. Admittedly, we will not find any forms that are 'ideologically pure': detective novels and Westerns, for instance, are authoritarian epics portraying the (violent) enforcement of justice, but at the same time they often show that nobody's hands are completely clean and that those in office are often failures. Westerns also show the settlers' hatred of the indigenous population and its dangerous consequences. As for the genre of horror, the sadistic motifs are clear, yet the stories do reveal the uncanny nature of a world that cannot be mastered by technological means. In the case of comedy, the laughter can be turned around to ridicule the dominated, but even then it will not leave the dominant completely unscathed. Comedy can make the dominant seem ridiculous in a way that is far more demoralizing for them than straightforward insurgency.

Of course, we should not assume that the pre-bourgeois 'entertainers' such as Hanswurst and Mr Punch et al. would ever be able to stage a return. If this were possible, it certainly would not take place through a return to recent forms of entertainment such as the circus. We would have to look back much further than that. To conclude, I will discuss two examples of this.

The first example concerns the Roncalli – a newly established circus whose performances have been enjoyed by many and whose acts have been deemed 'suitable for children' even by today's anxious parents. However, at the show that I attended, there were countless children (most of them boys) who found the circus too 'cute' and too 'boring'. In fact, I myself also experienced a growing sense of unease – what I was watching was not a circus, but something quite different. It was then that I noticed the general absence of bad smells and unsightly sweat. There was nothing sensational about the performance, and it did not seek to inspire fear. All of a sudden it dawned on me that all that was missing was the remote control – the performance was taking place as if behind a screen. It was a live TV show – a performance designed to look as if it was being featured on a wide-screen colour TV. These days, circuses maintain their popularity by adapting themselves to the format of the television show.

My second example also features a circus troupe. Some time ago, somebody at the theatre in Frankfurt decided to move the kids' performance into a circus marquee during the run-up to Christmas. The idea was to set up the 'big top' in the middle of town, so as to make it easily accessible to the Christmas shoppers. This new location led those involved to start concocting plans for the inclusion of circus-like elements within the performance. Somebody knew of a family who owned a small circus, and it was arranged for the marquee to be hired out in exchange for an appropriate fee.

This was a good business arrangement for the circus, for it came at what was usually a very difficult time of year. Normally, the whole circus would be forced into 'hibernation', which meant no income yet substantial expenditure. In this particular year, the theatre company was able to commandeer the marquee, together with the whole circus experience of caravans and animals. The company, however, was to be disappointed. The idea of borrowing elements from the circus met with polite astonishment from the troupe, and it soon became clear that the performers had very little to offer. They could do a bit of tightrope walking and could get their horses to run around the ring, but that was about the sum of it. What is more, the representatives from the theatre company were unwilling to compromise their standards in terms of the technical apparatus, which eventually meant that enormous constructions were erected and the atmosphere of the circus utterly ruined. This left only one challenge for the actors – how to act in the ring, that is, without a backdrop. This was largely resolved by limiting the action to a particular section of the ring, a move which ensured that the performance remained fairly conventional. In the end, the circus atmosphere was simulated through the inclusion of a troupe of clowns and street-players. Of course, this was more in the tradition of the Commedia dell'Arte or political street theatre than that of the circus. Stylistically, it was incongruous, but it benefited from the intimate atmosphere of the circus, and was entirely successful in practice.

When today's dominant media try to convey the impression that they are enriching themselves by drawing on elements of the less respectable art forms, they have no choice but to simulate these elements. The media cannot 'enrich' themselves by drawing on what they have already destroyed.

Culture as advertising – advertising as potlatch

Culture industry and advertising are inextricably linked in a variety of ways. Their shared mode of production is the strongest connection between the two. Large-scale advertising and commodified entertainment came into being only with the advent of Fordism, a regime in which consumer goods are produced on a mass scale, while the populace is obliged to persist in purchasing them. This connection between culture industry and advertising also led to elements of entertainment being incorporated into adverts. The noisiness of the early ads is very reminiscent of the county fair, which traditionally served as a space in which goods, entertainers and citizens (keen to see and be seen) could be brought together. We have only just rediscovered the idea of consumption as an entertaining experience in itself, but this is really only a matter of re-emphasizing one particular element of consumption that has always been a part (albeit of varying importance) of the act of buying goods. Ever since Toulouse-Lautrec started producing his posters, one of the major uses of art has been in creating advertisements. In any case, since the advent of Bohemianism, art (and even bourgeois art) has once more been linked closely to the business of entertainment.

Culture industry and advertising are also linked by the use of self-promotion. Self-promotion can be achieved by sponsoring art (in traditional terms 'patronage') or by organizing entertainment for the masses. Hosting public festivals and throwing in something for everyone is an old trick. It is a sign that you have got money to spend, and it indicates that your business clients may well benefit from remaining loyal. At one time, owning an art collection and exhibiting it in a purpose-built (and suitably named) museum would have been evidence of successful colonial looting. Nowadays it testifies to the owner's careful and not wholly egoistical use of his or her oversized fortune. Interestingly enough, academics still seem to pay more attention to this kind of sponsorship than to donations earmarked for the purchase of new medical equipment etc.

It is not surprising that recent exhibitions have turned to examining and documenting these links between advertising and culture industry. It all began in 1990–1 with the exhibition 'High and Low: Modern Art and Popular Culture' at the Museum of Modern Art in New York. This coincided with the exhibition 'Art et Publicité' [Art and advertising] at the Centre Pompidou in Paris. More recently, there has been 'Die Kunst zu werben' [The art of advertising] (1996–7 Munich and Hamburg) and ''68 – Design und Alltagskultur zwischen Konsum und Konflikt' [1968 – Design and everyday cultural life: consumption and conflict] (1998 Düsseldorf and Frankfurt). No doubt there will be more to follow. In the meantime, the successful publicist Michael Schirner has declared that 'Advertising is Art', and there are now annual prizes for the best and most artistic advertising ideas. The profession of the 'art consultant' has sprung up, and its salutary effects have been documented in books (or more specifically, in art books) such as *Art and Business*.[12] In the world of painting, the corporate demand for collectable art has been met by the emergence of a kind of art that can best be described as 'foyer art' (large-scale, decorative, abstract or minimalist art – the type of art that can also be found on a smaller scale in hotels.)

In Europe, the 1980s saw the start of the programmatic cultivation of art as a 'locational factor'. Big cities competed with one another in an attempt to persuade banks, business HQs and other service industry enterprises to settle in their area. This led to a rash of ambitious construction projects, some of which vastly overstretched the budgets of the city councils involved. (See in particular the case of Frankfurt and its string of museums along the embankment of the River Main.) Now cultural institutions are experiencing more difficulty in obtaining funding, and they are having to work hard to find the money that they need for buying new artefacts and putting on new exhibitions. These days they have to make themselves accessible to a wider public – once they manage to attract large numbers of people, they can finance themselves with income made from selling advertising space. This is something that has been going on in North America for some time, due to the stronger tradition of 'sponsoring' there. It is a more viable way of financing culture, and so far the consequences have been notable: exhibitions have taken on a new importance, and the more sensational they are the better. In connection with this, a whole new range of jobs has been created – from exhibition manager or art insurance salesman to specialist art transportation crews. Glossy catalogues now accompany the exhibitions, and the museum shops and cafés have become more important than the exhibits themselves. Twenty years ago, the fine arts were still covered in the must and dust of previous eras. Now they are caught up in the wheel of fortune that is culture industry. Advertising has played a key role in this process (whether in the form of advertising for the cities that have ornamented themselves with cultural attractions; or as advertising for the sponsor companies behind cultural establishments; as advertising for art exhibitions; or even in the publicity that art galleries generate for their owners – in most cases, large firms).

It is still quite common for this link between art and advertising to be thought of as a kind of contamination and to be treated with a degree of contempt – people seem to assume that art should have no need of material foundations. However, art has always been dependent on material considerations, and it always will be, for as long as people continue to specialize in and make a living from its production and presentation. The mere fact that art is linked to commerce says nothing in itself. We cannot use this as the basis for a critique of art and its institutions. In the past, the link between art and commerce has taken on many different forms. It is the task of a critical theory of culture (as outlined by Adorno in the 'Culture Industry' chapter) to analyse these forms and to describe their effects on production and reception.

The 'Culture Industry' chapter makes frequent reference to 'advertising' and 'propaganda'. This is pulled together thematically in section 7 (pp. 161–7) and at the beginning of the continuation to the manuscript ('The Schema of Mass Culture'). However, advertising is a recurring motif throughout the entire text. What it is that is being advertised in culture industry (or, to put it more precisely, what culture industry *advertises*) is stated most pointedly at the very beginning of the chapter: culture industry is an advertisement for the 'triumph of invested capital' (p. 124). For Adorno, it is not the attempt to sell individual products that is important, but rather the way in which the mere existence of culture industry and its products allows capitalist-industrial domination to glorify and promote itself – it allows it to present itself as an inevitability, and as an inevitability that is also 'fun'.

As consumers, we have long since learnt to be distrustful of the adverts for individual commodities: 'Value judgements are taken either as advertising or as empty talk' (p. 147). We know that somebody is always trying to sell us something and that it will eventually turn out to be 'rubbish'. On the other hand, we are forever on the hunt for a new 'bargain', with which we will be able to get one over on the sales staff and emerge victorious over our fellow consumers. In the case of televised adverts, we often use the commercial break to get up and go to the fridge or toilet. We are usually quite grateful for the pause. On the occasions that we do stay to watch the adverts, we examine them with professional interest, looking out for the latest tricks that are being used to grab our attention. This is an example of real mutual instrumentalization – each party is engaged in an open attempt to outwit the other. It is just like the fairground games that practised players delight in playing, even though they know that the cards are fixed. Nonetheless, it is only beginners and idiots that lose anything over the (structurally determined) odds. Adorno summarizes this situation in relation to radio: 'The illusion/robbery was made possible by the profits of the united automobile and soap manufacturers, whose payments keep the radio stations going – and, of course, by the increased sales of the electrical industry, which manufactures the radio sets' (p. 159).

In 1947, Adorno substituted the word 'robbery' [*Nepp*] for 'illusion' [*Täuschung*], thus playing down the economic dimension and emphasizing the subjective angle. But what if we are aware of the sizeable profits behind the 'Toscanini broadcast' (pp. 158–9) that was available 'free' for all to hear on the radio? And what if we are not even outraged by the existence of these profits? This kind of reaction is probably even more common now, in our age of 'cynical reason', than it was in 1944 – there is no need to create an illusion for us, since we already accept and agree with what is going on. Adorno's theory of 'illusion' may be inadequate, but this need not stop us from conceding that the type of advertising he describes has been successful: 'It strengthens the firm bond between the consumers and the big combines' (p. 162). At this point in the text, Adorno describes a second economic mechanism of advertising that is based in competing industrial capital and that strengthens the development of monopolies. This mechanism is rather more interesting than the somewhat banal talk of 'robbery' or 'illusion':

> Only those who can pay the exorbitant rates charged by the advertising agencies, chief of which are the radio networks themselves; that is, only those who are already in a position to do so, or are co-opted by the decision of the banks and industrial capital, can enter the pseudo-market as sellers. The costs of advertising, which finally flow back into the pockets of the combines, make it unnecessary to defeat unwelcome outsiders by laborious competition. . . . Advertising today is a negative principle, a blocking device: everything that does not bear its stamp is economically suspect. Universal publicity is in no way necessary for people to get to know the kinds of goods – whose supply is restricted anyway. It helps sales only indirectly. For a particular firm, to phase out a current advertising practice constitutes a loss of prestige, and a breach of the discipline imposed by the influential clique on its members. (p. 162)

In this passage, Adorno describes a possible effect of advertising that is rather more plausible that the supposed 'manipulation' of unsuspecting consumers. According to Adorno, advertising campaigns are designed to show that the firm in question can afford the expense – they serve to demonstrate that it is in the 'premier league' of 'global players'. The cost of advertising is enormous, and no one can be sure how it works out in terms of its effect on the individual consumer – it would certainly be difficult to justify the expense on the basis of a straightforward business decision. For some time now, shrewd observers have been pointing out that for a brand to be successfully marketed, the same campaign would have to be used year in, year out. Of course, this would be extremely tedious for the people in charge, and so it never gets done that way. This means that (1) we are still unclear as to the effect that advertising has on consumers (extensive research has gone into this, but we still do not know if the profit justifies the cost); and (2) we are not even using the kind of advertising that would actually be most likely to work. All in all, it seems that we have been asking ourselves the wrong questions about the impact of advertising: advertising does not act upon consumers, but on the firm and its competitors. The huge sums of money that are spent on advertising with no clear proof of their effect are designed to work on the same basis as 'potlatch': the sheer extent of the 'wasteful' expenditure demonstrates the importance and power of the firm in question. When you advertise, you advertise yourself. Advertising is the (self-)portrayal of domination.

This means that there is no clear distinction between economic and political propaganda – it is very easy to switch from one to the other:

One day the edict of production, the actual advertisement (whose actuality is at present concealed by the pretence of a choice) can turn into the open command of the Führer. In a society of huge Fascist rackets which agree among themselves what part of the social product should be allotted to the nation's needs, it would eventually seem anachronistic to recommend the use of a particular soap powder. The Führer is more up-to-date in unceremoniously giving direct orders for both the holocaust and the supply of rubbish. (p. 160)

The inference here is that fascist dictatorship represents the political form of monopoly capitalism – the Führer's rule is just the political version of the economic dictatorship perpetrated by monopolies. Although Horkheimer and Adorno took care to remove the term 'monopoly' and replace it with 'system', the thrust of their thought remains clear. There is also reference to Horkheimer's theory of rackets, which describes how in fascism 'capital' (which has long since lost its organizing function) is replaced by predatory gangs. Like Mafiosi despoilers, these gangs divide up and live off the bounty. As we have seen, the analysis of advertising leads straight into a discussion of politics, and it is this that is taken up in the subsequent passage.

At this point, I would like to stress once more that the superficial effects of advertising (such as the way in which people are 'manipulated' into purchasing products) play a fairly insignificant part in Adorno's argument. In Adorno's view, the way in which advertising affects society is more complex and far-reaching than this. Adorno argues that when firms lavish money on presenting themselves to the world they are demonstrating domination in the same way as political domination is demonstrated through the presence of troops or the public enactment of punishment. According to Adorno, the target of this demonstration is not simply the populace, but also (and perhaps primarily) any rival or aspiring forces of domination.

This is where the question of sexism in advertising comes into play. Adverts, of course, are often accused of being sexist.[13] Just as in other forms of entertainment, the relationship between the sexes is used in advertising to attract our attention. It is played out for us, and it is used to sell services (including sex). More importantly, the way it is presented forms a part of the demonstration of domination. Adorno does not actually deal with this question in his work, but we can still use his general analysis of advertising in order to see that what is significant here is not the indecent way in which bodies are represented, but the effect of instrumentalization. When pictures of naked or semi-clad women appear in the unerotic and competitive environment of day-to-day business, the people forced to confront these images are made slaves to a drive that they cannot give in to. Furthermore, the female observers and the women who appear in these adverts are made to recognize themselves in the pictures – they are forced into using sex appeal even though the situation is such that they are unwilling and unable to do so. In addition to this, advertising standardizes sex appeal on the basis of a visual norm that is unimportant in terms of real sexuality and that only becomes significant in the context of a market that is driven by 'possession' and 'conquest', that is, by competition and spoils. This is not only misogynistic, but also more generally misanthropic – it is certainly not just the increasing use of nude males in advertising that makes the latter harmful to both men and women!

Adorno's approach enables us to extend the analysis of advertising to include the question of sexism. It allows us to see sexism in advertising as a way of demonstrating domination that goes beyond straightforward misogyny. In fact, adverts are sexist because they show us instrumentalized sex appeal in relation to both men and women. They succeed in turning eroticism and sexuality into questions of power and performance, whether for the participant or the observer. Prudishness, however, would not solve this problem, but would merely turn all the 'subjective' pros and cons of competition into abstract entities. Indeed, prudishness would only universalize competition.[14]

If (as we have just argued) advertising is a demonstration of domination, we can use the changes that advertising undergoes in order to find out more about the state of domination and the nature of competition within the ruling class. In this way, we can see that the recent 'aestheticization of advertising' is an indication that competition is now characterized by 'taste' and 'luxury' and that domination is working via 'exclusive membership'. It is not a matter of providing perks to attract and encourage consumption, nor a question of promoting the goods as being 'good value for money' – it is about 'communication' between sophisticated yet approachable firms and us – their happy and individual clients. Whether in the normal everyday sense of the term or in the wider context described by Adorno, advertising does not work by manipulating or seducing us – what it does is to entertain us and make us complicit.

In his analysis of advertising, Adorno was struck by the way in which the distinction between representation and day-to-day reality was becoming blurred. These days, this blurring is a principle of domination. We are all involved in domination, and we are all part of its combine – the idea is that we should never achieve a critical distance. We participate in culture industry's competitions and games, but our involvement is by no means limited to this. In fact, we are also responsible for actively helping to create culture industry, as we take part in radio phone-ins or make appearances on talk-shows. We are also involved through the family sitcoms that recreate our everyday lives in only slightly exaggerated form (while the dubbed-in laughter draws attention to the show's fictional status). We are even implicated via the documentation of our reactions ('the voice of the ordinary people') to accidents or criminal activities. Of course, the latter are also documented in 'reality TV' – a form of television that sometimes disguises itself as 'news'. Clearly, TV does not report on a reality that is taking place 'out there' beyond the screen. On the contrary, TV is reality.

However, the reality of television increasingly coincides with our own small-minded everyday reality. We look on in admiration at the efficient globalization of the media – at an unimaginable cost, the media now cover all the world, the skies and the seas, yet what they bring back to us is nothing but our own reality. They return from outer space with nothing but a glossy version of our own unexciting obsessions. Despite the organizational and technical weaponry, all that we are left with is a kind of universal chitchat. Vast quantities of time and money are spent on entertainment, yet what we get from TV and the net is no different from small town gossip. We could have spared ourselves the trouble and never ventured any further.

5

The conditions of belonging: the appropriation of the audience

'Ironically, man as a member of a species has been made a reality by the culture industry [monopoly capitalism]'

When studying section 4 of the 'Culture Industry' chapter (pp. 144–9), it is worth taking a closer look at the revisions made by Horkheimer and Adorno between 1944 and 1947. These revisions are characterized by the replacement of words such as 'monopoly', 'capital' and 'class' by terms that are more theoretically neutral. As Willem van Reijen and Jan Bransen have shown, this was not simply a matter of the two exiles reacting with caution to the anti-communist witch-hunts that were taking place at that time in the US.[1] In fact, the change in vocabulary also signals a shift in Horkheimer and Adorno's analysis of Nazism, the Soviet planned economy and US capitalism. What was originally an economic theory (of 'monopoly capitalism') becomes a political theory (of 'state capitalism'). Before we investigate this further, we should start off by examining the contents of this section.

The theme in this short section is that of the appropriated individual. Individuals have been appropriated in that they have learnt to see themselves as being insignificant and replaceable. They have come to realize and accept that they are expendable. This section opens by linking the instrumentalization of the individual to the principle of amusement (the theme of the previous section). For Adorno, what we experience when we are being 'entertained' is above all 'helplessness': 'Pleasure always means not to think about anything, to forget suffering even where it is shown. Basically, it is helplessness. It is flight; not, as is asserted, flight from a wretched reality, but from the last remaining thought of resistance' (p. 144). However, it is not simply a matter of entertainment violently repressing us and forcing us into a life of drudgery. It is not that the misery of our lives is simply made to seem unavoidable. On the contrary, attaining personal happiness is made to appear perfectly possible, and indeed desirable. The only problem is that happiness is not presented to us as something that we could work towards or 'earn'. It does not seem to be something that we could reasonably expect to attain at the peak of a great career. Instead, personal happiness is equated with 'luck' – it is made to look as if it comes to us by chance. We are trained to see ourselves as mere statistics, and, statistically, we would have to be very lucky in order to succeed (and become famous) or to enjoy an enviably fulfilling private life (and a glamorous wedding). We know at once that the chances of this happening are infinitesimally small, and so we are happy to settle straight away for vicarious success. We content ourselves with watching and sharing in the success of others.

This way of thinking is a kind of culture industry *perpetuum mobile*: while we watch, we are shown that watching the success of others is the best that we can do for ourselves. We are led to conclude that watching is the only available form of fulfilment, and that it is not just a substitute for something that we could actually attain for ourselves in life: experiencing real success would be far too exciting for us, and it would only serve to confuse things. Culture industry demonstrates something that Oscar Wilde and Karl Kraus were already aware of: it is life that imitates art, and not the other way round. Actual sex is just a poor substitute for masturbation and fantasy. The reality of the media is a reality of its own, and it has its own pleasures. It is not necessarily related to external reality.

In Adorno's view, this absence of any link to a reality beyond that of the media is determined and disguised by probability:

> Ideology conceals itself in the calculation of probabilities. Not everyone will be lucky one day – but the person who draws the winning ticket, or rather the one who is marked out to do so by a higher power – usually by the pleasure industry itself, which is represented as unceasingly in search of talent. (p. 145)

Of course, it is hardly necessary to point out that game shows are an important genre of both radio and television broadcasting. There are countless shows in which you can try your luck in order to win money, or even friends, love and at least adventure. (In the early days of

Fordism, these prizes often took the form of commodities, but nowadays this is much less common.) Game shows are a significant sector of the entertainment industry to the tune of countless billions. They are often combined with other kinds of entertainment, and in particular with sport, through a multitude of competitions all with their own particular rules. Games of luck and chance are also related to the stories of winners and losers that feature in books and journals (from Dostoevsky to the tabloids) and in films and TV. In these stories, the 'winner's' luck does not usually last for long, and it ultimately appears as misfortune. It is customary to link 'luck' and 'happiness' to questions of character, and to tell stories in which the gambler is contrasted with the steady worker, or the speculator with the 'productive' entrepreneur who creates jobs (as in the cinema hit of 1990, *Pretty Woman*).

As Adorno explains: 'This changes the inner structure of the religion of success' (p. 146). It is no longer possible to earn happiness – you have to wait patiently for it to be bestowed on you. Nevertheless, you still have to keep paying into the lottery if you are to be in with a chance. In the extremely unlikely event that you do become successful, it is not an achievement, but a kind of prize. We are no longer dealing with an entrepreneurial model of success, where sacrifice and hard work lead to a financial breakthrough that is eventually consolidated in the steady growth of a family business. On the contrary, the current model of success is exemplified by the employee – by the worker who has the fortune to be picked out from the rest and who is then allowed to join the clique of more senior employees. It is no coincidence that it is often private secretaries and personal assistants (the workers who are closest to the boss) who are particularly susceptible to being 'co-opted' into the ranks above.[2]

Adorno links these conditions to rationality (in this instance 'planning'), and so reveals another case of dialectic of enlightenment: 'Chance and planning become one and the same thing, because, given men's equality, individual success and failure – right up to the top – lose any economic meaning' (p. 146). What Adorno is showing is that individuals are entirely expendable, even those who are right at the 'top'. (It is this inclusion of *every* worker that makes the claim original. Naturally, proletarian workers have always been aware of their expendability, for they have always been forced to compete with 'reserve armies' of replacement workers.) What counts is not the individual, but the overall statistics for the supply of labour power and purchasing power. Chance and planning have become identical, and as a result the form of rationality in operation is now characterized by the reproduction of the status quo. There is no longer any need to justify reality through reference to an external meaning or a higher purpose, for the existing world has become its own ideology. Adorno refers to this scornfully as the 'photological proof' (p. 148) – it is a system of evidence in which the mere fact that something exists is used to demonstrate its significance.

The text returns once more to the theme of 'realism' in culture industry, and Adorno now elaborates on the argument: 'The culture industry tends to make itself the embodiment of authoritative pronouncements, and thus the irrefutable prophet of the prevailing order' (p. 147). The conditions of production have developed in such a way that it is now impossible to justify the positions that people hold within them. It has all become a matter of chance. This forecloses the issues of meaning and significance, and it shuts out any possibility of a way of thinking that ventures beyond the empirical. 'Positivism' (the type of thinking that accepts reality as immutable and that remains within the limits of what already exists) corresponds to the social reality of domination that cannot be justified and that circumvents any need to do so.

The idea that reality is immutable is reinforced by the threat of destruction. The cult of the real is linked to a sense of amazement that we are all still here even though we are expendable. We are amazed that things can continue:

> That this goes on, that, in its most recent phase, the system itself reproduces the life of those of whom it consists instead of immediately doing away with them, is even put down to its credit as giving it meaning and worth. Continuing and continuing to join in are given as justification for the blind persistence of the system and even for its immutability. What repeats itself is healthy, like the natural or industrial cycle. The same babies grin eternally out of the magazines; the jazz machine will pound away forever. (p. 148)

The eternal cycles of nature and technology justify the system of domination and at the same time confirm its inevitability. Adorno illustrates this by referring to a movie that was of considerable importance to him – Chaplin's 'Hitler film', *The Great Dictator* (1940).[3]

Nature and technology are made to seem modern, and Adorno describes how they are:

> mobilized against all opposition ... we have a falsified memento of liberal society, in which people supposedly wallowed in erotic plush-lined bedrooms instead of taking open-air baths as is the case today, or

experiencing breakdowns in prehistoric Benz models instead of shooting off at the speed of a rocket from A (where one is anyhow) to B (where everything is just the same). (p. 149)

This last dig is surprisingly light-hearted for Adorno, and it emphasizes the idea (subsequently edited out of the text) that 'liberal society/liberalism' is the enemy of 'modern' forms of domination: 'The enemy who is already defeated, the thinking individual [liberalism], is the enemy fought' (p. 149).

In this sentence, as in the sentence that I have selected as a subtitle for this section (see above, p. 119), the change effected by the deletion of 'monopoly capitalism' and 'liberalism' is far more profound than the impact of the revisions elsewhere. In both cases, the sentence's subject was originally an economic, political and social formation, that is, a mode of production. In the first, this was 'monopoly capitalism' and in the second, 'liberalism'. In their original form, the sentences describe how domination was contested in the *economic* sphere, with one mode of production pitted against another. Monopolies are shown to gobble up the small entrepreneurs and to destroy their independence, while monopoly capitalism is seen to perfect the system of administration and planning and to erase the significance (economic and otherwise) of the individual. These are processes that take place in the basic mechanisms of social integration. They are sometimes portrayed in Hollywood films, but they are certainly not in any way dependent on the latter – they are far too powerful for that.

The seemingly harmless changes subsequently made to these sentences had a profound effect on the logic of the argument. In the revised version of the text, the processes are shown to take place within *society*. In place of 'monopoly capitalism' and 'liberalism', we have 'culture industry' and the 'thinking individual'. Culture industry appears as a specific institution of social formation that defeats and destroys the 'thinking individual'. To put it more strongly, the effect of the revisions is to replace structural argument with conspiracy theory. In their original form, the sentences analysed a mode of production, but in the revised version blame is apportioned to an economic institution. This change in meaning admits the possibility that it would be feasible to make 'better' films. In fact, it suggests that we could limit the damage to the 'thinking individual' just by altering the nature of films. This kind of thinking is akin to that of the social pathologist who recommends using censorship to combat pornography, representations of violence and any other kind of material liable to 'corrupt' the young. This attitude may bring about some change in an everyday practical context, but it is simply not an appropriate basis for theory. (In fact, it is more likely to form part of the subject-matter *for* theoretical analysis.) It is a kind of thinking that is entirely alien to Adorno, but (as we have seen from the above examples) it was able to slip into the text via the process of editing and self-censorship. In any case, we certainly should not allow it to distract us from the main thrust of Adorno's theory.

Field notes IX   Can we find Hitler funny?

The Great Dictator (1940) was the anti-fascist film that Charlie Chaplin felt driven and obliged to make. It was also the film in which he attempted the difficult transition from silent film to sound, finding his voice with an incomprehensible yet expressive fictional fascist dialect. With the exception of Ernst Lubitsch's *To Be or Not to Be* (1942), *The Great Dictator* was the only film of the World War II period that attempted to use comedy in order to tackle fascism.[4] For his 'Hitler' film, Chaplin once again takes on the role of the anti-authoritarian 'tramp', this time playing a Jewish barber in a ghetto. However, when Chaplin's character treats the Nazi Brownshirts in the same way as the 'tramp' treated the relatively harmless policemen of the earlier films, the comic limits of the role are revealed. We can no longer be amused by Chaplin's childlike anti-authoritarian antics, for fear silences our laughter.

The film also has a second strand of comedy, consisting of Chaplin's grotesque portrayal of 'Adenoid Hynkel' (the Hitler figure). The element of the grotesque is particularly strong in the scene where 'Hynkel' dances a joyful and narcissistic *pas de deux* with a globe, as well as in the scenes featuring 'Hynkel's' public speeches, for which Chaplin adopts a barking and rasping tone. At the very end of the film, Chaplin calls upon the normal language of sound film to make a democratic and humanist propaganda speech.

This concluding speech marks a formal break in the film. It is at this point that Chaplin tries rather clumsily to integrate the techniques of the 'talkies' into the forms of representation that he had developed in his silent films. The speech is a statement of political loyalty that is designed to stir the audience, yet its moralizing tone and exaggerated pathos make it most embarrassing to witness. In any case, what Chaplin is attempting to achieve in the speech has already been accomplished much more convincingly by the film's grotesque comedy and slapstick. It is like having to sit through a long-winded and sentimental explanation of a joke that we have already laughed at.

It is this last part of the film that is criticized in the 'Culture Industry' chapter, for Adorno takes issue with the images of 'healthy' nature that are shown in connection with the speech. There is no doubt that these images are indeed reminiscent of fascist aesthetics, just as Chaplin's anti-fascist speech is itself a piece of propaganda. Irrespective of their message, these scenes make for uncomfortable viewing. Adorno observes that the images of crops etc. portray 'nature' in 'healthy contrast to society' (p. 149): 'The ears of corn blowing in the wind at the end of Chaplin's *The Great Dictator* give the lie to the anti-Fascist plea for freedom. They are like the blond hair of the German girl whose camp life is photographed by the Nazi film company in the summer breeze' (p. 149).

Adorno chooses to identify Chaplin's speech with specific features of Nazi propaganda, but we can arrive at a more general (although at the same time more accurate) analysis of the scene if we describe it in terms of a change in the working alliance. As the speech begins, the anti-authoritarian working alliance of comedy is replaced by the working alliance of political propaganda. The form and content of the speech mean that the film shifts into precisely the kind of working alliance that was parodied and made to seem ridiculous within the comic scenes. Earlier in the film, the tramp critiques domination by exposing it as 'self-importance'. He shows how domination's claim to heroism, superiority, power and tragedy crumbles due to human weakness: the claim to power breaks down when it is confronted by someone who refuses to react in a sufficiently subordinate manner. (In fact, people and things that have a 'will of their own' are also well suited to undermining domination.)[5] However, in his own speech, Chaplin draws on the very characteristics that were previously being satirized, calling on ideas of heroism, superiority, power and tragedy. Chaplin's good intentions do not make up for the problematic nature of his means of representation. On the contrary, the form of his speech thwarts its message.

The potential for a critique of domination via comedy is fairly limited in the face of a regime that is prepared to physically destroy its opponents. If Chaplin or Lubitsch had known about the Nazi death-camps and mass killings, they would not have been able to make the kind of film that they did. This is why Mel Brooks's remake of *To Be or Not to Be* (1983) is so fascinating. The grotesque humour of the film is particularly successful due to Brooks's characteristically tasteless comedy, as well as to the film's critique of culture industry and the way in which it deals with 'Hitler'. However, the target is no longer Nazism, but its representation in culture industry.

Brecht's play *Schweyk in the Second World War* (1943) demonstrates the limits of comedy for the theatre. Schweyk can only survive for a certain amount of time by playing the role of the clown. During this kind of war, even tongue-in-cheek opportunism and a readiness to adapt to the new circumstances cannot save the ordinary people. (This theme is also played out in another of Brecht's plays, *Mother Courage and her Children*, as the mother's opportunism fails to save her family.) The terror may have its limits, but this is of little real use, for we will not survive to see its end. The SS 'exterminate' the anti-authoritarian working alliance. Luck is the only means of survival. The limits of comedy in Brecht's play demonstrate what Adorno was saying about the end of the individual.

What can the public want?

'It's good to see you here in such numbers tonight!'

At one time, newspapers and radio broadcasts were produced for particular groups of likeminded people. Now that this is no longer the
case, the media have a vested interest in trying to find out about the
composition of their 'readership' or 'audience'. However, this interest
is not fuelled by a desire to adapt the media's products to consumers'
needs. The revenue gained from selling newspapers or magazines now
plays a fairly insignificant role in the media business. Indeed, in the
case of radio or television (with the exception of pay TV), there is no
direct revenue from consumers. In fact, the media's interest in its audience actually stems from its desire to gain advertising clients. The audience is important not because it buys products, but because it can be
sold. Each medium sees itself as a market with a particular clientele
made up of specific social groups. This is what attracts firms to the
medium, for they can use it to promote their own products and so buy
into this 'market'.

   All this explains why the most extensive and frequent surveys are
conducted in the form of 'media analysis': tens of thousands of people
are questioned in interviews lasting several hours about their knowledge and use of various types of media. In addition to this, there is the
research conducted into TV viewing figures that allows us to evaluate
the popularity of each programme from one day to the next and that
now includes an ever increasing number of different channels. An
unbelievable amount of effort (and cash) is put into finding out about
'the audience', yet 'getting to know' the viewers primarily involves
attempting to count them. In fact, this kind of research takes place
solely in the interest of the media and is therefore extremely one-sided.
The media are only interested in the viewers as statistical units and
saleable goods. How an audience feels or what it experiences are seen
as completely irrelevant. Nonetheless, 'channel hoppers' give cause for
some concern, perhaps because they mess up the sums, or perhaps
because it is slightly insulting to think that some people would rather
surf the channels for interesting pictures than watch the programme
that has been designed for them. The fact that people switch between
channels is never linked to the content of the programmes, but is seen
as a sign of the audience's apathy and its inability to concentrate.

   The very concept of 'the audience' (or 'the readership') has been
shaped from the perspective of the media. When we go to the theatre
or turn on the TV, we do not do so as members of 'the audience' but

as individuals or in a group of friends. It is for this reason that the greeting 'It's good to see you here in such numbers tonight' is so comical, not to mention embarrassing. In most cases, it tends to be the amateur entertainer and not the professional who adopts this mixture of intimate address and delight in bulk numbers.[6] Nonetheless, whenever I am greeted in this manner, I cannot help but register that I am never 'here' (nor anywhere else) in any number other than one. The interest in quantity is played out in the opposite direction in the case of demonstrations, where people participate in order to be counted (whether by the police or by the media). It is important that the number of demonstraters seems as large as possible, so that the 'ratings' for the protest will suffice. It is already clear from these two examples that the relationship between the media and the audience is problematic. In fact, its basic structure ensures that the two parties are never on the same wavelength.

The title of this section was chosen in order to reveal the flawed process of interaction that takes place between the producers of culture and their audience. This same problem is in evidence in the advertising techniques used by the media. These techniques seek to bind the customer to the product and the brand. Each person is to be drawn in individually and enouraged to participate. The use of door-to-door sales reps is an attempt to create this personal link via an actual employee. The same technique is used in politics as candidates rush to shake people's hands or call on one household after the next. 'Mingling with the masses' has now become a speciality of political campaigns, which fits in somewhere between 'spotting the stars' and 'being accessible to the ordinary people'. (Of course, there is an obvious comparison with the way that people rush to touch saints and sacred relics. Indeed, it is quite rewarding in general to analyse 'fame' as a secularized form of worship.) The odd combination of anonymity and intimacy that is used when addressing the audience can also be explained with reference to the situation of the speaker. When introducing or announcing something, fears of an unpredictable reaction can be conquered by addressing the audience in a personal fashion. Speakers can present themselves as the representatives of an organization and identify with the latter. While speaking, they *are* the organization – the organization cannot be pleased about the number of people in attendance, but it is dependent on them. The intimate tone converts this dependence into a pseudo-personal advert.

Those familiar with culture industry often use their understanding of all this to conclude that the producers and performers of culture are always trying to sell them something. Many people assume that the makers of culture are *dependent* on our favour and that they are desperately eager to perform for us. They come to believe that cultural producers and performers are obliged to exert themselves in order to please us and that they are reliant on us watching and appreciating their products. However, this is only really true of live performances, where the actors are understandably quite keen to avoid being booed off stage. But even in this instance, the attitude towards the audience is often rather scornful; it is commonly felt that 'you can show people whatever rubbish you like because they have not got a clue about it anyway.'[7] The situation is even more curious with regard to pre-recorded or electronically transmitted material, for the latter precludes any possiblity of responding directly. What was once a direct (although of course largely anonymous) relationship is split into an abstract purchase for the audience and a one-off process of recording for the performers. It becomes a projective relationship for both parties.

Each party tends to assume rather too much goodwill on behalf of the other. In reality, cultural producers and performers seldom have a good word to say about their audience. Indeed, even when they are trying to ingratiate themselves with the public, the attempt to win favour is usually accompanied by a feeling of rage at their situation of dependency. The role of the producer or performer is quite similar to that of the domestic servant, for even when they are trying to impress us, the relationship is still one of distance and power. There is a sense that they are attempting to catch us unawares or trying to get one over on us. There is also an element of fear: it is always possible that we will not be flattered or impressed by their efforts. We may show our disdain and scorn by refusing to pay attention, by revealing our boredom or by rejecting their offerings. If we refuse to be impressed, producers and performers can look very foolish. In every instance, their narcissistic pride is at risk.

On the other hand, our attitude towards the producers and performers of culture is also marked by scorn and aggression. It is true that we admire these people and that we worship their products, yet at the same time there is nothing we enjoy more than watching them forget their words, trip up or make mistakes. We take pleasure in remarking that 'a child could do better' than a modern artist or sculptor, and we are quick to talk down the latest best-selling novel. We look up to the stars for their wealth, but we refuse to see why they should be so highly paid. Our interest in the problems of the rich and famous is never motivated wholly by pity, but is usually tinged with at least a little spite or schadenfreude.

All in all, we can be sure that the producers of culture and their audience are locked into a fundamentally ambivalent relationship in which aggression and scorn play no small role. This mutual antagonism is sometimes exploited, particularly in some forms of televised entertainment. There are programmes that consist of clip after clip of famous people tripping up or forgetting their lines. There are also shows that revolve around a hidden camera and that aim to catch the famous off their guard. Even the figure of the clown is designed to satirize 'established' performers (although of course the clown's very 'clumsiness' is a sign of artistic skill). On the other hand, there is the genre of programme that is designed to show up the audience and to make it seem slow-witted and helpless. Most televised quiz shows and game shows are driven at least in part by a vindictive desire to make the candidates (usually members of the audience) look ridiculous. Such malice is barely concealed in the talk-shows where people are made to reveal the monstrous goings-on in their private lives. It is an integral part of the viewer's fun to watch these people expose themselves and their intimate emotions.

The fundamental relationship in culture industry is that of mutual instrumentalization. Any relationship between a buyer and a seller is based on the desire of each party to get the better deal. In this instance, the instrumentalization is absolutely mutual: one the one hand, there is the audience (representing both purchasing power and a saleable commodity), and on the other, there are the entertainers (who have to exert themselves if they are to receive our precious cash). There are the masses (who are only really interested in scandals and sensations, but who are foolish and hungry for entertainment); and there is the huge entertainment industry that consumes vast amounts of financial resources and technical expertise in order to impress a public that often fails to take notice of its efforts and that is sufficiently cold and hardened to use the media for its own private needs. When we hear tales of cultural producers meeting with failure and financial ruin in their competition for our purchasing power, we feel no compassion and sometimes more than a little malice: if you are going to play the game, you have to be prepared to lose.

Culture industry's impact on consumers

In the field of Media Studies, Adorno's work on culture industry is often thought to be based on a diagnosis of total social delusion: it is generally assumed that what Adorno is describing is the utter manipulation and stultification of consumers by the media. Those who (mis)read Adorno in this way tend to argue for an alternative model of the relationship between the media and consumers in which the latter are active recipients of culture who use their common sense and reason in order to decide which media influences they are willing to expose themselves to. In this model, consumers are able to read more into the cultural products than the 'manipulative media' intend. Adorno is criticized for being an 'elitist' and for having 'failed' to acknowledge that not only connoisseurs of high culture, but also ordinary fans of popular culture might be capable of an active response to culture in this autonomous fashion.[8]

However, the very idea that a social institution can have this kind of impact on consumers is far too simplistic for Adorno's complex theory. Simplistic models of the relationship between the media and consumers abound in Media Studies, where they often appear in schematic form, such as 'sender–medium–receiver' or 'signal–transmission–decoding by receivers'. (Since these models do not actually work, there has been much research devoted to making them more complicated. Now, there is the theory of the 'two-step flow of information', for which we have to thank the advertising companies' preoccupation with 'endorsers'.) This kind of one-dimensional thinking was entirely alien to Adorno.

In this section, we shall examine Adorno's text in detail with the aim of finding out exactly what is said about how consumers receive culture. In order to do this, it is best to identify and sort through all the relevant passages. There are relatively frequent references to notions of culture consumption and manipulation, but the majority of these are clustered around pp. 123–7, 133–9, 144–8, 152–5, 160–2, 165–7 of the 'Culture Industry' chapter and on pp. 56, 70–1 and 77–83 of 'The Schema of Mass Culture'.[9] A glance through these passages makes it clear that what Adorno is talking about is not the isolated impact of specific programmes, genres or themes, but a far-reaching process of social integration. Adorno is writing about people in a capitalist formation and the way in which they are used and administrated as labour power and purchasing power. These people are also people 'with leisure' (p. 124) who have contact with the institutions and content of the 'culture' that is being produced for their education and entertainment. This also means that people are pressurized by culture industry, for the latter is intent on selling its products. There is a clear correlation: culture industry produces saleable goods, and it is these goods that the consumers are demanding. It is not a question of cause and effect: the workings of supply and demand are explained in the context of a social formation, the main mechanism of which is 'commodification'. Thanks to technological progress, there is far more labour power available than society can use or pay for. This situation is summarized very concisely (although somewhat pompously) in the following passage:

Whereas today in material production the mechanism of supply and demand is disintegrating, in the superstructure it still operates as a check in the rulers' favor. The consumers are the workers and employees, the farmers and lower middle class. Capitalist production so confines them, body and soul, that they fall helpless victims to what is offered them. As naturally as the ruled always took the morality imposed upon them more seriously than did the rulers themselves, the deceived masses are today captivated by the myth of success even more than the successful are. Immovably, they insist on the very ideology which enslaves them. The misplaced love of the common people for the wrong which is done them is a greater force than the cunning of the authorities. . . . The industry submits to the vote which it has itself inspired. (pp. 133–4)

There are various other passages in which it is clear that this is not a matter of simple manipulation. A few pages later, Adorno explains: 'It is quite correct that the power of the culture industry resides in its identification with a manufactured need, and not in simple contrast to it, even if this contrast were one of complete power and complete powerlessness' (p. 137).

The aforementioned passage about 'chance and planning' (p. 146) also makes it clear that it is not the rationality of culture industry, but that of society that has led to individuals becoming interchangeable. This development is shown to be reflected in the products of culture industry. These products can sometimes make hard rationality appear quite benevolent. Adorno remarks:

Higher up the scale, in fact, a kind of welfare state is coming into being today. In order to keep their own positions, men in top posts maintain the economy in which a highly-developed technology has in principle made the masses redundant as producers. The workers, the real bread-winners, are fed (if we are to believe the ideology) by the managers of the economy, the fed. Hence the individual's position becomes precarious. Under liberalism the poor were thought to be lazy; now they are automatically objects of suspicion. Anybody who is not provided for outside should be in a concentration camp, or at any rate in the hell of the most degrading work and the slums. The culture industry, however, reflects positive and negative welfare for those under the administrator's control as direct human solidarity of men in a world of the efficient. No one is forgotten; everywhere there are neighbors and welfare workers, Dr Gillespies and parlor philosophers whose hearts are in the right place and who, by their kind intervention as of man to man, cure individual cases of socially-perpetuated distress – always provided that there is no obstacle in the personal depravity of the unfortunate. (p. 150)

This is a fair description of the workings of long-running soap operas such as *EastEnders* or *Days of our Lives*. More importantly, it reveals how the products of culture industry are given an ideological edge: culture industry has a 'personalizing' effect. Culture industry has trouble representing purely functional relationships; if it tries, it becomes unbearably didactic. As Adorno observes, 'Monopoly scorns art' ('Schema', p. 57).[10]

We can examine the intensity of the pressure that culture industry is supposed to exert on consumers by studying the use of verbs within the text. In most cases, it is a question of something 'having to' or 'being expected to' happen, yet there is seldom any mention of whether this actually occurs. There is frequent reference to culture industry 'training' consumers or 'accustoming' them to something: Cartoons *accustom* the senses to the new tempo (p. 138), while consumers *learn* from the thrashings meted out to Donald Duck (p. 138). Consumers are *deprived* of their individuality (pp. 144–5), and they are *shown* 'the condition under which this merciless life can be lived at all' (p. 152). Each consumer is a 'recipient of gifts', who is given *training* (p. 161): 'the apparatus *trains* him to appear well-informed' ('Schema', p. 71). Elsewhere, consumers have denial *demonstrated and inflicted* upon them (p. 141). Culture industry *issues* them with an *invitation* to identify (p. 145), and they are *assured* that they are 'all right as they are' (p. 146). Culture industry *presupposes* 'the most recent characteristic of society' (p. 149), as well as *providing* things for the consumers and *comforting* them (p. 151). The 'fragility of society' is *reproduced* in culture industry (p. 155), while viewers are *persuaded* of the merit of their own 'averageness' ('Schema', p. 59). Consumers are *encouraged* to recognize what is offered to them ('Schema', p. 70).

None of this is particularly aggressive or underhand. Indeed, the excerpts largely confirm the idea that Adorno's culture industry is a mechanism that reproduces and reinforces the domination that has its roots elsewhere. On the other hand, there is no indication that culture industry actually has anything to do with enlightenment.

Adorno's consumers actively surrender to culture industry: they are by no means simply passive victims. In fact, they participate in their own oppression, and consent to discipline and instrumentalize themselves:

> Inwardness, the subjectively restricted form of truth, was always more at the mercy of the outwardly powerful than they imagined. The culture industry turns it into an open lie. It has now become mere twaddle which is acceptable in religious bestsellers, psychological films, and women's serials as an embarrassingly agreeable garnish, so that genuine personal emotion in real life can be all the more reliably controlled. (p. 144)

The way in which a girl accepts and keeps the obligatory date, the inflec-
tion on the telephone or in the most intimate situation, the choice of
words in conversation, and the whole inner life as classified by the now
somewhat devalued depth psychology, bear witness to man's attempt to
make himself a proficient apparatus, similar (even in emotions) to the
model served up by the culture industry. (p. 167)

The less the system tolerates anything new, the more those who have
been forsaken must be acquainted with all the latest novelties if they are
to continue living in society rather than feeling themselves excluded
from it. . . . The satisfaction of curiosity by no means serves only the psychological economy of the subject, but directly serves material interests
as well. Those who have been thoroughly informed lend themselves to
thorough utilization. ('Schema', p. 72)

It is only towards the end of 'The Schema of Mass Culture' that
Adorno provides a clear description of the pressure to conform that
culture industry is bound up with:

The old slogan of bourgeois entertainment, 'But you must have seen this',
which just represented a swindle in the market place becomes a matter
of deadly seriousness with the elimination of amusements and the
market alike. Formerly the supposed penalty merely lay in not being able
to participate in what everyone else was talking about. Today anyone
who is incapable of talking in the prescribed fashion, that is of effort-
lessly reproducing the formulas, conventions and judgements of mass
culture as if they were his own, is threatened in his very existence, suspected of being an idiot or an intellectual. Looking good, make-up, the
desperately strained smile of eternal youth which only cracks momen-
tarily in the angry twitching of the wrinkles of the brow, all this bounty
is dispensed by the personnel manager under threat of the stick. People
give their approval to mass culture because they know or suspect that
this is where they are taught the mores they will surely need as their
passport in a monopolized life. This passport is only valid if paid for in
blood, with the surrender of life as a whole and the impassioned obedience to a hated compulsion. This is why mass culture proves so irresistible and not because of the supposed 'stultification' of the masses
which is promoted by their enemies and lamented by their philanthro-
pic friends. The psychological mechanisms involved are secondary.
('Schema', pp. 79–80)

Culture industry does not just 'do' something to consumers that they
are then forced to do to themselves. Instead, culture industry products
familiarize consumers with the appearances that they will have to keep
up if they want to avoid being excluded. In this passage, Adorno
describes the need to conform as a pressure that must be obeyed in

order to preserve mere existence. This was certainly not a far-fetched claim in 1944, and it has become plausible again today. We are shown to be conscious of the pressure to conform – we experience it as a 'hated compulsion'. It only appears temporarily as a manipulative or seductive force in the short-lived period of Fordism, described here in terms of 'consumer society' and 'affluent society'.

Consumers are not passive and ignorant victims, and they are certainly not helpless and unsuspecting pawns. In fact, they know all about culture industry – it is just that there is little opportunity for them to act on this knowledge. As a result, they participate in culture industry in an ironic or even semi-serious manner. Adorno comments:

> That the difference between the Chrysler range and General Motors products is basically illusory strikes every child with a keen interest in varieties. (p. 123)

> The rate at which they [the consumers] are reduced to stupidity must not fall behind the rate at which their intelligence is increasing. (p. 145)

> Everyone knows that he is now helpless in the system, and ideology has to take this into account. (p. 151)

> The defenceless person [who] has swallowed his rebelliousness. (p. 154)

> One could certainly live without the culture industry, therefore it necessarily creates too much satisfaction and apathy. (pp. 161–2)

> Consumers feel compelled to buy and use [the culture industry's] products even though they see through them. (p. 167)

> the reduction of the work of art to empirical reason is already capable of turning into overt lunacy at any moment, a lunacy which the fans who send trousers to the Lone Ranger and saddles to his horse already half affect. ('Schema', p. 56)

It is fair to say that what Adorno is referring to here is by no means serious and heroic resistance. However, it is also important to note the conscious effort of will-power that Adorno ascribes to the consumer. Adorno's consumers have no illusions about the reality of the situation they are in: they are aware of the pressure they are under and they know they must swallow their feelings of protest. Adorno's consumers participate in culture industry, but only half-heartedly. They are not 'sovereign individuals', yet neither are they products of manipulation – their state cannot be approximated to that of the 'amphibians' (p. 36).

In Adorno's view, consumers have little opportuntiy to resist culture industry. Nonetheless, the basic theoretical model that Adorno uses (whereby the dominated have to participate in their own domination) means that the possibility of refusing to participate is always open. For the media, thinking subjects only exist in reified form as 'the audience', and, if at all possible, they are completely left out of the equation. However, Adorno's theory succeeds in acknowledging the role of the thinking subject, even while it mourns the death of the individual.

Analysing 'the audience' from the audience's perspective

Our existing concept of 'the audience' is bound up with an idea of instrumentalization, but if we try to think round this, it soon becomes clear that we actually need a whole range of different concepts for the various relationships and forms of interaction that link cultural suppliers and performers to consumers of cultural artefacts and services. Our existing concept of 'the audience' reifies these relationships, but if we are to find more appropriate ways of describing them, we will have to treat these various reifications reflexively and analyse the working alliances in which they occur. Before we examine any of the working alliances in detail, we can begin by grouping them into two main categories: those in which artefacts are presented to the audience, and those in which an event is organized and physically represented. The relationship between the two differs according to the various cultural genres and productions. Ballet and improvised jazz are primarily events, while newly published books or public monuments are first and foremost artefacts — they are simply there, 'waiting' for us to find them. If no one takes the time to open the book and start reading, its contents will remain latent. If no one stops to examine the monument, it becomes an 'obstacle', and people will only take note of it as something that is blocking their path.

The primary category of working alliance is that involving an event. Even in the case of artefacts, an event has to occur at some point during the process of reception, otherwise nothing would happen. Cultural artefacts are always presented in such a way that the event that *should* occur is already prescribed. In some instances, we are then left relatively free to decide what we would like to make of it. It is generally the 'private' types of media that grant us this kind of freedom. Once you have taken your book home, you can read it out loud, you can start at the end or you can throw it away. Once you have bought a CD, you can play it softly in the background, sing along to the music or nail the disk to the wall. If you tried behaving this way in an art gallery or a concert-hall, you would be pursued as a vandal or a philistine. Some institutions might treat you rather more gently than others, but there is little doubt that you would be swiftly and decisively punished. By imagining these and other misdemeanours, we can easily work out the rules set down by the various working alliances about how we should consume culture in public contexts.[11]

The two main categories of working alliance can be divided into further subcategories:

A	(Working alliances for cultural artefacts)	B	(Working alliances for cultural events)
i	The literary or 'work' model	iv	The performers' model
ii	The news model	v	The (self-)representation of domination
iii	The propaganda or publicity model	vi	The roller-coaster model

The 'literary' model and the 'performers'' model both deal with 'extra-ordinary' material that is explicitly fictional – the artefact or event is produced and received autonomously, and it demands to be admired and respected. The 'news' model and the '(self-)representation of domi-nation' both foreground the connection to a 'real' reality beyond the medium. The 'propaganda' model and the 'roller-coaster' model come into play in relation to material that is intended to be sensational – the emphasis is on the artefact or event overwhelming the audience. The 'literary' or 'work' model is the working alliance of European high art. Looking at an abstract painting that is hanging in a gallery would be a good example of this. The corresponding model from the second cat-egory of working alliances (category B) is the 'performers'' model. This might involve singers and dancers, but it is not only high culture to which it relates, for it is also linked to tightrope walkers, clowns, jazz players and famous footballers. As for the 'news' model or the '(self-)representation of domination', when these working alliances are taken to extremes, the medium loses all significance and the focus is entirely on the information that is being conveyed. The event or artefact becomes 'pure' signal. (This is an ideal that instruction manuals are always striving to attain!) Of course, this goal of 'pure' informa-tion is never really attainable, especially in the case of the '(self-)representation of domination', where there are always other elements of expression or persuasion involved. The 'purest' representation of domination is probably attained in images of the sublime in nature, that is, in the sight of a majestic mountain range or (to quote Adorno's famous example from *Aesthetic Theory*) in the unperturbed singing of the blackbirds after the storm. As for the 'propaganda' model and the 'roller-coaster' model, extreme versions of these could be found in the political pamphlet and the fairground ride. The political pamphlet denounces society and harangues its rulers, aiming to fill us with a sense of outrage and disgust. The fairground ride turns our stomachs and pushes the air out of our lungs, sometimes making us shriek.

It is actually quite difficult to find extreme examples for these models, but this is because they usually appear in combination. In reality, working alliances rarely function in complete isolation from one another. As confused teenagers, we have all used novels and films to learn about 'love' and what it means. Even in the world of art, some of the most famous paintings have been treated like pornographic pictures and viewed in the context of the 'roller-coaster' model. And there is certainly an element of sensationalism to most items of news and propaganda, both of which are also usually linked to the representation of domination. There are plenty of opportunities for examining these and other combinations of working alliance, and we can begin by observing our own reactions to different artefacts and events.

It is also interesting to look at what happens when people confuse one genre with another.[12] This usually gives rise to misunderstandings and misplaced concerns. The distinction between action films and narrative cinema is a relatively common cause for confusion – particularly among more 'cultured' viewers. Detractors of the action film tend to have little understanding of the pleasure to be gained from long and drawn-out car chases, or from well-choreographed but brutal punch-ups and frequent and excessive violence. However, their inability to see the attraction of all this probably lies in the way that they are bound up with the conventions of narrative cinema (that is, with the 'literary' model) – they do not understand that action films should be viewed according to the 'roller-coaster' model. If you have been brought up with 'literary cinema', it is easy to forget that films started out as fairground sensations with terrifying and baffling scenes such as that of the steam train heading straight towards the audience. Slapstick comedies and cartoons were two of the most important genres in the next generation of films, and it was only with the advent of the 'talkies' that 'literary' cinema gained its hold. These days, 'literary' cinema is in decline: James Bond (and in particular the James Bond of the recent films) and *Die Hard* have much more in common with Tom and Jerry than with *High Noon* or Maigret.

Understanding horror films can be similarly fraught. There is plenty of evidence to suggest that the real fans of horror treat the films according to the 'roller-coaster' model: for them, it is a matter of steeling themselves and keeping calm so as to prove their strength and manliness to their anxious companions or competitive mates. However, if horror films are treated according to the literary model, the story is usually so thin that you have to ask yourself what the scary moments and nasty scenes are actually supposed to achieve. Those concerned for the education of our youth often insinuate that horror films are watched as instruction manuals or for information purposes (but this is usually how parents or teachers would wish their own utterances to be treated!).

All this is further complicated by the fact that viewers rarely treat films etc. with the seriousness, patience, concentration and alertness that their producers would wish. When we are watching something, we often have our own intentions. We frequently put products to quite different purposes, and these are predominantly social: when we go to museums, cinemas, concert-halls, exhibitions, theatres and operas we usually do so in company. It is only when we are jogging with our headphones on or snoozing in front of the TV that entertainment is a truly solitary pleasure. In most other cases, we enjoy looking at pictures or listening to music in the company of others, and we find ourselves eager to discuss what we have just seen or heard. The contact with other people becomes more important than the actual works of art. This is of course regrettable for those who have put so much effort into producing the artefact or arranging the event, but it is an important feature of culture industry. (It was also a feature of bourgeois culture, where intensive individual engagement with high culture was probably the exception rather than the rule.) Adorno discusses this decline in our attentiveness to culture (what Benjamin terms 'distraction' [*Zerstreuung*][13]), and he links it to the 'worthlessness' of culture industry products:

> Those who spent their money in the nineteenth or the early twentieth century to see a play or to go to a concert respected the performance as much as the money they spent. The bourgeois who wanted to get something out of it tried occasionally to establish some rapport with the work. . . . Criticism and respect disappear in the culture industry . . . Consumers now find nothing expensive. (pp. 160–1)

In the present day, this process appears irreversible. From a sociological perspective, our task is now to analyse the workings of cultural reception; to examine how many different forms of reception can be used in relation to certain artefacts and events; and to investigate what these forms of reception might presuppose.

Field notes X   Total control of your life

In sociology, there is a way of looking at people's lives that sees them as a series of 'choices' or 'decisions'. Each 'choice' determines the range of subsequent opportunities and decisions. This model has the charm of being fairly obvious (if not actually tautological), but it also serves to set out exactly what it means to plan life in a disciplined fashion: it stresses how important it is to remember that your future prospects can be permanently damaged if you let yourself slack for only one moment. Those who fail to plan ahead will surely be punished by life – at some point in the future. The idea of 'the beyond' is no longer quite so compelling, but our 'careers' demand of us the same kind of discipline that was once inspired by our desire to please God. (Of course, we are all familiar with the concomitant negative example: those who cannot bring themselves to put off immediate gratification will not have a career and will only have themselves to blame!)

One group of researchers in New York used this model in order to analyse people's 'life stories' and the meaning of 'love' within them. Unsurprisingly, the study showed that within this context 'love' has nothing to do with 'adventure' and very little to do with 'passion'. On the contrary, love appears as the fusion of two careers. It is a decision that should not be taken lightly – if it is to work out well, it must be of benefit to both partners. In any case, it should always include a get-out clause, so as to enable escape when the arrangement is no longer proving useful. The problem faced by people taking this 'decision' is that they always run the risk of attaching themselves to a 'loser'.

In our society, it is always important to be 'popular'. For a single woman, this means having numerous 'options' for weekend dates. For a man, it means not being left to sit around alone on a Friday night. This kind of thing does not just affect young people, but also matters to many successful career women. I have heard countless conversations about the correct etiquette for dating: if it is already Thursday, and you are asked out on a date for the following evening, you can be sure that you are not his first choice. If you are confident enough to do so, you should show that you are offended, and you should certainly turn him down. Once you get to the first date, it is only right for the man to pay. (At the start of the relationship, it is usually the man who is expected to take the risks.) By the second date (if you get that far), it is OK to split the bill. This means that the woman has no obligations, while the man never had any anyway. (The woman's 'obligations' are still sometimes an area of confusion, although thanks to 'fc' (feminist correctness) misunderstandings of this kind are becoming increasingly rare, especially as far as students are concerned.) One academic once informed me that in her view, Valentine's Day had been invented solely in order to fuel single women's obsessive concern with their own 'popularity' (thus encouraging them to sometimes send a little something to themselves).

When someone is 'available', their friends and acquaintances often take the opportunity to set them up on 'dates'. Woody Allen's films have made us all too familiar with this scenario. People's 'availability' (or 'unavailability') is something that is gossiped about when their names come up in conversation – there is simply no point in wasting your charms (and money) on hopeless cases where the person in question is already 'attached'. A casual acquaintance of mine once gave me the address of one of his friends in New York – since I was passing through, I should give her a call. She was 'between partners' and would appreciate being looked up. I was too embarrassed to act on the tip, but it was evidently seen as an 'option'.

Indeed, it was every bit as much of an 'option' as hanging around in singles bars or turning to 'Telepersonals' – a telephone dating agency that specializes in memorable commercials. In one such advert, a man and a woman in their late twenties are dining in a restaurant. They have obviously known each other for a long time, and the man tells the woman that he has a new girlfriend – someone he met through 'Telepersonals'. The woman responds by asking him if he is not yet fed up with seeing 'losers', but the man praises his new 'love' and explains how 'Telepersonals' works – there is no chance of meeting 'losers', it is just a reliable way of finding good dates for people who are short of time and fed up with the bar scene. The man advises the woman to give it a go – she has not been particularly successful with her latest few 'catches' at the bar. The woman looks at him sceptically but with an obvious glimmer of hope in her eyes. The advert closes as the telephone number for 'Telepersonals' appears on screen.

What is noticeable about these commercials is the way they try to shake off the reservations that we have about the rational approach to dating. It is clear from the commercials that our wariness of dating agencies stems not from any moral concern, but from the implication of social failure. It is thought that successful people should not need to 'work' at being popular and that they should not have to admit that they have trouble making contact with others. Escort agencies do not seem to be affected by this problem, or at least it is not something that is addressed in their commercials. It seems that hiring an expensive woman is not interpreted as a sign that you could not come by one any other way. On the contrary, it is taken as proof that you have the money to afford such luxuries. 'Escorts' are aimed at a different class of businessman. They are intended for the powerful (and more elderly) managers and directors, while the 'Telepersonals' system is clearly targeted at a lower rank of employee. 'Telepersonals' comes at the junction in life before the all-important decision over 'love' and the fate of two careers. Escorts, by contrast, are part of the 'bounty' you can enjoy once you have made it – all major credit cards accepted.

The best solution to the problem of 'love' would be a return to the custom of arranged marriages, where both sets of parents agree to bring their offspring together in order to secure their financial and social stability. However, these days many parents would not be able to provide much of an 'inheritance', as they have already spent most of their money on equipping their children with a good education. In any case, the majority of parents do not know enough about their children's careers and they do not have access to the right 'contacts'. In some instances, the parents are long dead or vanished. All in all, this means that 'arranged marriages' now have to be organized indirectly, that is, by choosing the right school and financing the child's education. This narrows the range of possible partners, but even so the child is likely to be too busy to be able to get a good overview of the 'market'. In any case, the decision is far too important to be taken without guidance or 'coaching'. The simplest way out would be to consult one's friends, but friends are often unreliable and inexperienced, and they may turn out to be rivals or 'losers'. What is more, nurturing friendships takes time, and this is already in short supply.

Fortunately, help is at hand in the form of 'psychic friends', as advertised on TV. (The first phone call is free, and you will also be sent a special Brazilian energy crystal – while stocks last.) Psychic friends are advisers and fortune-tellers who can tell you how things will work out. Apart from winning the lottery, the best news that you can ever get is that Prince Charming is on his way, riding towards you to the sound of wedding bells. Just as with 'Telepersonals' you are spared the embarrassment of any direct contact with this mysterious person. (If you wanted to actually meet an 'adviser', you would probably choose to visit a 'psychic' instead. In New York, there would be ample opportunity to do so, as there are innumerable 'psychics' in private practice.) It is evidently seen as an advantage of the service that you can just pick up the phone and dial – it is possible to confide in someone without ever having to meet them. Of course, we are all aware that long distance prognostics and advice can only be accurate if the person behind them has supernatural powers. And so it is that these people are credited with such abilities – they overcome our initial doubts by telling us some detail that is supposedly 'private'. On the other hand, we are continually reassured that nothing is really predetermined – it is only the different signposts that are apparent. Whatever you do, it is essential to remain in 'total control of your life'.

The enlightened drive to lead our lives in a rational and disciplined way leads to the search for advice and guidance in the realms of superstition and delusion.

6

Culture industry politics

Structural populism

In 1936, Max Horkheimer wrote a lengthy article entitled 'Egoismus und Freiheitsbewegung. Zur Anthropologie des bürgerlichen Zeitalters' [Egoism and the liberation movement: on the anthropology of the bourgeois era].[1] By then, the Nazis had already forced the Institute for Social Research into exile, but the article was published in the Institute's journal, which was edited by Horkheimer himself.[2] The title of the article suggests that Horkheimer is discussing a specific philosophical problem, namely 'human nature' and the familiar and misguided question as to whether humanity is good or evil. On the very first page, Horkheimer makes it perfectly clear that he is not interested in questions of ontology, but in different forms of politics: Horkheimer's interest is in domination and repression and in the possibilities of liberation.

In this article, Horkheimer raises some specific questions about the form of bourgeois politics of liberation. Horkheimer asks why this form of politics has always tried to appeal to people's morality, rather than relying on people to follow their own economic interests (as is the principle of capitalism). He questions why the preachers of bourgeois liberation attempted to rouse the people with fanatical speeches, rather than depending on them to act in their own political interest. If you were offering people liberation and a better life, then surely it would be enough to appeal to their egoism? The bourgeois politics of liberation, however, is based on the assumption that people must be forced into doing what is best for themselves. Does this indicate that there is something wrong with this notion of liberation?

Horkheimer conducts a historical examination of this question. He analyses the fourteenth-century Roman uprising under the leadership of Cola di Rienzo, as well as Girolamo Savonarola's attempt to establish democracy in Florence in the late fifteenth century. He also draws on the French revolution of the eighteenth century and particularly on the role of Robespierre. Reference is made to Calvin and Luther, while some of Horkheimer's more abstract statements seem to refer to the coups that were carried out by the fascist mass movements of the twentieth century.

Horkheimer's conclusions can be summarized as follows: the bourgeois struggle for liberation relies on the support of the lower classes, whose only recompense consists in the bourgeois freedom of property (although the lower classes owned none) and the freedom of the market (although they had only themselves to sell). If the lower classes had been led by their own egoistic reasons, they would have turned against bourgeois liberation, which for them meant domination. In order to prevent this from happening, everyone had to be encouraged in their duty to the whole. It was important to intervene and to stop the emergence of social forces organized around class interests. This was achieved through the use of demagogy and via the appeal to 'morality'. Nowadays, this would be referred to as 'populism' – it is a form of bourgeois politics that takes place when different elite groups compete against each other and draw on fanaticism to stir up the masses for use as a battering ram. These days, this kind of fanaticism exists in more muted form among the readers of a particular newspaper or the members of a particular political party, and it represents merely a potential threat.

In the 'Egoism' article, Horkheimer describes and analyses the central mechanism of 'dialectic of enlightenment' in politics: (bourgeois) liberation leads to a new form of domination. He also points to the conflicts that arise between the economic bourgeoisie and the educated classes. Bourgeois revolutions are based on a new economic form that is already in part established at the time of the uprising. Their aim is to create new political and administrative institutions that will fit in with and promote the emergent economic form. As Horkheimer writes:

> Unlike social revolutions, they [bourgeois revolutions] do not directly affect the economic base, but tend to develop and enhance the bourgeoisie's position already secured in the economy by opportune changes in the military, political, juridical, religious, and artistic spheres. The most bitter struggles are fought to renew the body of functionaries in these realms, to replace an earlier 'elite', an old stratum of bureaucrats and

intellectuals, with one better suited to the new tasks and to create more appropriate institutions. ('Egoism', p. 83)

This is why bourgeois revolutions appear as struggles between competing intellectual fractions. Those in favour of modernization (in most cases, the younger generation) clash with the more conservative-minded over the fate of culture and its institutions. Thus the 'Enlightenment' started out as the struggle between secular intellectuals and the church for control over the education of the rulers and of the people. Horkheimer describes this in relation to mid-twentieth century society by referring to monopolies:

> With the consolidation of a small stratum of monopolists brought about by concentration and centralization, cultural activity takes form more and more exclusively as domination of the masses. Although the culture is addressed just as much to the rulers and is held in especially high esteem by them, they sometimes sense very well that this is its main function in their system. . . . Deep contempt and indifference to the spirit is a trait of the ideal type of the modern bourgeois . . . They make religion, ideal values, and sacrifice for the nation into the highest goods of humanity, praise the success of the giants of art and science without any reference to the content of their accomplishments, and characteristically remain atheistic out of intellectual prudery, vulgar materialists incapable of any real pleasure. ('Egoism', pp. 83–4)

What Horkheimer is saying is that there is no possibility of using culture to 'refine' the abstract and anonymous economic interests of the 'global players'. In liberalism, these interests could be refined and restrained, for the owners of the means of production were personally identifiable. Indeed, in liberalism, culture was supposed to limit competition within the bourgeoisie and to keep the exploitation of labour power and nature to a socially acceptable level. Nowadays, the moral efforts of the intellectuals are no longer directed at the owners of the means of production, but at the members of the lower classes, who are being bound against their interest to the whole. This change has meant that influential members of society now treat intellectuals with disdain, regarding them as servants and entertainers whose activity is of no relevance to the lives of the powerful.

None of this is set out explicitly in the 'Culture Industry' chapter, although it is helpful to bear it in mind when trying to understand and contextualize the references to advertising and political propaganda. For Adorno, advertising has much in common with dictatorship, and he describes how 'totalitarian advertising bosses enforce[d] the general lines of culture' ('Culture Industry', p. 165). Naturally, this affects the consumers of culture, but it also and primarily affects its producers. In culture industry, intellectuals who are happy to follow economic dictates succeed at the expense of those who wish to remain autonomous. There is a sharp distinction between those who welcome advertising as a convincing and successful way of representing domination, and those who have no truck with the 'fraternal millions' ('Schema', p. 60) and who privilege 'enjoyment' over attending the 'right' events and 'keeping up' with what is going on; who are not interested in merely seeking prestige; and who value the 'relaxed self-surrender to all kinds of association and happy nonsense' over 'elevated pleasure' ('Culture Industry', p. 142).

The political situations described in the 'Culture Industry' chapter are not as dramatic as those referred to in 'Egoism and the Liberation Movement', for the focus of the 'Culture Industry' chapter is on everyday domination. The influence of the populist mechanism is as great on everyday domination as it is on bourgeois revolution, but it is not as noticeable. In everyday domination, populism is evident in the preoccupation with ratings, in the jubilant yet unobtrusive celebration of domination and in the mobilization of passive participation. It also creates a division among the public, pitting the 'fraternal millions' (in this case, the willing consumers) against those who question domination. Once again, the 'fraternal millions' are misled about their own best interests, this time via amusement. They are kept in line through the pressure to be disciplined and to behave in a 'moral' way. They subject each other to this pressure and are in turn subjected to it. There is a voyeuristic pleasure to be had in observing the disgraceful lack of morality of those at the very top and bottom of society. The populist notion of the enemy is always twofold: it targets the decadent upper classes, as well as the depraved lower-class foreign enemies who unite with and are protected by the former.

Adorno and Horkheimer link the form of politics that relies on agitation, demagogy and moralizing to its corresponding medium. Populism takes place in public gatherings, speeches and sermons. During the French Revolution, it was conducted through the use of festivals, public tribunals and executions. Adorno and Horkheimer also describe the medium of populism in fascist Germany:

> The radio becomes the universal mouthpiece of the Führer; his voice rises from street loudspeakers to resemble the howling of sirens announcing panic – from which modern propaganda can scarcely be distinguished anyway. The National Socialists knew that the wireless gave shape to their cause just as the printing press did to the Reformation. The metaphysical charisma of the Führer invented by the sociology of religion has

finally turned out to be no more than the omnipresence of his speeches
on the radio, which are a demonical parody of the omnipresence of the
divine spirit. The gigantic fact that the speech penetrates everywhere
replaces its content. (p. 159)

The forms of political propaganda used by agitators are analysed by
Adorno in several of his texts, as well as by Leo Löwenthal and N.
Gutermann.[3] However, it is more interesting to analyse the form of the
working alliance with the public, since this is more generally applicable. Indeed, what happens in populism is that the public is overpowered: it is overpowered by omnipresence, by the intensity of the
appeal and by the excitement of being part of the masses and of
responding with disciplined, subservient and ritualistic answers.
(These days, the most striking form of such attempts at self-integration
can be found in the phenomenon of the Mexican wave.)

Radio can only create this kind of working alliance when there is a
group of people listening or when the programme is broadcast to a
public assembly. This used to happen regularly in Nazi Germany, but
it is now no longer the case. Moreover, the fact that we watch television in the privacy of our homes means that this medium is equally ill-
suited to the populist working alliance. For political agitators such as
Haider (of the right-wing Austrian Freedom Party) and Le Pen (president of the French National Front), this has necessitated a return to the
medium of mass gatherings. In any case, the medium of television
tends to present the figure of the agitator in one of two ways: on screen,
agitators are either made to resemble harmless minuscule dolls, or
else are filmed so close up that the sight of their stubble, skin problems,
wrinkles and grimaces makes it difficult for them to overpower
the viewers. Domestic TV is not the best medium for ensuring that
the audience will be overpowered. In order to achieve this effect, you
need to be able to transmit your speeches in a pompous and public
manner – you need to recreate the situation of the traditional mass
gathering.

The false sense of proximity created by TV has had an enormous
effect on politics, changing politicians into actors, as well as actors into
politicians. We now participate in politics in the same fake way as we
become members of the great economic powers through advertising.
In both cases, our participation is passive rather than active, and so it
is necessary to offer us something to ensure that we stay. Political activity has to be made visible to us, but this is much easier in a military
dictatorship than it is in a democracy, where the whole point is to avoid
'memorable times' and to keep things 'boring'.

The attempt to represent politics in democracy results in endless shots of limousines pulling up in front of various governmental or official buildings. We are then shown the pompous figures who emerge from their cars and brush past the waiting journalists, refusing to give anything away until their discussions are complete. Representing politics in democracy involves press releases and press conferences, as well as all the other forms of political announcement that take place via the journalistic apparatus. Only occasionally does anyone ever ask a question that is not entirely predictable or that has not been 'cleared' beforehand, and when they do, it usually happens in the course of an interview or a political talk-show. In order to make politics look exciting and dramatic, political activity has to be represented in a way that takes in conflicts and controversies, plans and counterinitiatives, schemes and the struggles to implement them. Above all, it is important to show personal rivalries and bitter power struggles. Politics has to involve catastrophes, surprises, successes and failures. It is quite rare for any of this to actually happen, but the idea is to keep it at the forefront of people's minds.[4]

Political journalists have become 'insiders', and they are treated as a kind of courtly entourage. They are invited to all the important events, and have themselves turned into politicians. Journalists are political players, for they have power over a particular resource. They control access to an audience, and the size of this audience determines the extent of their power (just as it does in other types of advertising). In fact, the type of news broadcast or interview in which journalists put questions to each other may at first appear disconcerting, but it is not actually as illogical as it might seem. In politics as in advertising, everything that matters takes place within a closed circle. The importance of a politician appearing on TV or in the newspapers lies primarily in the fact that it causes other politicians, important officials and journalists to take note of what is being said and to respond to it.[5]

As anonymous potential voters and, in the worst-case scenario, potential demonstrators, strikers and campaigners, we are of merely secondary importance. We are only of interest due to the threat that we might pose. (In the sixties, the authorities' response to demonstrators and campaigners was rather heavy-handed, but since then protest movements have been handled in a far more flexible and laid-back manner.) In the normal run of events, we are only of significance when we can be used to reinforce political arguments, as politicians back up their policies with lines such as 'On a recent visit to X, one woman pointed out that . . .' We are reified into the statistics of various surveys, and we are frequently the object of supposition and pure fantasy, with politicians making remarks such as 'Of course, ordinary men and women won't be able to appreciate any of this . . .' It is practical for political actors to rely on structural populism without any exact information. Of course, this can lead to politicians 'losing touch', but that never seems to have troubled them too much anyway.

The false sense of proximity created by the media personalizes politics and turns politicians into celebrities. Articles and reports about politicians now resemble publicity slots for pop stars and actors: the politicians are being brought closer to us as people. Political reporting is nothing but amusing gossip, and we all know that gossip does not have to be true in order to have an effect. People are becoming more and more apathetic about politics, but this may be because they have stopped confusing culture industry politics with 'news'. Perhaps people have realized that political activity consists of a series of performative acts that take place in a closed circle from which we are excluded. The fact that we have nothing to do with it leads us to view it as entertainment. We have stopped kidding ourselves that we are part of the circle of political rulers, and we no longer engage in heated debates about 'what should be done'. Instead, we have come to see politics in an unemotional manner as a distant power struggle that is carried out in our name but at our expense.

This means that the working alliance that comes into play when we are presented with politics no longer involves any respect or engagement. Unlike the population under feudal rule, we are not taken in by displays of power and glory, yet neither do we have any illusions about participating in the bourgeois power struggle. We do not want to have to rely on the protection and the goodwill of the powerful, but we no longer believe that we can participate in an effective way. We do not have any faith in the bourgeois model of the reasoning public sphere, according to which everyone with a voice can join in. Our political education has taught us that we should take our right to self-determination seriously, and we know that we have the intellectual ability to join in the discussion. Nonetheless, we are also aware that nobody is interested in our opinions, and that the administration has arrogantly taken it upon itself to decide everything for us. Politicians are deaf to our interventions and try to palm us off with sound-bites, making themselves look ridiculous in the process.

The 'public sphere' (as described by Habermas) is vanishing before our eyes. Habermas's public sphere is an ideal type of bourgeois politics of reason, in which everyone takes part in the discussion about the best way to shape the whole, and in which individual interests must be generally applicable if they are to be accepted. Habermas describes the transition to 'manufactured publicity' and the 'manipulated public sphere', yet the change that is occurring is far more profound than this.[6]

It is interesting to note how *The Structural Transformation of the Public Sphere* (originally written by Habermas as his Habilitationsschrift in 1961) sets out the kind of analysis of culture industry politics that is missing in Adorno's work. However, even though this book draws closely on Critical Theory, Habermas goes his own way and finally finds himself at great distance from the fundamental precepts of Critical Theory. In setting down a substantive theory of democracy (and by extension ethics), Habermas draws on linguistic theory to arrive at a concept of communicative recognition (whereby in consenting to discuss something with somebody, I recognize that that person has an equal right and capacity to participate in the discussion). Yet this means that Habermas's model of the public sphere is clearly one of intellectual politics. The reasoning public sphere is a 'permanent panel discussion' (as I heard it termed rather polemically many years ago). However, the way that politics is conducted is not through intellectuals debating with each other in the *Guardian* and *New York Times* or on TV. Habermas takes what is essentially an intellectual's ideal of politics and attempts to apply it universally, transforming it into a political norm.

In actual fact, this type of intellectual politics is now conducted by the media, for the latter represent a powerful economic force and are part of the game of global capital. This is not due to the content that the media transmit, but to the possible gains and losses. This is particularly evident in war reporting, for how the war is documented is part of the way in which it is fought. War reporting also brings in vast amounts of money for those selling pictures or reports. Wars have always been wars of propaganda, but since Vietnam politicians and the military have learnt to use professional PR when presenting the pictures. CNN's market share reached its peak during the Gulf War. Films such as *Tomorrow Never Dies* and *Wag the Dog* play on the idea that media giants create and then orchestrate wars in exchange for power and money. In thematizing media power in this way, such films are far ahead of the intellectual critique that comes from the more 'serious' and predominantly literary branches of culture industry.[7]

In enhanced culture industry, there is something touchingly nostalgic about the idea that democracy could be based on public communication among intellectuals (not to mention among the population as a whole). On the other hand, the old fear that we might be entirely manipulated by the media also seems a little outdated. These days, the media subject themselves to constant self-criticism, and media content is in any case viewed with a degree of distance. The notion of the 'public sphere' as a democratic place in which people can engage in rational debate about different political policies has lost much of its credibility. Since the 1970s, it has become increasingly clear that politics 'from above' takes place either as behind the scenes diplomacy or as populist political show, while politics 'from below' assumes the form of discrete independent projects (from the hobby subculture to alternative lifestyles) or of public displays of dissatisfaction and rebellion. The latter, of course, are more likely to provoke an 'official' political response.[8]

If we are to take culture industry seriously, we will need a way of analysing and theorizing democracy that is radically different from the bourgeois model of a 'public sphere' characterized by rational debate. Trying to adapt this model or to reinstate some of its elements only results in helpless moralizing.

Field notes XI   Why Princess Diana's death was so moving

> Cynics would diagnose a bad case of mass hysteria, but right now there are no cynics; for a decent interval they have all gone to ground. (Anthony Lane, 'Last Rites')[9]

In Britain, the accident involving the Princess of Wales, her Egyptian playboy lover and her bodyguard met with mass demonstrations of public grief. There was a peculiar pressure to join in the mourning for the couple whose death had taken place in the car of a drunken chauffeur, under a storm of flashlights from the cameras of professional celebrity stalkers. At the insistence of the tabloid press, the Queen was forced to express (and in all probability thus experienced) emotional distress. Until that moment, the Queen had always seemed the very model of the British aristocracy's traditional reserve, and this was now shattered by populist pressure, which ruled that the entire nation should appear shaken by the news of Diana's death. No one was to be excused from this public mourning, least of all the family of Diana's divorced husband. (This is the family against whom Diana had waged a PR war. Since her divorce, Diana had enlisted the help of the tabloid press and had fought her campaign by declaring her loyalty to us – the ordinary people and voyeurs.)

From the very beginning the incident is intriguing due to its reflexive nature. Members of the press induced an accident involving a celebrity victim and then reported on it, at the same time mobilizing every possible expression of disgust to condemn the predatory behaviour of the press sharks (press piranhas is a more appropriate metaphor). Attitudes towards the incident only began to change when it became apparent that the vehicle's driver had been heavily under the influence of alcohol. Those paparazzi members who had initially been imprisoned were then released, while those who had been quick to call for laws against intrusive journalism fell silent. In a counteroffensive, the question was raised as to the credibility of Diana's desperate flight. Does not the joint appearance of two celebrities in August on the Côte d'Azur and in Paris constitute an invitation for reporters to follow them? As the German newsmagazine *Der Spiegel* suggested, could this not be construed as a kind of unofficial press conference designed to make the relationship public? It would have been possible for the couple to hide, if this had been their real intention. Yet there is something almost flirtatious about trying to hide in Nice or Paris. In accordance with this interpretation, the Princess's legendary shyness could be understood to be part of the self-image that Diana herself was attempting to project. In this way, Diana's timidity appears to be a ploy to make herself interesting and to use the press to her best advantage. In addition to this, the macho struggle between celebrity hunters and protectors could be seen to provide the final element to the drama. In this struggle about who can fool whom, it was the driver from the Ritz who finally succumbed.

It is not difficult to grasp that what we are dealing with here is a mesh of accusations and counteraccusations. Blaming others helps us to deal with mishaps and accidents, but it does not serve to clarify an event's significance. Nevertheless, we can still get a good handle on the matter if we examine what lies behind such attempts to attribute blame. This leads us to the insight that the two opposing camps of interpretation were divided over Diana by one fundamental issue: the question as to whether celebrities should be allowed to create and control their own self-image, or whether this task should be left to the media. The Princess of Wales was clearly very good at controlling her own media image. She went to the press in order to ensure that her divorce would proceed in the way that she had intended. In fact, she succeeded in arranging a financial settlement that was really rather generous. (This matter is never mentioned, but it is surely a contributory factor in the royal family's less than friendly feelings towards Diana. It seems that Diana had made rather a hole in their pockets.) After the divorce, Diana succeeded in presenting herself as an elegant lady who did not shy away from contact with the ordinary people and who immersed herself in charity work. When not shopping or at a party, Diana, it seemed, was burdened with the suffering of the world. This image was projected by Diana in part through organized photo shoots, that is, with the help of press photographers. Her association with Mother Teresa was a last touch of genius that reached its coincidental and intolerable climax when the two women died within the same week.

In both cases, however, the image of the saint was merely superficial, and in Diana's case, it was simply the result of a ridiculous misunderstanding. Nevertheless, through their care for the poorest of the poor and for the dying, both women conveyed the same message: that official and state support for these people is inadequate or non-existent, and that the only thing that can help us in this miserable world is pure and selfless compassion. Admittedly, the majority of us (the voyeurs) are at least partially protected from such misery by our social status, yet we remain affected by the notion of human kindness, knowing that someday we too will have need of it. Both women (the beautiful British aristocrat with her financial fortune and model looks, and the diminutive, old, impoverished Albanian nun who lacked even a surname) embodied a reproach that brought shame upon the welfare state and the cold professionalism of organized charitable aid. All amateur and celebrity charity ventures live off their supposed contrast to the unfeeling professionalism of organized welfare. (Indeed, given their lack of expertise, this is, of course, their only trump card.) Ideally, welfare aid should consist of both professional help and personal care. The dying, however, are beyond the reach of professional help, and it is for this reason that they become a suitable object for amateur aid. It is hardly necessary to make specific mention of the fact that all over the world governments are trying to save money by mobilizing amateur aid. For these governments, the photos of caring celebrities are a welcome form of inexpensive propaganda.

The press, however, is also governed by its own interest. It is not simply a PR agency for the famous, and it does not merely assimilate and transmit the self-image that celebrities would wish to portray. Even if it often engages in such activities (for the press, cooperation often proves the simplest, cheapest, least demanding and in the long run most profitable way of dealing with celebrities), there will always be people who decide to break away. The task of propagating a celebrity's self-image can be extremely boring: there is little chance of finding an exclusive scoop, and little opportunity for reporters to exercise their skills. In any case, it is not only love that we feel for our celebrities. On the contrary, we often complain about the undue attention that their overly affluent and slightly ridiculous lives receive. In short, we enjoy it when they fall. Behind the chic facade, we want our celebrities to engage in different, more everyday activities. We want them to experience the problems that we experience, to commit the mistakes that we have committed, and to suffer from the fears, failures and insecurities with which we are familiar. We like to watch our celebrities as we view a soap opera, following the details of their messy lives and observing their highs and lows. Without all this, what reason would we have to bother with them at all?

Those who mourned Princess Diana's death will have followed her life with interest, scrutinizing the 'indiscreet' photos of Diana and Dodi and eager to know more about the couple's romance. We can be sure that they were impressed by Lady Di's struggle against the cold-hearted royal family, which clearly also played a part in her latest misalliance. It is always possible that if the affair had developed any further, it would eventually have provoked a public outcry against racial prejudice. Alternatively, it may have ended by revealing the difficulties of intercultural relationships. Either way, the outcome would have been interesting to follow. In fact, there is no doubt that the whole thing would have brought humiliation on the royal family, especially if William and Harry had found themselves with a new half-brother or sister. It is not surprising that the press was already full of rumours about the Princess's alleged pregnancy, or that the perspective of the Al Fayed family was almost entirely ignored.

When we talk about the 'paparazzi', we mean those photographers who refuse to stick to the self-image that celebrities would like to present of themselves. What the paparazzi do is not so much to infringe anyone's right to privacy, as to inhibit people's power to control their own image. They are after photos that do not fit in with the picture that celebrities strive to promote of themselves. In this respect, there was nothing to 'uncover' or 'reveal' about Diana's romance with Dodi, for it already corresponded to the image nurtured by the Princess. In fact, it merely added a new dimension to the existing drama, which pitted Diana against the royals. Seen in this light, the couple's flight from the press was unnecessary, and the fatal crash was just a drunken accident. It was only its aristocratic component that made it stand out from countless other such incidents.

The widespread sorrow at Diana's death was made up of various elements. In the first instance, it stemmed from regret at the premature conclusion to the soap opera and revenge drama of 'Snow White and the cold-hearted Stepmother, plus her rather clumsy Son'. (Nonetheless, the press continued to exact revenge on the royal family by pressurizing the Queen to make a public show of emotion at Diana's death.) Secondly, the sorrow derived from our desire to be cared for by the young, rich and beautiful and to win their sympathy for our lives in this era of cold (and failing) bureaucracy. (Of course, as we all know, only a saint could grant us this wish!) Thirdly, the mourning was bound up with the wonderful feeling of belonging that we experience when we gather around the coffin of a rich and prematurely deceased woman: the mourners became a community united by borrowed feelings of outrage and sorrow. The secret of the tabloid papers' success lies in the way that they effectively manufacture these emotions.

It is now customary to stress that all these various types of 'emotion' are perfectly acceptable. We are supposed to defer to people's fears, concerns, problems, sadness and 'sorrow and anger', as well as to their religious rituals and taboos and their nationalistic or racist affinities or antipathies, not to mention their protests of superiority or discrimination. We are expected to accept all this and be prepared to put it to populist purposes. The ideologues of communal emotion seize on any event, however unlikely (from war to student strikes and from racism to youth culture) in order to identify the desire for shared emotion as the original cause of the phenomenon (or at least as a welcome by-product of it). We are supposed to take all this seriously – and presumably we should have treated the popular enthusiasm for Hitler's speeches in a similar manner. It is expected that we will treat it as a matter of genuine emotion.

To suggest that such emotion is not real but merely borrowed is definitely p.i. (politically incorrect), yet we should question exactly what it is that we are doing when we go to the cinema in order to cry at a sentimental film or when we watch wrestling so as to make ourselves feel macho. We need to examine what it is that is going on when we attend political meetings in order to edify ourselves by rubbing shoulders with the heroes of liberation or when we join in with others in professing our faith or expressing our disgust, as appropriate. In all of these scenarios, we experience real emotions – we feel genuine sadness, outrage, disgust or enthusiasm. However, we need to remember that we deliberately put ourselves in such situations *in order* to experience such emotions. We manipulate ourselves in order to induce genuine emotions by identifying with something or by deciding to oppose it. Culture industry aims to enable us to indulge in such pleasurable emotional outbursts without danger or consequence. The real question is why all this should be of any significance (apart from as a possible threat to security) to the public sphere.

There is also the question as to how we should treat situations in which emotions are used to justify political decisions. In such situations, whether the emotion is 'genuine' or 'profound' is of no importance – it does not matter whether it really exists, or why it exists and how many people share in it. In any case, if it really came down to it, the emotion could probably be induced. Yet all this is irrelevant, for what is really decisive is the act of instrumentalization, in which emotion becomes something more than a signal pointing towards an objective state of affairs that we could then discuss rationally. The existence of emotion is presented as proof positive that there is an objective problem that should be dealt with. This overlooks the question as to why the emotion should be treated as something that is of public and political relevance (other than for populist politicians trying to whip up some support). Irrespective of whether or not the feeling is genuine, it is again a case of borrowed emotion that is being selected and put to use as appropriate. When we claim that these emotions are of public importance, we make ourselves look as childish as most politicians and journalists already think we are. Indeed, it is both insulting and patronizing if politicians promise to take these emotions 'seriously'.

In the case of Lady Diana Spencer, it is not enough to say that the nation (if not the whole world) was overcome by emotion and self-pity at the news of her death. It is important that we also draw attention to those who were responsible for this state of affairs. A list of those responsible would include tabloid journalists and PR pros such as Elton John and Tony Blair (who were quick to make the most of the opportunity presented to them), but it would also include ourselves, for we were keen to find out all we could about Diana. Indeed, we were determined not to miss out on such a 'beautiful corpse'.

7

Intellectuals in the supermarket: perplexed

Professional and lay critics of media and society

Wrong television cannot be viewed rightly

Adorno's shrewd critique of culture industry was based on his understanding of autonomous art at the turn of the century. In Adorno's view, art had failed to develop from that point onwards, and he identified in twentieth-century art nothing but the progressive advance of culture industry. For Adorno, 'culture industry' could only be thought of in critical terms, since his understanding of art and culture placed the latter in opposition to the social order. Adorno had arrived at this conception of art via a historical analysis according to which bourgeois society is divided between the opposing spheres of culture and the economy. According to this model, the cultural sphere was set up in distinction to the economic sphere in order to allow men and women to escape their lives as functionaries and to regain their humanity. It had been the task of the artist and intellectual to defend this alternative sphere and to extend its scope. The goal was to secure autonomy for culture, for it was thought that culture should be governed by its own rules alone: only then would it be able to fulfil its task in providing critique and innovation and in revealing new possibilities. Thus culture was to provide a niche for all that was beautiful, good and true, for all humankind's more elevated desires, for its capacity for thought and indeed for its humanity – in short, for all those qualities which, as the bourgeoisie were well aware, had no place in the everyday business of competition and economic necessity. After all, even those caught up in the hectic business of making money were grateful for those times in the evening, at the weekend or on high days and holidays when they could sit down and reflect on God, the universe and themselves – times when they could regain the humanity that they were otherwise forced to forfeit due to the form of production. It was thought that the proletarian workers were in particular need of such cultural respite, for the ennoblement of the working classes was to occur by way of bourgeois culture, albeit administered in carefully measured doses. The only solution seemed to lie in the autonomy of art and culture.

A highly cultured man, Adorno was of course too reflective to fall for the bourgeois conception and business of culture. As an incisive critic of domination, he was familiar with the cynicism inherent in the bourgeois model of functionalized culture, yet he was able to identify the remote possibility of using the bourgeois concept of cultural autonomy to critique bourgeois culture. He found a historical alternative to culture industry in the 'autonomous work of art' of the kind created by Schoenberg, whose brief period of success and subsequent fall he observed and articulated. Based as it was on this contrast with the concept of autonomous art, Adorno's theory of culture industry was necessarily bleak, for it pointed to the end of art, the end of a public political sphere and the end of the individual.

Adorno was astute in his observation of the way in which culture industry was expanding, yet he did not anticipate the change in the critical function of art that this entailed. Art cannot operate in isolation from culture industry. On the contrary, it can only exercise its critical function from within the apparatus of culture industry and its products. Thus critique is limited to localized resistance and to subversion from within, taking the form of irony, ridicule and derision and working by undermining the privileged status of 'serious' and 'high' culture and of supposedly 'serious' information and 'cultured' debates. Consumers either overlook or pay no serious attention to culture industry. (This failure to take matters seriously is, of course, a widespread phenomenon whose existence we customarily lament, citing cultural ignorance or political apathy.)

This extension of the culture industry theory should have obliged Adorno to withdraw from and indeed renounce his own public role as a prophet of doom and a preacher of repentance. However, by the 1960s, Adorno had himself become an object of and a player in culture industry. (In fact, Adorno's assimilation into culture industry can be dated back to the success of *Minima Moralia* (1944/1951).) For culture industry, 'Adorno' was an instance of moral authority. This authority built up around Adorno's name in West Germany during the 1960s, but it was dismantled towards the end of that decade and particularly after Adorno's death in 1969. In the end, Adorno was dismissed as an 'elitist man of high culture', and the matter was left at that.

Adorno's status was not (and indeed is not) that of the many professors capable of writing and speaking in a language that is sophisticated and complex. On the contrary, Adorno has been seen as a man who has something to say about the way we should live our lives. This is clear even in the face of what is perhaps his most famous aphorism, an aphorism in which Adorno almost ventures a joke: 'Wrong life cannot be lived rightly' (*Minima Moralia*, p. 39).

In order to defend themselves against attacks based on Adorno's critique of jazz music, jazz musicians and contemporary composers still find themselves having to stress that Adorno clearly did not understand anything about jazz. Moreover, Adorno's remark that 'to write poetry after Auschwitz is barbaric' (*Prisms* (1955), p. 34) continues to circulate in various misleading guises. (I recently heard a literary specialist referring to the 'aesthetics of prohibition of the 1960s'!)[1] Aficionados of baroque music have had to come to terms with the diagnosis of authoritarianism that Adorno applied to them. Indeed, all those in favour of providing a musical education for the population have been forced to confront the charge that music groups and classes are for dilettantes. As listeners of music, we were expected to rise to the challenge of 'structural listening' (that is, of composing music anew as we listen). Unsurprisingly, most of us failed. In any case, we found ourselves unable to refute the charge of 'pseudo-culture'. Moreover, the 'authoritarian personality' had become a negative norm against which to compare ourselves. Those who attended Adorno's lectures still take pride in spreading the story that nobody ever understood anything of what he said for the first few semesters. Whether he liked it or not, Adorno was a public instance of arbitration over intellectual questions (including the crucial question as to how we should live our lives) 'after Auschwitz'.

Quite clearly, this relates to the way in which intellectuals in West Germany attempted to 'come to terms' with the Nazi past. People felt that they had to strengthen their moral character against prejudice and delusion. The general feeling was that the necessary political and institutional changes had already been taken care of by those responsible for creating the new German constitution.[2] What remained was for the change to take place in people's minds. Bold theories such as those of the 'authoritarian personality', the 'inability to mourn' and the 'fatherless society' located the problem within the individual and the family.[3] For the younger generation of Germans who had been brought up by ex-Nazis at school, university and perhaps even at home, this meant that they would have to try to change themselves: they would have to try to pull themselves up by the scruff of their necks from the mire of their socialization. There was a great demand for reliable role models who could provide guidance on how to deal with this terrible threat.

Those who read Adorno (not to mention other writers such as Freud, Camus and Sartre) in this manner had to devote themselves to their cultural education and to impose on themselves strict cultural discipline. They had to tackle the sheerest cliffs and the steepest summits of culture. Those who could claim not to have failed utterly in this task were already a step ahead of their teachers (who were less well or wrongly educated). The extreme nature of what Adorno was perceived to have demanded provided an excellent goal for the new generation of intellectuals to work towards, and it helped them to retain their advantage over the 'intellectual climbers', of which there was no short supply after the drive for increased access to higher education in the 1960s. Subsequent developments (for instance, the process of dogmatization that took place supposedly in the name of Marx, the formation of various different academic political sects, and the devaluation of the intellectual, etc.) can be understood as an attempt on the part of the intellectual climbers to establish new subject-matter and approaches that would definitively destroy the advantage held by the old school of intellectuals. This is particularly true of the devaluation of culture and theory carried out by feminists and ecologists, as well as of the contemporary culture of 'fun' in which an expertise in TV soap operas, sporting competitions, fashion and the latest commercials is considered more important than a knowledge of the work of unworldly philosophers and of the more rigorous arts, in which there is nothing much to laugh about.

Adorno's moral authority was forgotten because having an expert knowledge of high culture does not impress anyone anymore. Since the 1960s, the 'educated classes' have expanded, but they no longer define themselves in relation to high culture or avant-garde culture. To be more precise: the small cultural avant-garde that we have nowadays defines itself as a punk/rave/techno avant-garde. It is characterized by its wildness and by a wild determination to seek pleasure. It chooses to exhaust itself and to associate itself with trash. It expressly links itself to the products and possibilities of culture industry, and it is certainly not defined by esotericism and seriousness. The attitude of today's avant-garde is that of the PR expert who is cynically in search of a slice of the fame and who is keen to earn some easy money.[4]

The best way of explaining this change is through reference to the altered situation of competition between intellectuals. Traditionally, the market for high culture was small and elitist, in terms both of producers and consumers (who tended to take on the role of patrons and were therefore personally linked to the cultural producers). Now that ever more people are going into higher education, the market for high culture has become a mass market for both producers and consumers. This makes the production of high culture in the old sense of the word impossible. In fact, even the high culture that we have inherited has been either seduced or forced into adopting the imperative of commodification. This is particularly noticeable in the case of the art museum. Art museums used to have an elitist niche existence, but now they have been transformed into a mass medium. This change came about as they turned towards large-scale exhibitions and consumer friendliness, and as they became involved in city councils' policies to attract new business to the area. It was also a result of advertising and of the alliance between the different types of media, as exhibitions became the subject of TV documentaries and the content of catalogues and books, while art provided the content for films and for other kinds of merchandise.

Seen in this light, the whole discussion about 'postmodernity' can be analysed in terms of the way in which intellectuals have adapted their understanding of culture in accordance with the new situation of the market. In a mass market, the range of commodities on offer and the different consumer demands for products all have to be treated as if they were of equal value. Any concern for criteria other than the selling power of these products (such as a concern for enlightenment, liberation or critique) only interferes with the market. Such concerns or commitments would lead to 'eliminatory' competition, and this is felt to exacerbate the situation quite unnecessarily, while also endangering the consumer-friendly atmosphere of 'fun'. It is much better for the market if there is a random variety of styles and forms that are able to co-exist happily, so long as they all get their share of attention. It is for this reason that producers and consumers alike bade farewell to the rigours of 'modernity'.

This also explains why Adorno is still the target of caricature and disrespectful anecdotes (which are then rejected with horror by the Adornoites who have made it their task to keep the memory of Adorno sacred). There is usually no need to poke fun at philosophers, but mocking Adorno does help people to deflate the heavy moral challenge that they are unable or unwilling to meet. This is particularly true when this challenge does not simply remain on the abstract level, and instead requires intellectuals to engage seriously with the everyday and political context that they need for their task.

Social criticism and culture

Those who boast that sociology (or the particular branch of sociology they are working in) is a 'critical' discipline thoroughly deserve the dismissive smile with which their claims will inevitably be greeted. These days absolutely everything is 'critical'. Journalists show no mercy in spreading the news of politicians' failings, while incidents such as industrial accidents are the subject of condemnatory commentary for days on end. In fact, there is a tone of distinct outrage about almost all news broadcasts and even about the weather forecast. Protest groups of all kinds campaign against the deplorable state of affairs in relation to any number of different phenomena, and we are all concerned about the mistreatment of 'our' rainforests abroad. Even pop-music is accused of brutalizing adolescents and predisposing them to violence.

The spread of 'critical' attitudes has resulted in the term 'critical' losing its distinctness of meaning. The term has been trivialized, and it is no longer clear exactly what it describes. This has come about not only as a result of the general lack of confidence in the social system and political leadership, but also, and more seriously, as a consequence of the way in which voices from the right have joined in the chorus of complaint. The 'critical' voices have come to include populist racist and anti-Semitic sentiment: the 'anti-capitalism of the unthinking' is once again finding expression. The situation is not helped by the fact that social criticism is also being conducted 'from above', as the population is criticized for its insatiability and laziness, as well as for its tendency to violence and its reluctance to make sacrifices. In 'criticism from above', as well as in racist 'criticism', it is not a matter of criticizing domination, but of condemning a sector of the population and attempting to exclude it from society. Moreover, even the criticism of domination can be manipulated in order to drive out or 'do away with' particular groups that are alleged to be dominant or privileged.

'Criticism' appears in whatever guise it chooses, and it is the expression of a discontent that is bound to the 'critic's' interests. This corresponds to the approach of 'social problems theory', according to which everyone has the right to participate in the social struggle in order to get their interests or moral preoccupations recognized as constituting a 'social problem', in other words, in order to secure state resources. To what extent people succeed in securing acknowledgment and resources depends on their skill and on other such factors, not to mention on the input of journalists hungry for a good scandal.[5]

These days, there is not much point in engaging in social criticism, particularly if you are a sociologist. There are professionals there to do the job for us, for we now have a fully developed industry of scandal based on the alliance between politics, entertainment and journalism. The scandal industry keeps society whipped up into a continual state of outrage. The objects of this outrage change with regularity, and are wheeled out again and again. The public is confronted with corruption or with the privileges enjoyed by officials and politicians. The slips in safety standards in production are revealed, and we are presented with instances of negligence in relation to the helpless. (Such stories can cover anything from the inadequacy of the measures designed to combat unemployment to the accounts of old people being found dead in their flats.) There are reports about male violence (especially in the case of young men and when the violence is directed towards women) and about the disadvantages experienced by various groups of people (the teachers/students/policemen/women/local population/foreigners/old people/young people/transport unions/lorry drivers and people who live near airports or motorways, etc., etc.). We perennially hear about the unjustifiably high profits that are made in certain businesses (and, as players and gamblers, we are as fascinated by this as we are outraged) and about health risks and murders. When we are told about these things, we are encouraged to contact the police, the opposition group, the governing body, the campaign group or the individual in question. Sometimes even the government draws on scandal and proclaims the existence of a crisis to keep its own apparatus in better control or to persuade the population to accept certain measures. It is of no real importance if these announcements are pure fabrication – even the attempt to deny them (which is seldom necessary) is itself newsworthy.[6]

From time to time, academics and intellectuals are also brought into play – providing, that is, that their work lends itself to being presented in a sensational way. In this context, intellectuals cannot count on people actually wanting to understand their work. In fact, the general atmosphere is almost diametrically opposed to the culture of reflection and consideration that is at the heart of intellectual life. Intellectuals are called on to provide the cues, or are instrumentalized for use as a battering ram. One particularly popular strategy involves setting up two intellectuals (or one intellectual and one practitioner) to argue against one another. That way, the public can enjoy following their ruses and their flowery insults, as well as taking pleasure in the occasional strike 'below the belt'.

Social scientists entering these debates with thoughts of a 'reasoning public sphere' soon discover that the strength of their theories and arguments is of no importance whatsoever. Instead their success will be measured by the force with which they advance their arguments and on the sang-froid with which they launch their counterattacks and deflect reprisals. In this kind of public tussle, there can be no victory in terms of content. In fact, victory consists merely in triumphing over the personality of your interlocutor. The only reward for such success is an invitation to appear once more in front of the microphone as an intellectual/actor.

Social 'criticism' has proliferated in recent decades in the form of protest movements of various kinds. These movements have become increasingly professional, especially those connected with animal rights or environmental protection. Here the multinational protest organization Greenpeace is at the fore. In fact, the environmental movement's professionalism in the field of criticism and PR work makes other protest groups such as the peace movement and the anti-nuclear movement look comparatively homespun. Local protest is by its nature amateur protest, and it acquires professional elements by the coincidental local availability of such resources. All in all, however, the skills involved in PR work and criticism seem to have undergone a democratization. This is linked to the fact that the educated classes have increased in numbers, but it is also a result of the ubiquity of the media. TV is particularly instructive in this regard, for it often broadcasts reports and documentaries from which we can find out what it is that makes for the success of a campaign.

It is not only 'alternative' protest movements that are critical of society. In fact, right-wing movements are similarly critical, and their forms of protest (up to and including acts of arson and violence) should also be understood as political statements or as PR work. Indeed, such actions are targeted at social forces and politicians that the perpetrators believe will be able to respond.

So, what do we have to complain about? The world, it seems, is full of social criticism. Admittedly, not all of it is as comprehensive and as theoretical as we might like, and it is often bound up with people's immediate interests. Nonetheless, there is always an inherent awareness that there is plenty of discontent about numerous other things and that this is not the first or last time that society will be criticized. This awareness is a first step towards theorizing social criticism.

This theorizing of social criticism often implies the existence of a kind of conspiracy theory that assumes that the administrative and political systems are both incompetent and corrupt. The social democratic parties in particular seem to have lost their credibility as representatives of the 'ordinary people'. Instead, small populist fractions are moving into the foreground and voicing their pseudo anti-authoritarian creed of force. Within the environmental movement, the conspiracy theory is accompanied by apocalyptic fears.[7] This minimum of theory is enough to underpin the themes of social criticism.

It is useful to examine the women's movement in order to see how social movements can come to adopt the political tactics of moralizing and sensationalizing, rather than aiming to represent their adherents' interests. This occurs when the movement has to encompass a broad range of heterogeneous interests. Among other things, the women's movement has had to try to bring together career woman and housewives with children. Of course, in practice, many women fall into both of these categories, yet the interests of the career woman are very different from those of the housewife or mother. Career women need to be protected against the discrimination that may block their path to advancement, and they need help in overcoming the 'old boy's network'. Women with children need to be able to be independent from their partners and need help in raising their children. They need to be able to work shorter hours, to take a break from their careers, and to have the opportunity to cease their work as housewife and full-time mother: they need nursery schools, a supportive work environment and the opportunity to return to their jobs. This divergence of interests is made all the more complicated by the fact that women from different social classes have very different interests. On top of this, there is a further category of women who still believe that it is the right and proper duty of all women to try to civilize men, whom they deem to be naturally brutal, irrespective of whether they are soldiers, manual labourers, office workers or investors. The disparity of interests within the women's movement is overcome through campaigns against violence, pornography, sexual harassment and cruelty to children, etc. Here, as in other heterogeneous movements, the best way of overcoming difference is to pick a common foe. Political campaigns that rely on moralizing and sensationalizing are one way of overcoming conflicts of interests that cannot otherwise be dealt with.

In this context, 'criticism' is a rather opaque mixture of various things, ranging from the only barely disguised promotion of a particular group's interests to the impossibility of ever identifying any common interests, let alone energetically pushing them forward. In every instance, however, it takes on the form of scandal and sensationalism, a form that is very effective in media terms and that relies on exaggeration, outrage and moral agitation. Creating a scandal involves valuing effect over truth. It sometimes leads to the neglect of the very people who are affected by the problem, and it tends to cloud our understanding of what is going on. The form of the media being used corresponds to the structure of the politics involved.

In this climate of permanent overexcitement, it is becoming increasingly common for sociologists to intervene with warnings against exaggerations and generalizations. They have come to take on the task of dedramatizing the situation and appeasing the various parties. As the accusations fly, sociologists find themselves trying to point out that there is always another side to the story, and that it might help to listen to it. At the same time, sociologists are also filled with concern (and sometimes contempt) for the state of the world (and in particular the part of the world that falls into their specific area of expertise), and so, like others, regard affairs with a profoundly 'critical' attitude. It would be absolutely impossible to make yourself stand out from the rest by being particularly 'critical'. 'Social criticism' is now as much a part of the business as 'cultural criticism' was at the time that Adorno was writing his essay on 'Cultural Criticism and Society' (1949).

In this situation, the only way of making a serious contribution is by drawing back from the tendency to sensationalize social problems. We need to analyse this tendency and to hold on to the philosophical tradition of 'critique'. In this tradition, 'criticism' does not mean that there are things that the thinker does not like or agree with. In this context, 'criticism' means reflexivity, and it refers to a way of thinking that must be learnt and then practised. The title of Kant's *Critique of Pure Reason* is not meant to indicate that there was something about reason that Kant and his followers were not happy about. Similarly, in his *Critique of Political Economy*, Marx does not quibble with capitalism, but analyses the leading economic theory of his time in terms of 'false consciousness'. 'Criticism' is always about the circularity that arises from the fact that we always have to work with the (conceptual) tools of domination and that we always have to be wary of concepts due to their abstractness and their link to ideology.

'Criticism' is the reflexive analysis of our conceptual tools (concepts, theories and methods). It is the self-criticism carried out by intellectuals as part of their scholarly and scientific work, and it is the analysis of intellectual products as culture industry events.

Critical theory in enhanced culture industry

Early forms of critical theory were characterized by the 'modern' attitude of intellectuals in the context of 'public aloofness'. However, this attitude was itself a last-ditch attempt to preserve intellectual autonomy in a world that was already in the grip of culture industry. Critical theorists were confronted with extreme examples of the exclusionary side of capitalism in Nazi Germany, World War II and the politics of extermination. At the time when Horkheimer and Adorno were writing *Dialectic of Enlightenment*, European society was being divided radically in two, as one section of the population was drafted into the *Volksgemeinschaft* and the other was excluded and physically destroyed.[8] Culture industry played an important role in all this: mass assemblies were stage-managed and became the subject of films; Hitler's speeches were broadcast on the radio; and malicious propaganda was circulated about internal and external 'enemies'. On top of this, forward-looking culture industry pleasures were used to tempt the population. Thus the Germans were offered organized leisure activities through the 'Kraft durch Freude' programme (the 'Strength through Joy' scheme offered holidays and cultural activities to the working classes, and was designed to increase the productivity of the labour force), the *Volksempfänger* (inexpensive radio sets that were produced with the intention of ensuring that Nazi propaganda reached every German home) and the Volkswagen (many Germans invested in purchase schemes hoping to own their own model of the 'people's car', but, during the war, production in the Volkswagen factory had actually switched to military vehicles). However, at the same time, the fascist state singled out culture industry and culture industry intellectuals for attack. Journalists, artists and entertainers were kept under close observation. Many were persecuted for being 'degenerate' and 'subversive', and were then replaced by 'reliable' workers. Moreover, the emphasis placed on creating a working and fighting 'racial community' meant that people were actively encouraged to discriminate against intellectuals, as well as against Jews and Communists.

In the 1950s, Horkheimer and Adorno returned to Germany, where they attempted to revive and strengthen the little that remained of the possibility of securing intellectual autonomy. They set out to save reason by way of a particularly demanding way of thinking and by increased reflexivity and increased individuality. However, according to their own analysis of the situation, this was no longer possible: Horkheimer and Adorno's work was a contradiction in terms. Yet it is this ability to work with contradictions and in contradiction to itself that lends Critical Theory its power. The real achievement is to maintain clarity of theory, despite having to compromise in life; and to preserve theoretical pessimism, even though each day you have to get up and get on with things as normal, since there is no guarantee that the apocalypse will occur tomorrow.

'Public aloofness' has long since been appropriated. The Dadaist tactic of subversion is not suited as a general model, and it only succeeds very occasionally. Intellectuals now make up a large social class, which is split in various ways in enhanced culture industry. Culture industry has gained huge economic significance, and its substratum of communications technology has become *the* technology of the future. In the 1950s, fantasies of progress were bound up with outer space and nuclear energy: these days they focus on the internet. Of course, this kind of technology is mostly used for computer games and for unnecessary mobile phone conversations, but it is also linked to globalization. In this respect, communications technology is responsible for creating a new computer-wise upper class of people who have access to all kinds of information and who live and work in a way that transcends regional boundaries. It is also creating a new lower class of people that is made up of homeworkers and the irregularly and precariously 'self-employed', as well as of those who only ever have contact with this kind of technology in the form of game consoles. While the information upper class makes use of the different time zones in order to conduct its business transactions on an international scale, the lower class is confined to one place and remains unemployed. Whenever a new form of cultural technology is introduced, the social differences resulting from differing levels of education are exacerbated, for the well educated and the young are the first to pick up on the new technology. (Besides, now that education involves mastering the latest technology rather than appropriating a tradition, the 'well educated' tend to be young.)

This division of society into an information upper and lower class also occurs among intellectuals. Intellectuals can now be separated out into those who look to the international scene and have international communication networks; and those who stick to their local context. The two groups have very different resources and forms of competition. The 'international' intellectuals publish their work in the 'important' journals, and meet up at international conferences and on panel discussions. (These usually take place in hotels that closely resemble airport terminals. In fact, the hotels are often a part of the airport. In any case, the conference venues all look exactly the same, regardless of whether they are in Colorado or Honolulu. Indeed, even the temperature is regulated to the same degree.) Some 'international' intellectuals also become media figures, who work to provide the public with bite-sized chunks of information. This often involves participating in media criticism or describing the unbelievable and marvellous advantages of the latest in communications technology.

'Local' intellectuals tend to express concern about current developments. Their familiarity with the big wide world of globalization is limited largely to the pictures on their TV screens, and they are usually troubled by the effect that globalization might have on their children and on other defenceless beings. (In the globalized world, the local context is inhabited primarily by children, old people and women (especially women with children). This is particularly true in places that are short on resources, that is, within the lower classes and in rural areas.) 'Local' intellectuals are served by a constant stream of media research and media pedagogy that never has any real effect. Again and again, the same old self-contradictory conclusions are broadcast on their screens for discussion (and entertainment). Of course, the children grow up regardless of all this, and eventually elude the control of media pedagogy.

In both the global and the local context, 'media philosophy' (or 'media criticism' and 'media theory', as practised by writers such as Marshall McLuhan, Neil Postman and Vilém Flusser) should be seen as part of the problem experienced by intellectuals when their means of production develop. 'Media philosophy', on the whole, does not deal reflexively with culture industry, but is a part and symptom of it.

Reflexivity has become much more difficult to achieve, not least because culture industry is itself very often reflexive. Culture industry imparts to us knowledge of culture industry. Culture industry does not get to work on us behind the scenes: it takes pains to show us exactly how much effort is being lavished on us. In what Peter Sloterdijk terms 'cynical reason', ideologies are delivered to us together with their critique. The traditional task of the critic has been assimilated into the production and packaging of ideologies. Culture industry has become reflexive in the sense that it readily reveals its intention to manipulate us.

The fact that culture industry goes to great lengths in order to manipulate us is seen as proof of our own importance. The way that culture industry tells us about this effort is equivalent to the ringmaster's announcement that 'no effort or expense' has been spared in preparing the performance. As sophisticated viewers, we would not be taken in by subliminal effects, yet we do like to be treated like a king – and kings are rarely told the truth. Being treated like a king means being treated with excessive respect and being lied to 'politely'. As customers and 'kings', we love to be shown the enormous effort that culture industry expends on taking us in and in making us buy a product or vote for a particular candidate or issue.

There are other ways in which we learn about how culture industry works. Media such as theatre, newspapers, film, TV stations, advertising agencies and presidential campaigns, etc., are a most attractive milieu for plays, reports, movies, TV plays and even advertisements. Moreover, there are media spin-offs attached to every successful product. In most cases, magazines and books will provide information for the fans, and on occasions there are even supplementary film or TV productions. The phenomenon of the 'star' depends on fake information as to how the objects of our desire live, love and go about their daily business. Yet even if the information is false, it still results in a close acquaintance and even intimacy with celebrities. Indeed, we rarely know as much about our 'real' neighbours and colleagues as we do about certain 'stars'. In any case, we know from other sources (other books and magazines, etc.) that the information is fake, and we are aware that it is made up expressly to please us or to provoke our envy or glee. Culture industry is happy for us to know this, providing that we keep buying the product and then the spin-offs. Besides, we derive pleasure from this knowledge of culture industry, for it means that we can continue to indulge in culture industry products while sitting smug in the feeling of our superiority over those who are so easily entertained.

Both deliberately and unintentionally, culture industry produces a particular kind of reflexivity. Media consumption teaches and presupposes a large amount of knowledge about the media, as well as a great deal of experience about our relation to the media and vice versa. However, this kind of reflexivity is not reflexivity as *critique*, but rather reflexivity *turned affirmative*. The same kind of affirmative understanding of reflexivity is evident in the social sciences. Indeed, Ulrich Beck and Anthony Giddens draw on a systems theory model, and use 'reflexive' to mean the opposite of 'traditional' or 'taken for granted'. In this sense, 'reflexive' (as in the title of their book *Reflexive Modernization*) really means nothing more than 'self-monitoring'.[9]

Critical reflexivity involves analysing the domination that inheres in our concepts and ways of thinking, and examining the regime of domination that prevents societies and individuals from realizing their potential of freedom, equality and solidarity. (Of course, the failure to achieve freedom, equality and solidarity is due not least to the presence of domination in our concepts and ways of thinking.) By contrast, *affirmative* reflexivity describes an advanced form of domination: it refers to a system of regulation that works by constant feedback and anticipated feedback on both the administrative and individual level. The fact that media presentations contain self-referential traits does not mean that the media *are* critically reflexive – but at least they provide us with the material for engaging in critical reflexivity.

Culture industry is gaining influence and power over other intellectual fields, including that of politics. What happens in the public sphere (especially in the case of political or intellectual debate and art) gets restructured in anticipation of and in line with its eventual presentation in the media. New professions have arisen in order to manage these contingencies and to consult, produce and mediate: there is a whole host of roles of varying usefulness, including advertising experts, agents, PR specialists, campaign managers, designers and people who specialize in organizing 'sensational' exhibitions. Culture industry is growing in scope and in intensity. To mark the contrast with Horkheimer and Adorno's culture industry of fifty years past, this new situation can be termed 'enhanced' culture industry. The determining trait – commodity form – remains the same.

Intellectuals are dependent on culture industry, not least because it provides them with their income. Most intellectuals can be placed in one of two opposing groups, depending on how they view new developments in their field of production. The first group stands in opposition to new means of production and new demands, deeming them to represent the end of high quality intellectual work. The other group enthusiastically embraces new possibilities, and turns out ardent fantasies of the wonderful new world that is arising as a result of the internet etc.

These days, this latter group of intellectuals is fascinated by a whole new socioeconomic phase, namely the post-Fordist 'knowledge economy' that has taken over from the 'industrial society' of the nineteenth and early twentieth centuries.[10] These intellectuals conceptualize (and celebrate) several features of this brave new world of productive knowledge. In their view, hard labour of the type prevalent in heavy industry is being (or perhaps has already been) replaced by the application of knowledge, and the application of knowledge is seen to generate value. The traditional work ethic of physical strength, determination and pride in workmanship is consequently held to have become outdated, together with the old egalitarianism of straightforward proletarian solidarity and solidity. For those intellectuals who celebrate the 'knowledge economy,' such values are thought to exist only in neo-fascist, xenophobic and nationalist forms. The whole labour–capital relationship is shown to be subject to dramatic change, as we move from wage labour to universal self-employment. The 'labour-power entrepreneur' is held up as the new model for the future. Of course, the internet start-up crash of the late 1990s somewhat dampened the atmosphere of excitement. We are no longer confident that any smart business-school student could turn to risk-capital investors (so-called 'angels') and issue shares in trendy computer programming ventures, in order to make their first million before graduation. Nonetheless, there remains the basic conviction that our main productive activity now consists in producing cultural goods or cultural services. This idea is well established in the 'educated classes', and is still propounded by its ideologues.

Clearly, in this context 'culture industry' takes on a new meaning. The clearest indication of this shift in our understanding of the concept lies in the widespread use of the term 'culture industries'. Adorno's concept of 'culture industry' does not allow for the plural form, for in his usage 'culture industry' is the mode of capitalist commodity production and the subsumption of culture under this form.[11] These days, the term 'culture industries' (*plural*) is simply used to distinguish the various different products and their genres of production. It refers to the publishing industry, the music industry, the film industry and more rarely the opera industry, the museum/gallery industry and the architecture-and-building industry. Such distinctions are necessary for empirical economic studies, and are also essential in establishing the new academic field of 'culture management' in business schools and universities.[12]

This kind of radical shift in the understanding of culture industry is presented by Lash and Urry in their relatively early description of the 'information' or 'knowledge economy'. In that description they claim to turn the argument around:

> Even in the heyday of Fordism, the culture industries were irretrievably more innovation intensive, more design intensive than other industries. The culture industries, in other words, were post-Fordist avant la lettre. We are arguing . . . against any notion that culture production is becoming more like commodity production in manufacturing industry. Our claim is that ordinary manufacturing industry is becoming more and more like the production of culture.

Further on in the text, this is set out more specifically:

> What (all) culture industries produce becomes increasingly, not like commodities but advertisements . . . In their loss of a manufacturing function, in their advertising function, in their taking on of mainly a financial function, the culture industries are becoming increasingly like business services.[13]

What is happening in this text is a variation of something that regularly occurs in literature on the 'knowledge economy': Lash and Urry take up Horkheimer and Adorno's argument, but render it positive. What was originally a philosophical critique becomes nothing more than an empirical description of *how* cultural commodities are produced. Lash and Urry even argue that the specific characteristics of cultural production represent the future of all commodity production. However, cultural commodities are not any 'less' of a commodity than those of heavy industry. Indeed, the modernization of commodity production does not reduce the commodity character of the product. As for cultural 'services', these involve a different kind of self-instrumentalization of its operators than in commodity production, but they do not bring about any fundamental change; it is really just a rather more intense stage of all-round commodity characteristics.

In the world of media and entertainment studies, the switch to 'culture industries' (*plural*) is often hailed as a decisive advance over Adorno and Horkeimer's 'simplification' of the situation. People argue that culture is now extremely diverse and that it offers something to suit everyone and their particular taste.[14] Our understanding of culture has now been pluralized so as to include the mechanical (or rather electronic) beats and harmonies of popular music and the somewhat vulgar entertainment of soap operas and talk-shows, in addition to the most exquisite and refined pieces from Europe's aristocratic heritage. For the time being, we have ensured that all this is available to whosoever should care to partake in it: there are no longer any entry restrictions in place at art galleries and concert-halls. Indeed, it is all supposed to be good, clean fun, whether for the hard-working broker or consultant, or for the couple from the mid-West and the youngster from the ghetto.[15]

Intellectuals in the 'knowledge economy' are in no easy position. On the one hand, criticism and reflexivity have become much more demanding – not least because critique is now a genre of entertainment itself. On the other hand, intellectuals are always faced with the prospect (and sometime even the opportunity) of giving up their role as social critics and becoming highly paid experts instead. For media experts, this involves a thorough acquaintance with contemporary popular culture – there is still the expectation that the experts should know something of high culture, but this alone is no longer deemed sufficient. It seems highly likely that criticism no longer has a place in society. In fact, it is possible that the role of the intellectual is being absorbed into one or other of the culture industry professions, and that it is thus being neutralized.

However, there is certainly more to criticism than this. Intellectual and reflexive attitudes exist as part of a thinking person's approach to life, irrespective of how they make their living. (In fact, there is a good argument for deprofessionalizing and thus democratizing artistic as well as other kinds of intellectual production.) Having a clear awareness of culture industry as we experience the ubiquitous 'novelties' and 'sensations' of contemporary culture and politics makes life with these exclusive 'once in a lifetime' offers really exciting. Culture is not simply 'out there'; it is in the eye of the (culture industry sophisticated) beholder.

Field notes XII   Woody Allen's Manhattan operettas

Manhattan, and especially the 'Village', is packed with tourists from all over the world. Visiting New York is definitely 'in', and for people who are 'cultured' and wealthy, it is almost compulsory. Of course, this has something to do with the unbelievably low prices of transatlantic flights, but I cannot help suspecting that Woody Allen is also in part responsible. Nowhere is the romantic image of Manhattan propagated more convincingly than in Woody Allen's films. A tourist board would not be able to compete with the unfailingly consistent portrayal of this image. Allen's films have been repeating the same simple message year after year: Manhattan is a place where dreams can come true, even for middle-aged men who are wrapped up in their work, who feel insecure about their masculinity, and who have become disillusioned with relationships. What is more, the fairy-tale unfolds among Manhattan's fountains, roof gardens, elegant apartments, art-deco skyscrapers and jazz bars. It draws on the flowers in Washington Square, the wealthy window-shoppers in Madison Avenue, the chic autumnal tristesse of Central Park, the square in front of the illuminated Met and Brooklyn Bridge by night.

Two films mark the launch of the advertising campaign that was to turn the 'Big Apple' into a city of romance, *Manhattan* and *Annie Hall*. With these films, the genre of the 'Woody Allen film' was created. The fairy-tale plot featuring hopeless and sentimental relationships in a mad, old-fashioned place called Manhattan came into being.

In his films, Woody Allen often combines his Manhattan fairy-tales with genre parody. Allen's most successful genre parody is *Zelig*, a film that parodies documentaries. Once you have seen *Zelig*, it is impossible to find documentary films in the least bit believable. (Allen tried something similar in his earlier film, *Take the Money and Run*, but in *Zelig* he truly perfects the technique.) *Broadway Danny Rose* is Allen's ironic take on the Italian-American mafia, and it forms the most melancholy of his genre parodies. However, the parody is at its most complex in Allen's reworking of Chekhov in *Hannah and her Sisters*, and at its most frantic and seemingly 'moral' in the 'crime' movies *Crimes and Misdemeanors* and *Manhattan Murder Mystery*. In addition to this, there are the two 'period pieces', *Radio Days* and *Bullets over Broadway*, whose nostalgia makes the Manhattan of our dreams utterly irresistible.

Allen can be counted on to recreate this kind of atmosphere and to engage with fairy-tales and take-offs. Moreover, he can be relied on to bring out a new film almost every year. As soon as we hit January, we start waiting for the latest 'Woody Allen'. The rest of the world listens expectantly for the news from New York. Each year, we find ourselves wondering which genre Allen will choose to parody. Each year, we ask ourselves whether the films can get any more ironic. Allen does not always manage to raise the ironic stakes, but he certainly did so in 1996, with a film that also succeeded in going up a notch or two in reflexivity.

Allen's use of the Greek chorus in *Mighty Aphrodite* prepared the way for his parody of the musical film in *Everyone Says I Love You*. In this film (starring Julia Roberts, Goldie Hawn, Drew Barrymore and, of course, Woody Allen) the characters satirize the conventions of the musical by suddenly (and ridiculously) switching over to song and dance. In addition to this, the film presents us with an image of ourselves, the fans of Woody Allen's films. Allen did this once before in *Stardust Memories*, but the effect in *Everyone Says I Love You* is rather different: it becomes clear that those of us who have followed his ironic films loyally and with enthusiasm are actually nothing but sentimental fools. The genre of the operetta is made to seem ridiculous by the actors (including Woody Allen) who can neither sing nor dance, but who readily engage in both activities. This last twist demonstrates that the films that we have been watching all these years are in fact Manhattan operettas – the films portray the unimportant worries and the sentimentality of the wealthy, yet we found them not only ironic, but also enjoyable. *Everyone Says I Love You* forces us to acknowledge that the genre of the 'Woody Allen film' has much in common with the musical, even when it does not involve any singing or dancing. It also reminds us that many of Allen's other films, such as *Hannah and her Sisters*, *Alice* and *Annie Hall* also revolve around the adolescent yearnings and dreams of grown-ups. *Everyone Says I Love You* acts as a kind of negative commentary on Allen's earlier films, as it highlights their ridiculous nature and forces us to recognize the sentimentality of their supposedly enlightened and cynical audience.

In fact, *Everyone Says I Love You* does not have a plot as such: there is an upper-class version of 'boy meets girl, loses girl and finds her again', but that is about all there is to it. The story line is no more challenging than in any musical or operetta. In terms of the film's content, the only highlight is the despicable nature of the affair, which starts up as a result of the man ('Joe' played by Woody Allen) gaining inside knowledge of the woman's ('Von' played by Julia Roberts) secret desires through his daughter (the narrator) who is eavesdropping on Von's therapy sessions. The way that the affair ends is also of interest, for when the woman's desires are actually fulfilled, the attraction comes to an end. The second story line is generally rather silly and tends towards romantic cliché. It involves a wealthy and foolish young girl falling for a lower-class crook. It is amusing in the way that it shows how the family's concern for status takes priority over any supposed affinity with bleeding heart liberalism, yet this is really nothing new.

All this is presented in a far more reflexive manner in *Purple Rose of Cairo*, which explicitly features the movie-watching public and the film industry. This film is set in New Jersey, where 'anything is possible' and where New York appears from across the Hudson River as a place of dreams (or nightmares). However, the added attraction of *Everyone Says I Love You* is that Woody Allen actually sings. Indeed, with the help of modern film technology, he is even able to outdo Fred Astaire and Ginger Rogers in his final scene with his old love 'Steffi' (played by Goldie Hawn).

It is becoming ever more obvious why Woody Allen's films have to take place in New York. New York is clearly associated with cities of the past (such as Paris) or cities in decline (such as Venice). (The action of *Everyone Says I Love You* is split between these three locations.) New York is a city of yesteryear: it represents modernity in decline, showing the gradual loss of 'progress' and wealth. Young and energetic people can feel at home in this city, provided that they are able to come to terms with the neurotic effect that it is liable to have on them. In order to feel at home in New York, you also have to be rich. If you are not, you will have to settle for the dreams you find in movies.

The dreams presented in Woody Allen's films once seemed quite modern, but they are now becoming clearly and self-consciously nostalgic. *Radio Days* seemed to be an exception, but *Bullets over Broadway* and *Everyone Says I Love You* made the nostalgia explicit. With the release of these two films, it suddenly became clear that Allen's supposedly 'contemporary' films in fact take place in a romanticized New York of yesterday. They are set in a New York inhabited by wealthy people who live in old-fashioned elegance and who engage in neurotic relationships that seem to belong to another era.

It is this that makes the films realistic, at least for the tourists. Unlike the Dadaists at the beginning of the twentieth century, educated Europeans no longer go to New York in order to experience the exciting shock of being in a society that is at the summit of technological achievement and progress. It is now clear that the summit of progress must be found elsewhere. Either that, or progress actually means that things are falling apart. What people are looking for in New York is in fact something entirely different: they are not seeking the shock of modernity, but the charm of past modernity. New York is an old-fashioned city, and it is this that makes it so attractive.

New York's skyscrapers are the most obvious demonstration of this. The art-deco Chrysler Building remains a cult construction, but there are also the numerous and usually nameless historic buildings that are adorned with smooth turrets stretching up out of view. Such constructions come complete with pseudo-gothic ornamentation, including merlons, oriels, arches, ledges, crests and Doric pillars – they are utterly kitschy, yet striking in the sheer absurdity of their assertion of wealth and power. You will not find skyscrapers built of bricks in the business districts of European cities. New York also boasts the attraction of multistorey apartment blocks with ladders running down the outside. These were intended as fire-escapes, but they also made the job of burglars far easier here than anywhere else in the world. The blocks often have decorative roofs like the patrician houses in Florence. On top of this, New York also has its quaint old brownstones in the quieter streets. These buildings take you back a hundred years, although there is also a more recent variety dating back to the twenties and thirties. They are marble floored and have stucco ceilings. There are very few European cities that can compete with all that.

Woody Allen's films always feature sightseeing tours of Manhattan in which the old-fashioned beauty of the city is shown in its proper light and in the best possible camera perspective. This is done most explicitly in *Hannah and her Sisters*, as well as in the introductory sequence of *Manhattan* that has now become something of a classic. The cycle of seasons, sometimes striking and at other times banal, is used as a structuring device in *Everyone Says I Love You*, as well as in some of the earlier films. However, in *Everyone Says I Love You*, the way that Manhattan is linked to Paris and Venice heightens the romantic appeal of the city. Manhattan comes to resemble an ancient European city that is gradually becoming submerged in water, just like Venice. It is turned into one of those places that is able to ironically transfigure our memories. Now that the status of the film as an operetta has been made explicit, our pleasure in following the trials and tribulations of the wealthy becomes an embarrassment. In *Everyone Says I Love You*, Allen has created a genre parody that targets his own kind of film. The parody, however, is benevolent, and it only ever subtly offends the fans of the genre.

Parody is the truth of culture industry: New York represents the romanticism of past modernity that can now be put to contemporary purpose. As for the educated and ironic tourists and Allen fans who visit New York, they are hopelessly bound up with this progress of yesteryear – they are committed to this past modernity that was built robustly, but that is falling into decline and neglect.

Notes

The bibliographical data for texts by Adorno and Horkheimer are to be found at the back of the book in the select bibliographies of the two authors' works. The bibliographical data for texts by other authors referred to in this study are listed in the notes below.

Where no English language source is given for extracts in the text and notes, translations from the German are by the translator.

Introduction: the pleasures of criticism

1 See the initial note above and the Select Bibliography.

1 Approaching culture industry: recommended equipment

'Field notes I: Why are you smiling, Leonardo?', in this chapter below, was originally published in my preface to Christine Resch's *Kunst als Skandal. Der steirische herbst und die öffentliche Erregung* (Verlag für Gesellschaftskritik, Vienna, 1994).

1 'Culture Industry: Enlightenment as Mass Deception' is one of the chapters in Horkheimer and Adorno's *Dialectic of Enlightenment*, written during the authors' Californian exile and first published in a run of 500 private copies in 1944. The revised print version came out in 1947 in Amsterdam (published by Querido). Copies of that edition were still available in the early sixties. An Italian translation came out in 1962, yet the text was not reprinted in German until 1969 (published by Fischer Verlag, Frankfurt am Main). John Cumming's English translation (*Dialectic of Enlightenment*) was published in 1972, and is still in use. It was last reprinted in 1999, and this is the text that is referenced here.

There are voluminous German editions of the writings of both Horkheimer and Adorno. See Max Horkheimer *Gesammelte Schriften*

[Collected Works, 18 vols] and Theodor W. Adorno *Gesammelte Schriften* [Collected Works, 20 vols]. There is a well-funded and well-staffed Adorno-Archive and a less well funded but more easily accessible Horkheimer-Archive in Frankfurt. The publication of Adorno's work (letters, lectures, diaries and unfinished or unpublished manuscripts) is still in process, and a further twenty volumes are planned. *Dialectic of Enlightenment* is volume 3 of Adorno's *Gesammelte Schriften* and volume 5 of Horkheimer's. I recommend that German readers consult the latter: it contains text variants and an editorial commentary, and there is also a very valuable epilogue written by the editor, Gunzelin Schmid Noerr. A continuation of the 'Culture Industry' chapter was written, but not published during the author's lifetime. It was found in the Adorno estate and first published under the title 'Das Schema der Massenkultur' in volume 3 of Adorno's *Gesammelte Schriften*. The English translation, 'The Schema of Mass Culture' is to be found in Adorno, *The Culture Industry: Selected Essays on Mass Culture* (Routledge, London, 1991), pp. 51–84.

2   In terms of supplementary reading, the other chapters of *Dialectic of Enlightenment* would be first choice. Adorno's other essays and articles related to the topic of culture industry are collected in *The Culture Industry*. The debate about culture that Adorno had with Benjamin in their correspondence in 1936 and 1938 may also be of specific interest. See *The Complete Correspondence: 1928–1940*, ed. H. Lonitz, trans. N. Walker (Polity, Cambridge, 1999).

   There is also a considerable amount to be read about Critical Theory. Despite the fact that it could be described as a 'family saga', Rolf Wiggershaus's *The Frankfurt School: Its History, Theories and Political Significance* (trans. M. Robertson, Polity, Cambridge, 1994) is a comprehensive general introduction to the subject. Deborah Cook's *The Culture Industry Revisited: Theodor W. Adorno on Mass Culture* (Rowman and Littlefield, Boston, 1996) deals specifically with culture industry. Douglas Kellner's *Media Culture* (Verso, London, 1995) and Max Paddison's *Adorno, Modernism and Mass Culture* (Kahn and Averill, London, 1996) both discuss Adorno's work at length.

   In general, recent books on Critical Theory have tended to focus on aesthetic theory rather than on the theory of culture industry. It is characteristic of the wider discussion that a term informed by business management studies – 'cultural industries' – has now gained general currency. In May 1997, New York University hosted an international conference on Research Perspectives on the Management of Cultural Industries. During this conference, the name 'Adorno' barely entered the discussion. Even in an introductory text as generally commendable as Diana Crane's *The Production of Culture* (Sage, London, 1992), the reference is to 'culture industries', while Adorno is dealt with in a single paragraph of the introduction. Culture industry has moved on from 'Culture Industry'. However, this does not mean that we should abandon either the concept or the text.

3   Niklas Luhmann's work is similarly reflexive, but the current, more functionalist, versions of systems theory are often not.

4   Unfortunately, Horkheimer and Adorno are not entirely consistent in this usage. Usually, when they use the term 'culture industry' without the article, it means 'commodity-form culture'; and when they use it with the article, it means 'factories'. However, there are some cases where the article is used, but the term refers to 'commodity-form culture'.

5   See Martin Scorsese's *Taxi Driver* for an example of one such social gaffe. In this film, the confused Travis thinks that a porn film constitutes a suitable form of entertainment for dating and courting.

6   I have based these case studies on extracts from my earlier publications, from my notes, and from the jottings that I make to keep myself on my toes. I present my methodology in the section on 'Analysing the working alliance', but the best way to get to grips with it – bar taking on your own project – will be to look at the case studies themselves.

7   See *The Village Voice*, 8 Mar. 1994, p. 87. This article provides us with an interesting insight into the strange social position of the cultured citizens of Manhattan. On their way to work, they daily pass by numerous homeless people and beggars, yet are only alerted to the latter's plight by a painting dating back to the year 1895.

8   The promise of exclusivity can never be realized within an actual relationship. In fact, within a relationship, exclusivity is destroyed and replaced by a much more tangible – or indeed physical – bond. If all goes well, this bond will bring us pleasure, but it will also bring us pain. There will be moments when it will appear both ridiculous and grotesque, and moments when it will provoke us into fear or anger. In any case, this type of bond is very different from the hesitant, secret and entirely reversible moment of mutual understanding that is based on the excitement of a possibility.

    At this point it becomes glaringly apparent that reactions to the painting have been heavily influenced by male fantasies. If we were to take our analysis any further, we would have to consider other reactions to the painting, including those from women and – taking into account the comments below – from the working classes.

9   In this section, I draw on Kenneth Clark's *Leonardo da Vinci* (1939; Pelican, London, 1989). When discussing reactions to the painting, I draw on A. Richard Turner's *Inventing Leonardo* (Knopf, New York, 1992).

10 Duchamp disfigured the face of the *Mona Lisa* by adding a moustache and a goatee. His alterations make the gender indecision of the face very visible: the *Mona Lisa* could well be a young man. The title of Duchamp's painting also contains a sexual pun: when read aloud, the five letters *L.H.O.O.Q.* give 'elle a chaud au cul'. In French, this is a crude reference to the woman's state of arousal. Thus, with *L.H.O.O.Q.*, Duchamp not only targeted an icon of tender feminity, but also attacked the venerability of high art. Duchamp's playful additions to the *Mona Lisa* were made possible by the ready availability of cheap reproductions of the famous painting: *L.H.O.O.Q.* was also a comment on the fact that the *Mona Lisa* had already been degraded to the status of an everyday object.

11 In his influential *Theory of the Avant-Garde* (trans. M. Shaw, University of Minnesota Press, Minneapolis, 1985), Peter Bürger merely repeats this claim about the supposed function of avant-garde art, failing to make any plausible argument to support it. For Bürger, therefore, the avant-garde was a historical failure. Bürger describes how art no longer existed in terms of oeuvres, and how montage and chance were being used for the creation of artistic pieces. He also notes how the historical emergence of the avant-garde led it to adopt the drive for autonomy championed by Dadaism and Surrealism. However, what Bürger fails to realize is that art had become reflexive. It is this reflexivity that should prevent us from declaring it a failure. Bürger's misinterpretation of the situation is the result of his over-estimation of the importance of the avant-garde's political engagement (and his overestimation of the importance of the claims made by the various artists concerned). This is altogether characteristic of the time in which his theory was written. Linked to Bürger's misinterpretation of the political dimension is the notable absence of any reference to culture industry.

12 See 'Excursus I', which deals with Odysseus' mythic journey past the Sirens. Using this story, Adorno comes up with an excellent illustration of the Hegelian/Marxian master–servant dialectic. It is for this reason that many critics have focused their work on this particular part of the text.

13 In Germany, post-doctoral students are required to produce a Habilitationsschrift in order to gain their *venia legendi* (the right to teach at university level). [Trans.]

14 'Use-music' (*Gebrauchsmusik*) is music written for practical use, as opposed to music conceived in terms of 'l'art pour l'art'. In contrast to the latter, use-music is not written for performance by professionals, but is intended for use by amateurs at home or at informal gatherings. [Trans.]

15 At the beginning of the essay, Adorno writes: 'The role of music in the social process is exclusively that of a commodity: its value is that deter-mined by the market' ['On the Social Situation of Music' (1932), p. 128]. This claim would seem to apply to music in general, yet in the course of the essay a distinction is made between 'art' and 'culture industry'. Naturally, Adorno never considers Schoenberg and his School in terms of culture industry. Even in his analysis of three other types of music ('neoclassicism', 'folklore' and 'surrealistic music'), it would never have occurred to him to treat the music of Hindemith, Bartòk or Weill as part of culture industry. Nevertheless, there would be nothing to stop us from considering those elements of Hindemith's music critiqued by Adorno (e.g. Hindemith's attempt to implement new fixed musical conventions, or to make some of his pieces more comprehensible and appealing to the public by organizing and structuring them through rhythm alone) as characteristic of commodification. Moreover, Adorno never uses the term culture industry to describe Richard Wagner's work, despite the fact that his own analysis of the composer all but demands that he do so.

16 Parts of Adorno's contribution to the project fed into the section 'Über die musikalische Verwendung des Radios' [On the musical uses of radio] in

'Der getreue Korrepetitor' [The faithful repetiteur]. One part of the project – the 'Analytical Study of the NBC Music Appreciation Hour' – was published in *Musical Quarterly*, 78 (1994), complete with an introduction by Thomas Y. Levin and Michael von der Linn. The first interim report that Adorno wrote on the project, entitled 'Memorandum: Music in Radio', can be found in the Lazarsfeld archive in Vienna. It dates back to June 1938 and consists of 161 A4 pages, many of them annotated with cutting comments from Lazarsfeld. Hans-Joachim Dahms quotes from the memo in *Positivismusstreit* (Suhrkamp, Frankfurt, 1994), pp. 232–53, and I am grateful to him for alerting me to the existence of this source.

17   See S. Kracauer, *The Mass Ornament: Weimar Essays* (trans. and introd. T. Y. Levin, Harvard University Press, Cambridge, Mass., 1995).

18   Gunzelin Schmid Noerr (the editor of *Dialectic of Enlightenment* as it appears in the German edition of Horkheimer's collected works) has written an epilogue that gathers together evidence on the nature of the collaboration. See in particular pp. 425–30 of Max Horkheimer, *Gesammelte Schriften*, vol. 5, ed. Gunzelin Schmid Noerr (Fischer, Frankfurt, 1987).

19   Two chapters in *Dialectic of Enlightenment* were written in the first draft by Adorno. Since the 'Culture Industry' chapter was one of these (the other was 'Excursus I' – the famous analysis of the *Odyssey*), it is usually referred to in what follows as 'Adorno's' text. Nevertheless, on occasions, the names of both authors will be used, to remind us of Horkheimer's part in the text.

20   See J. Habermas, *The Structural Transformation of the Public Sphere: An Inquiry into a Category of Bourgeois Society* (trans. T. Burger with the assistance of F. Lawrence, Polity, Cambridge and MIT Press, Cambridge, Mass., 1989).

2 On method: look carefully, think thoroughly, and do not let yourself be taken in

1   When I first read Adorno's text, I too had to ask one of my philosopher friends what 'Skoteinos' meant. It was then that I learnt that the term had originally been used in relation to Heraclitus.

2   Of course, it is impossible to tell how many people actually read Eco's novels, particularly the later ones. Moreover, after the first hundred pages, a book like *The Name of the Rose* can be read as a straight detective story (as is made apparent by the film of the same name). Like Woody Allen's films, Eco's novels have multiple layers of meaning and are open to vastly different interpretations – in the age of the 'open work' (as analysed by Eco), this is probably the prime criterion by which to judge a work's quality.

3   Horkheimer was a lot more hesitant – or perhaps even nervous – about this. As a result, his early essays first appeared in volume form in 1968, while *Dialectic of Enlightenment* was first reprinted in 1969. Until then, it had only been available in pirate editions or to those 'in the know'. In 1968, Horkheimer wrote of his earlier work that it was 'dominated by economic

and political ideas that should no longer be used without qualification' (Horkheimer, *Gesammelte Schriften*, vol. 3, p. 14). To put it simply,
Horkheimer had been actively distancing himself from his early Marxist
views ever since his period of exile in the US. One of the ways in which
he did this was by 'neutralizing' some of the vocabulary that he had used
in his early essays. (See, for example, the contrast between the American
version and the original German text of 'Vernunft und Selbsterhaltung'
that was circulated only among friends and colleagues.) There was no need
for Adorno to follow suit, for he had always been more of a Hegelian than
a Marxist. (Again, this is rather a simplification.) It is not really clear from
Adorno's biography at what point he first took an interest in Marx. Nor is
it clear exactly how (after his early introduction to Lukács by his friend
Siegfried Kracauer) he engaged with Marx's thought. In any case, in
Adorno's essays and lectures, the influence of Kant, Hegel, Kierkegaard
and Husserl is much clearer than that of Marx.

4   I have borrowed this term from Albrecht Dümling, who used it to describe
    Schoenberg's music. See Steinert, *Adorno in Wien. Über die (Un)Möglichkeit
    von Kunst und Befreiung* (Fischer, Frankfurt, 1993), pp. 67, 117.

5   It is plain to see that our current methods of sociological research
    have their origins in social domination. Opinion polls and the like
    are refinements of techniques used for census-taking, which originally
    served administrative purposes, if not political machinations. This is
    not to say that we should stop using these methods, although we need to
    be aware of the perspective of domination through which the data are
    filtered. Research methods do not guarantee any immediate insights into
    the phenomenon in question. All data need to be subjected to an
    interpretation that takes account of the method by which the results were
    generated.

6   This is how the promise of 'hermeneutics', the science of interpretation,
    is described in *Sozialwissenschaftliche Hermeneutik*, ed. R. Hitzler and H.
    Honer (Leske and Budrich, Opladen, 1998), p. 23. It is my impression that
    our reasons for preferring a particular method of interpretation are similar
    to those for preferring a particular brand of word-processing software –
    we tend to opt for whatever we learnt to use first. It is only when you try
    out the alternatives that you begin to notice the common principles that
    lie behind them all. Nonetheless, those methods of interpretation that are
    blind to countertransference are indeed very different from the rest, for
    these methods lead to dogmatic and non-reflexive readings.

7   See the screenplay, W. Allen, *Hannah and her Sisters* (Faber and Faber,
    London, 1988), p. 181.

8   See Hans-Dieter Seidel in *Frankfurter Allgemeine Zeitung*, 2 Oct. 1986, p. 25.
    This German film critic and the others who are quoted here are merely
    being used as exemplars of their profession. I do not think German film
    critics are exceptional (or were at the time). Culture criticism of all kinds
    has, due to its conditions of production, a tendency to be judgmental,
    superficial and generous in its neglect of detail or simple invention of
    contents.

9 See *Die Zeit*, 3 Oct. 1986, p. 59. This also leads me to the general observation that the reviews would be much improved if only the critics were to
   divert their attention away from the celebrity 'Woody Allen' and back to
   the actual film.

10 See *Frankfurter Rundschau*, 3 Oct. 1986, p. 29.

11 See *Der Spiegel*, 6 Oct. 1986, p. 238.

12 I would like someone to point out just *one* example of the 'Jewish self-
   hatred' that one critic found so striking about the film (Heike Kühn in
   Frankfurter Rundschau, 3 Oct. 1986, p. 29). I am afraid that I have not been
   able to locate one. In the film, all the *other* religions are in crisis. If the type
   of irony used in Woody Allen's films (a type of irony that also targets the
   self) has anything to do with 'Jewish self-hatred', then I wish that the critics
   would undergo a bout of it. As it is, the diagnosis of self-hatred has an
   unpleasant ring to it.

13 In his discovery of the 'talking cure', Freud came across a situation that
   was conducive to treating countertransference in a reflexive manner. He
   was thus able to find a use for countertransference in psychotherapy.
   However, in the context of our study, it is important to note that Freud and
   his early followers also used countertransference as a means of interpreting cultural artefacts. In his 'cultural analysis', Alfred Lorenzer has
   brought this line of research up to date. See Lorenzer (ed.), *Kultur-
   Analysen* (Fischer, Frankfurt, 1986).

14 Bestsellers may seem particularly suited to a reading that treats them as
   being 'symptomatic' of collective emotions. This is, however, an extremely
   problematic assumption. Of all our interests and desires, most bestsellers
   only manage to represent the lowest common denominator. This means
   that bestsellers are seldom very revealing. This is particularly true in the
   case of internationally successful action films, for the action sequences of
   these films are broken down to such a basic level that they can be understood by almost anyone, anywhere. This contrasts greatly with the situation in films by directors such as Woody Allen. In Allen's films, there is
   such a wealth of specific information about New York, intellectual life,
   European literature and American films that the potential audience is
   greatly reduced. In the case of an action film, we cannot find out much
   more about society than what I have already implied above: that society
   aims to produce goods that will achieve the best possible sales, and that
   its products must therefore be based on the lowest common denominator
   of our desires (e.g. a certain ideal of masculinity and the corresponding
   notion of femininity). I do not mean to sound dismissive about action films
   – they offer an interesting, important and useful way of analysing culture.
   However, this is not because they 'sell well', but rather because they often
   deal with a working-class notion of masculinity that is usually scorned in
   other cultural forms.

15 In his book *Faszination und Langeweile. Die populären Medien* (Enke, Stuttgart,
   1979), Dieter Prokop examines the spectator's interests and desires. These
   days, it is only children that openly admit to – and indeed determinedly
   pursue – their pleasure in repetition. Since the Renaissance, bourgeois

European art has accepted novelty as a cultural imperative. The principle of innovation is also a characteristic of market economies, in which each product has to surpass the rest. The importance of artistic innovation has been grossly exaggerated. There have always been schools of art, styles, variations and repetitions. Even artists, composers or writers must keep practising and repeating a piece until they have got it right. Only occasionally do they have ideas that are really new – this might happen only once in a lifetime, and all the rest is simply routine. A visit to the Picasso Museum in Paris would provide an indication of the extent of such repetition. (And that is in an artist who was really quite varied in his output!)

16   It is ironic that, as a result of this instrumental attitude towards texts, the interface between man and machine has now become a weak link in the system. These days, instruction manuals are a universal cause of complaint.

17   In qualitative sociological research, this is known as 'theoretical sampling'. Theoretical sampling means looking for cases that – according to the logic of our theoretical expectations – will either be particularly interesting or will fall at the extreme points of the distributions.

18   My thanks go to Christine Resch who dug out, read through and analysed all the German reviews of the film held at the Frankfurt Museum for Film.

3 The production of cultural commodities

The first section of this chapter is a shorter version of pp. 56–9 and 72–80 of my book *Adorno in Wien*. See Steinert, *Adorno in Wien. Über die (Un)Möglichkeit von Kunst und Befreiung* (Fischer, Frankfurt, 1993).

The quote in the title of the second section (p. 71) is from *Dialectic of Enlightenment*, p. 120.

'Field notes VI: Exoticism and music', in this chapter below, is an extract from my 1997 essay 'Musikalischer Exotismus nach innen und außen. Über die kulturindustrielle Aneignung des Fremden', in *Step across the Border*, Beiträge zur Popularmusikforschung 19/20, Coda, Karben.

1   Of course, it is very tricky to distinguish between artistic 'progress' and changing fashions. These days, people content themselves with the latter and do not demand 'progress'. This means that even yesterday's news can be successfully marketed, as is evident in pop-music or even in the popularity of 'classic' novels.

2   This observation dates back to a conversation that I had with Krenek, 17 Sept. 1985. [HS]

3   The fact that the artist is no longer dependent on direct patronage is generally viewed as a positive step towards liberation, and of course there is this dimension to it. However, in *The Court Artist: On the Ancestry of the Modern Artist* (trans. D. McLintock, Cambridge University Press, Cambridge, 1993), Martin Warnke puts forward a convincing argument that links the court artist to modern practitioners of art. Warnke argues that the court artists were able to free themselves from the traditional ties of the urban artisan-artists because they were seen to be 'unique' and 'special'.

According to Warnke, the court artists thus pursued the goals of individuality and self-expression shared by our artists today. In this way, the transition from patronage to bourgeois dependency is cast not so much as liberation as a change in the form of dependency.

4   Schoenberg, 'How One Becomes Lonely', in *Style and Idea: Selected Writings of Arnold Schoenberg*, ed. Leonard Stein (trans. L. Black, Faber and Faber, London, 1984), p. 51 (emphasis added).

5   Peter Schleuning, in *Geschichte der Musik in Deutschland. Das 18. Jahrhundert – Der Bürger erhebt sich* (Rowohlt, Reinbek, 1984), provides a detailed and well-argued account of the social history of music relevant to this section. My intention is to summarize some of the significant points in this history and to link them together as different manifestations of the attempt to achieve artistic autonomy.

6   Hans Mayer, *Richard Wagner in Bayreuth 1876–1976* (Suhrkamp, Frankfurt, 1978), p. 10.

7   Schoenberg's manuscript went for the highest price, while Berg's went for the asking price.

8   Arnold Schoenberg, 'Music', in *Style and Idea*, p. 370. This essay was written in 1919 for Adolf Loos's *Richtlinien für ein Kunstamt* [Guidelines for a Ministry of Art].

9   Some time ago, Peter Sloterdijk's *Critique of Cynical Reason* (trans. M. Eldred, Verso, London, 1998) was hailed as a literary sensation. The book is a detailed historical exposition of an idea that Adorno was already writing about back in 1944.

10   The term 'Fordism' was coined by Antonio Gramsci. There are numerous books that deal with the social history of Fordism, especially in the US. The following list contains merely a few examples of these: Stuart Ewen, *Captains of Consciousness: Advertising and the Social Roots of the Consumer Culture* (McGraw-Hill, New York, 1976); Marshall Berman, *All that is Solid Melts into Air: The Experience of Modernity* (Simon and Schuster, New York, 1982); Richard Ohmann, *Selling Culture: Magazines, Markets, and Class at the Turn of the Century* (Verso, London, 1996).

11   David Bordwell, Janet Staiger and Kristin Thompson in *The Classical Hollywood Cinema: Film Style and Mode of Production to 1960* (Routledge, London, 1985) focus on presenting the different market structures, audience structures and modes of production within the various genres and the individual products. This type of materialist analysis of culture industry thus evades the trap of explaining everything with reference to the economy.

12   See *Frankfurter Rundschau*, 30 May 1996.

13   See *Der Spiegel*, no. 6 (1996), pp. 178–80.

14   See *Die Zeit*, 31 May 1996.

15   Yodelling is defined in the notes to the next song as 'the call to other people in a deserted place'.

16   By this, I am not referring to the first missed entry, which, although clearly a mistake, still serves to unpick the banal melody. What I am talking about are the numerous instances of 'hanging back', a technique that Billy

Holiday also used to employ and which creates an inimitable sense both of building tension *and* release.

17 Clint Eastwood's well-intentioned and insufferably politically correct film *Bird* gets it wrong because it does not give the musical element enough emphasis, preferring to focus instead on the story of the unrecognized genius and on racial discrimination. It is a well-known fact, however, that these problems were not a factor in Parker's addiction to drugs. Parker's addiction started in his youth, long before there was any talk of his 'genius'. In later life, he still valued drugs as a form of painkiller, finding them more effective and cheaper than prescription medicines. Of course, the film was also handicapped by the fact that the actor had to pretend to be playing during the recordings. In fact, these scenes work admirably well, but they still cannot compare with those in *Round Midnight* in which Dexter Gordon plays 'Dexter Gordon' and performs the music live.

18 There is already a good deal of literature on the interesting – and for many styles (e.g. futurism, expressionism and new functionalism) important – link between World War I and art. I will simply mention a few of the more recent publications: K. Vondung, *The Apocalypse in Germany* (trans. S. Ricks, University of Missouri, Columbia, 2000); R. Cork, *A Bitter Truth: Avant-Garde Art and the Great War* (Yale University Press, New Haven, 1994); G. Watkins, *Pyramids at the Louvre* (Harvard University Press, Cambridge Mass., 1994); M. Ekstein, *Rites of Spring* (Doubleday, New York, 1989).

19 By 'event', I do not mean a 'party' or 'festival', a 'sensational occurrence' or a 'big occasion'. It is really a matter of emphasizing the process – a process in which artefacts (cultural or otherwise) may play a part. On the other hand, looking at a painting in a museum or in the 'white cube' of a gallery is also an event of a certain kind. We cannot simply disregard this type of event, nor can we claim that the artefact is the only significant element in it. (This would only be possible if we were to call on a specifically bourgeois understanding of art, i.e. if we were to fall for the bourgeois ideology of art.)

20 See D. D. Egbert, 'The Idea of "Avant-Garde" in Art and Politics', *American Historical Review*, 73, no. 2 (1967), pp. 339–66 for an alternative historical analysis of the term 'avant-garde'. See S. D. Hobbs, *The End of the American Avant Garde* (New York University Press, New York, 1997) for an account of the history of political and cultural avant-garde thought in the United States. Examples of the colloquial usage of 'avant-garde' to mean 'latest trend' can be found in B. Taylor, *Avant-Garde and After: Rethinking Art Now* (Abrams, New York, 1995) and F. Orton and G. Pollock, *Avant-Gardes and Partisans Reviewed* (Manchester University Press, Manchester, 1996).

21 Robert Morris is a particularly fascinating figure, since he belongs to both traditions. His work is 'modern' in its minimalism and 'reflexive' in the way that it draws on Duchamp and the happening. Jackson Pollock's work is also grounded in both the happening and in abstract art. In reality, the various working alliances are by no means mutually exclusive, and one

alliance often leads into another. Thus impressionist representation and expressive self-portrayal lead into abstract art (this transition is apparent in the portraits and landscape paintings of Richard Gerstl), while cubist abstraction leads into reflexivity etc.

4 What is wrong with consensual entertainment?

1   See W. Benjamin, *Charles Baudelaire: A Lyric Poet in the Era of High Capitalism* (trans. H. Zohn, Verso, London, 1997); W. Benjamin, 'Paris, Capital of the Nineteenth Century', in W. Benjamin, *The Arcades Project* (trans. H. Eiland and K. McLaughlin, Harvard University Press, Cambridge, Mass., 1999); S. Kracauer, *Offenbach and the Paris of his Time* (trans. G. David and E. Mosbacher, Constable, London, 1937).

2   See S. Kracauer, *The Salaried Masses: Duty and Distraction in Weimar Germany* (trans. Q. Hoare, Verso, London, 1997); Adorno, 'Those Twenties' (1962).

3   See H. M. Enzensberger, 'The Zero Medium or Why All Complaints about Television are Pointless', in *Mediocrity and Delusion: Collected Diversions* (trans. M. Chalmers, Verso, London and New York, 1992), pp. 59–70.

4   But why settle for an ordinary wide-screen TV? For only a few thousand or so, you can now get a plasma flat screen to hang on your wall!

5   See the section 'Adornos Psychoanalyse des Jazz' [Adorno's psycho-analytic reading of jazz], in Steinert, *Die Entdeckung der Kulturindustrie oder Warum Professor Adorno Jazz-Musik nicht ausstehen konnte* (Verlag für Gesellschaftsanalyse, Vienna, 1992). It would also be possible to produce a more subtly differentiated reading of laughter and irony than that arrived at by Adorno. See the chapter 'Lächerlichkeit, Tragik und Ironie' [Absurdity, tragedy and irony], in ibid.

6   The material that I deal with in this section is just basic literary history. You can read up on it in general surveys of the topic, or in more special-ized studies such as P. Burke, *Popular Culture in Early Modern Europe* (Scolar Press, Aldershot, 1994) or Mikhail Bakhtin's *Rabelais and his World* (trans. H. Iswolsky, Indiana University Press, Bloomington, 1988). Bakhtin's book is an analysis of the social institution of carnival that has inspired much debate and considerable further research.

7   I draw here on the entries for 'light fiction', 'pulp fiction' and 'trash' listed in Gero von Wilpert's *Sachwörterbuch der Literatur* (Alfred Kröner, Stuttgart, 2001). This particular dictionary of literary terms has been in use for half a century, and is still one of the most popular of its kind in German liter-ary studies today. (The book is now in its eighth edition and has been revised several times over the years. This makes the older editions very interesting to study, as the differences between the various editions reveal changes in the orthodoxy and canon.) Of course, Pierre Bourdieu's well-known study, *Distinction: A Social Critique of Judgement of Taste* (Harvard University Press, Cambridge, Mass., 1998), demonstrates empirically how different understandings of what constitutes 'high art' and 'good taste' in culture correspond to different class positions.

8   See the entry 'Künstlerdrama' [artist's drama] in von Wilpert, *Sachwörter-buch der Literatur*, p. 442. The Künstlerdrama is a type of play that was particularly popular in Germany and that has an artist (or writer/dramatist etc.) as its central character. The plot would trace the development of the artist from childhood to maturity. [Trans.]

9   'Sturm und Drang' or 'Storm and Stress' was a literary movement that flourished in Germany in the late eighteenth century. It anticipated many elements of Romanticism and is characterized by its emphasis on subjectivity and on inspiration over reason. Storm and Stress writers rejected neoclassical conventions and took up the themes of youthful genius and rebellion. [Trans.]

10   Hanswurst (in effect, 'John Sausage') was a descendant of the Italian Pulcinella and a relative of 'Mr Punch'. He was recognizable for his long nose, his coarse jokes and his violent reactions. [Trans.]

11   Ferdinand Raimund (1790–1836) was a Viennese actor and playwright. Johann Nestroy (1801–1862) was a prominent actor in the theatres of Vienna and Graz. [Trans.]

12   See M. Schirner, *Werbung ist Kunst* (Klinkhardt and Biermann, Munich, 1991) and Marjory Jacobson, *Art and Business: New Strategies for Corporate Collecting* (Thames and Hudson, London, 1993).

13   See, for example, E. Goffman, *Gender Advertisements* (Macmillan, London, 1979).

14   Adorno discusses the universalization of competition, contests and aptitude tests in relation to sport. See 'The Schema of Mass Culture' (1944/1981), pp. 74–8.

5 The conditions of belonging: the appropriation of the audience

The words in square brackets in the title of the first section of the chapter represent the original version of 1944 that was subsequently edited out of the book.

1   See the appendix to vol. 5 of Max Horkheimer's *Gesammelte Schriften* for Willem van Reijen and Jan Bransen's analysis of the revisions.

2   Naturally, what predestines an employee to be co-opted into the clique is usually their erotic promise rather than their professional skills. (Besides, these would be quite hard to quantify, given the anonymous nature of a secretary's job in a busy open-plan office.) This has been a popular theme of comedy ever since *Wife vs. Secretary* (1936, starring Jean Harlow). It is presented with varying degrees of malice from the bitterly ridiculous Jack Lemmon in Billy Wilder's *The Apartment* (1960) to the Coen Brothers' screwball comedy *The Hudsucker Proxy*, a parody of the genre released in 1994.

3   Adorno was aware that his negative assessment of Chaplin stood in conflict with the views of his friends, Siegfried Kracauer and Walter Benjamin. This difference of opinion was bound up more generally with their con-

trasting assessments of the value of film as a medium. Kracauer and Benjamin differed in the specifics of their analysis, yet they both saw in film the potential for arriving at a critical attitude towards culture and, by extension, the possibility of creating a proletarian consciousness. Adorno deemed this to be illusory, and he saw it as the result of a false analysis that was not sufficiently 'dialectical' in character. In relation to this, it is helpful to read Adorno's letter to Benjamin of 18 March 1936 in which he criticizes the latter's essay on 'The Work of Art in the Age of Mechanical Reproduction'. Adorno refers to Chaplin in order to dismiss the idea that the perspective of the camera allows the audience to become a critical instance: 'You need only to have heard the laughter of the audience to realize what is going on' (T. W. Adorno and W. Benjamin, *The Complete Correspondence, 1928–1940* (1994), p. 130).

4   Leo McCarey's *Once Upon a Honeymoon* (1942, starring Cary Grant and Ginger Rogers) is another comic film that deals with this period. However, in this film the comedy is kept within limits and the Nazis are not made to seem ridiculous.

5   In Howard Hawks's *Bringing up Baby* (1938) the inflated claim to power is brought down to earth in a particularly amusing manner. The clown figure (Katharine Hepburn as Susan, a mad-cap heiress) provides the comedy by consistently failing to react in a suitably deferential manner as she does away with conventional niceties and responds to situations in an unexpectedly 'logical' manner. The dog also provides for the comedy, as does the leopard and the dinosaur, for the two animals and the skeleton clearly exhibit a will of their own. (Cary Grant, playing a stuffy palaeontologist, spends most of the film desperately trying to reconstruct the dinosaur from a heap of bones.)

6   There is not actually any really suitable way of addressing a group of viewers or listeners. Conventionally, performances and shows begin with the presenter or compère respectfully addressing the 'Ladies and Gentlemen'. Equally conventionally, it is the audience's task to welcome the performance with applause. People only really start to communicate with one another when everything is over. Yet even at drinks receptions or when everyone is milling around after the final curtain call, people still avail themselves of ritualistic ways of introducing themselves and making contact. It is really a question of role-play, and the individuals remain nameless and impersonal.

7   The sociologist and jazz player Howard S. Becker was quick to recognize and describe this phenomenon (see chapters 5 and 6 on dance musicians in H. S. Becker, *Outsiders: Studies in the Sociology of Deviance* (Free Press, New York, 1997)), yet other sociologists working in the field of aesthetics showed little interest in the topic.

8   John Fiske is the most vociferous advocate of the idea that consumers are capable of subverting the content of the media to create their own meanings and message. See J. Fiske, *Understanding Popular Culture* (Routledge, London and New York, 1989) and J. Fiske, 'Popular Discrimination', in J. Naremore and P. Brantlinger (eds), *Modernity and Mass Culture* (Indiana

University Press, Bloomington, 1991), pp. 103–16. In *Loving with a Vengeance: Mass-Produced Fantasies for Women* (Routledge, London and New York, 1984), Tania Modleski created a stir by arguing that women can interpret soap operas in terms of female protest and strength. At one time, it was necessary to highlight the existence of 'active consumers', but we have now progressed from this stage, and we are able to criticize the way in which such overoptimistic estimations of consumer power often serve to excuse poor or reactionary media content. Jim McGuigan coined the useful term 'cultural populism' and set out this argument in detail in *Cultural Populism* (Routledge, London and New York, 1992).

9   It is not a bad idea in general to choose a particular theme and then go through the text and make notes on any relevant passages. This way you get a different perspective on the structure of the text.

10 Adorno illustrates this remark with an example that shows the impossibility of creating artistic representations of events such as company mergers: 'Even a radical film director who wished to portray crucially important social developments like the merger of two industrial concerns could only do so by showing us the dominant figures in the office, at the conference table or in their mansions' ('Schema', p. 57).

11 With hindsight it seems surprising that it took so long for audience research to free itself from the dictates of culture industry and to start looking at problems from the perspective of the viewers or listeners. This perspective takes for granted that every time we turn on the radio or TV we have our own intentions that do not necessarily have anything to do with the material being broadcast or the intentions of the broadcaster. Audience research had difficulty in accepting the idea of the 'active audience', and it took numerous attempts on the part of various theorists before the notion became established. For further reading on audience research see J. Hay, L. Grossberg and E. Wartella (eds), *The Audience and its Landscape* (Westview Press, Boulder, 1996); I. Ang, *Living Room Wars: Rethinking Media Audiences for a Postmodern World* (Routledge, London, 1996); V. Nightingale, *Studying Audiences: The Shock of the Real* (Routledge, London, 1996); S. Moores, *Interpreting Audiences: The Ethnography of Media Consumption* (Sage, London, 1993).

12 According to the theory of 'working alliances', identifying which genre a commodity belongs to is an important step towards understanding what is going on. However, it is also important in relation to the production of the commodity, as well as being a necessary stage in our attempt to analyse it. Examining a particular genre is interesting in that it leads us to describe the relatively detailed rules of the working alliance that is specific to e.g. the Western, the detective novel or the romantic comedy. This type of research is particularly well developed in film studies. For a good introductory text on the subject, see A. A. Berger, *Popular Culture Genres: Theories and Texts* (Sage, London, 1992).

13 See W. Benjamin, 'The Work of Art in the Age of Mechanical Reproduction', in *Illuminations* (trans. H. Zohn, Pimlico, London, 1999).

6 Culture industry politics

1 'Egoismus und Freiheitsbewegung. Zur Anthropologie des bürgerlichen Zeitalters' (1936) can be found in English translation in *Between Philosophy and Social Science: Selected Early Writings*. In this translation, the essay appears as 'Egoism and Freedom Movements: On the Anthropology of the Bourgeois Era'. However, Horkheimer's article clearly deals with the movement (singular rather than plural) towards liberation (rather than freedom).

2 In the 1960s, very few people knew about the articles published in the *Zeitschrift für Sozialforschung* [Journal of social research] or about *Dialectic of Enlightenment*. Horkheimer was reluctant to republish these texts, for they had been written in a very different historical context from that of ex-Nazi Germany in the postwar period and the new era of totalitarianism. 'Egoismus und Freiheitsbewegung. Zur Anthropologie des bürgerlichen Zeitalters' was eventually reprinted in volume 4 of Horkheimer's *Gesammelte Schriften*. For Horkheimer's analysis of the political situation in the late 1960s see 'Brief an den S. Fischer Verlag' and 'Vorwort zur Neupublikation' in volume 3 of *Gesammelte Schriften*.

3 L. Löwenthal and N. Gutermann, *Prophets of Deceit: A Study of the Techniques of the American Agitator* (Harper, New York, 1949).

4 A striking example of this is the perpetual discussion of 'violence' – even if we never actually witness this trend, we are always being told that violence is becoming more extreme and increasingly common.

5 Anyone whose name has ever been mentioned in the newspapers or on TV will know that this is the main consequence of being referred to in the media. If your name crops up in an article or broadcast, countless other journalists ring you up and ask you to repeat (sometimes in a different medium, e.g. radio) exactly what you were quoted as saying in the original report.

6 See J. Habermas, *The Structural Transformation of the Public Sphere: An Inquiry into a Category of Bourgeois Society* (trans. T. Burger, Polity, Cambridge and MIT Press, Cambridge, Mass., 1989). In the foreword to the new German edition of the book (1990), the author distances himself from the position that he took in 1961 when the book was first published. Recent debates are taking place under the banner of 'civil society', a concept that was borrowed from Gramsci, but that has now been detached from its theoretical foundations.

7 For further discussion of the 'news business', see J. Fallows, *Breaking the News: How the Media Undermine American Democracy* (Random House, New York, 1997). On the topic of journalism, it is often more rewarding to read embittered journalists' accounts of their profession than to study the warnings written by theorists of media and democracy. Criticizing culture industry is another branch of culture industry, and it takes place in various guises in fiction, entertainment, journalism, propaganda, empirical research and social philosophy.

8   The student movement of the 1960s and 1970s was analysed as a media event even at that time. See for instance T. Gitlin, *The Whole World is Watching: Mass Media in the Making and Unmaking of the New Left* (University of California Press, Berkeley, 1970). The student 'terrorism' of the 1970s and today's right-wing extremism would also be suited to such analysis, and could be examined as forms of PR and of culture industry politics. The collapse of the communist regimes in Eastern Europe and recent anti-globalization protests have shown that the street is still a politically effective mass medium – so long as the TV cameras are there, that is.

9   *New Yorker*, 15 Sept. 1997, p. 4.

7 Intellectuals in the supermarket: perplexed

1   Alongside the aphorism 'Wrong life cannot be lived rightly' (*Minima Moralia* (1944/1951), p. 39), Adorno's best known (and most frequently misunderstood) quote is probably his verdict that 'to write poetry after Auschwitz is barbaric. And this corrodes even the knowledge of why it has become impossible to write poetry today' (*Prisms* (1955), p. 34). This line is widely taken to be a prescriptive sentence: people interpret it as saying that to write poetry after Auschwitz is forbidden. Ironically, this misinterpretation of the line is in keeping with Bertolt Brecht's earlier lyrical reflection that to talk about trees has become almost a crime, since it involves keeping silent about so many horrors. (See 'To Those Born Later', in *Bertolt Brecht: Poems, 1913–1956*, ed. J. Willett and R. Mannheim with the cooperation of E. Fried (trans. J. Willett, Methuen, London, 1976), pp. 318–20. Fortunately, even the politically minded Brecht was not kept from writing love poetry by this insight.) Adorno's sentence, however, is a statement of a fact, a critique and a dilemma. The fact is that Auschwitz was the act of a nation that had always prided itself on its high culture. Accordingly, it may be this (specific German form of) high culture that was instrumental in making possible the ultimate barbarism. As critique, the sentence is an indictment of high culture's inability to prevent genocide from occurring. The dilemma is that, while the diagnosis is valid, the very act of talking and debating about poetry is part of that same high culture, and it gives poetry and high culture an importance that they cannot have 'after Auschwitz'. At the end of a long and drawn-out debate as to how to continue writing in a language forever corrupted and discredited by the Nazis and how to break with the cultural tradition that had led to Auschwitz, Adorno readily conceded: 'perennial suffering has as much right to expression as a tortured man has to scream; hence it may have been wrong to say that after Auschwitz you could no longer write poems' ('Meditations on Metaphysics: After Auschwitz', in *Negative Dialectics* (1966), p. 362). The most sarcastic retrospective contribution to this debate has come from Peter Rühmkorf, with his question as to whether, after Auschwitz, it is still possible to read Adorno (cf. Rühmkorf's poem of 1986,

'Vom Einzelnen ins Tausendste', in *Werke I. Gedichte* (Rowohlt, Reinbek, 2000), p. 412).

2 The 'Basic Law' [Grundgesetz] for the Federal Republic of Germany was promulgated on 23 May 1949, and took as its model the constitution of the US, but without the strong position of the President, for obvious reasons. [Trans.]

3 See Adorno's *The Authoritarian Personality* (1950); A. Mitscherlich and M. Mitscherlich, *Die Unfähigkeit zu trauern. Grundlagen kollektiven Verhaltens* (Piper Verlag, Munich, 1977); A. Mitscherlich, *Auf dem Weg zur vaterlosen Gesellschaft* (Piper Verlag, Munich, 1973).

4 Diana Crane examines this phenomenon in relation to American Pop Art and Neo-Expressionism. See *The Transformation of the Avant-Garde: The New York Art World, 1940–1985* (Chicago University Press, Chicago, 1987). There is no real equivalent that examines European culture. In European pop-music, the most obvious phenomenon is that of punk and rave music, in which machines and primitivism are used in order to provoke a reaction and to encourage sales.

5 After Dada and the tabloidization of political journalism, scandal became the main way of manipulating the public in a variety of arenas. See for example J. Lull and S. Hinerman (eds), *Media Scandals: Morality and Desire in the Popular Culture Marketplace* (Polity, Cambridge, 1997).

6 Professional journalists seem particularly liable to engage in this kind of revelatory and pedagogic 'social problems' orientated criticism, and in so doing they create an authoritarian working alliance. Journalists reporting on right-wing violence sometimes enter into an unwitting coalition with the skinheads and neo-Nazis they are filming, thereby unintentionally offering the latter a good opportunity to portray themselves to the public. Young people are sometimes quite keen to engage in such self-presentation. In a research project on youth gangs in Vienna, I found it easy to make gang members take part in group discussions, but the only way they could really understand what was going on was by comparing it to being interviewed on radio or TV. They were most disappointed by the fact that we did not have a video camera and that we were not planning to broadcast the tape recording. They talked enthusiastically about TV, radio and newspaper reports on gangs (and sometimes even on the gangs that they belonged to), and they were keen to take part in a similar kind of documentary. Evidently, even these gangs were eager to engage in some PR for their own cause. They wanted to represent to the public the violence of their clashes with other gangs in their wars with the far right and ethnic minorities. It was also a question of proving and dramatizing their manliness. In this way, it was not dissimilar to the case of those academics who parade in front of their bookcases for the camera, eager to further their particular cause *and* to show off their intellectual splendour.

7 It goes without saying that there is much more to the concerns about the environment than I have indicated here. What I am referring to is not the scientific research etc., but the protest movement, and the latter relies on alarmism. In short: I am not saying that the environmental movement

is wrong. I am only saying that it is short on social theory and that it obviously has no need for it.

8   Horkheimer and Adorno highlight the forced integration of opponents of the Nazi regime, as well as of sceptics and of supporters experiencing a crisis of faith (brought on, for example, by the knowledge of military crimes or by the prospect of imminent defeat). People in Germany and in the occupied territories were tempted by the promise of belonging to a magnificent 'master race' and by the real material gains that were to be had from 'Aryanization'. The process of integration was able to build on this, as well as on the long tradition of European anti-Semitism.

9   See Ulrich Beck, Anthony Giddens and Scott Lash, *Reflexive Modernization: Politics, Tradition and Aesthetics in the Modern Social Order* (Polity, Cambridge and Stanford University Press, Stanford, 1994). Interestingly, in this book the third author, Scott Lash, clearly notes the reduced character of 'reflexivity' as used by Beck and Giddens (cf. esp. p. 115). To this criticism Beck replies by pointing to his understanding of a paradox of modernization: the main point is 'unintended reflexivity in the sense of self-application, self-dissolution and the self-endangerment of industrial modernization' (p. 176). He thus confirms that in his understanding 'reflexivity' is feedback, the outcome of which is open: it can also be negative and self-destroying. Giddens agrees with this (cf. esp. p. 187), and in his turn repudiates Lash's counterconstruction of an 'aesthetic reflexivity' (p. 196). Both Beck and Giddens have departed from the enlightenment understanding of reflexivity as critique by reconstruction of the categorical limitations of our concepts and understandings – in a materialist theory deriving from and being part of the given regime of domination.

10 The 'information' or 'knowledge economy' is scarcely distinguishable from the earlier 'service economy'. Back in the 1960s, it was first referred to as the 'postindustrial society'. These days, it has become a byword among sociologists, journalists and politicians.

11 Adorno could still conceive of products that are not for sale or that are not custom-made for the purposes and demands of a market. In fact, this resistance to the imperatives of instrumentality is what distinguishes bourgeois art and what makes it stand in contradiction to the very society from which it emerges.

12 What we are dealing with here is a simple shift from a theoretical concept to a pragmatic classification of a field. In such cases, there is often only very limited understanding that a theoretical concept ever existed. (This is particularly true in relation to the study of 'culture industries' within business studies.) Moreover, even when reference is made to Horkheimer and Adorno's theory, the link to the empirical analysis is seldom acknowledged. See for example Keith Negus's introductory article on 'The Production of Culture' in Paul du Guy (ed.), *Production of Culture/Cultures of Production* (Sage/Open University, London, 1997), pp. 67–104. Negus begins by introducing the ideas of Horkheimer/Adorno, but he oscillates between the term 'cultural' and 'culture industry' (singular). When he gets round to discussing some more contemporary examples, he shifts to the

term 'culture industries' (plural) without comment. Eventually, the term 'industry' disappears from the text altogether and is replaced by micro descriptions. The text's treatment of 'culture industry' and 'culture industries' seems to suggest that we have now left the original (and allegedly outdated) concept behind.

13 Scott Lash and John Urry, *Economies of Signs and Space* (Sage, London, 1994), pp. 123, 138.

14 Jim McGuigan coined the very apt term 'cultural populism' for this orientation. See his book *Cultural Populism* (Routledge, London and New York, 1992).

15 Admittedly, some of these cultural experiences still come at considerable cost and effort (not least in terms of the advance planning). However, it is not just the visit to the ballet or opera that is liable to swallow up a worker's weekly income in admission alone, for Disneyland, Las Vegas or the latest West End musical are equally expensive. Surprisingly, the differentiation of visitors to different culture events and institutions is still extremely skewed, and the main determining factor (apart from age) is education.

Select bibliography of works by Adorno and Horkheimer

The initial dates of the works below (also cited on first mention in the text) are those of the manuscript or of first publication in any language. They are followed by the English language editions to which page numbers in the text refer.

For Adorno's collected works in German see *Gesammelte Schriften*, ed. Rolf Tiedemann, 20 vols, Suhrkamp Verlag, Frankfurt, 1970–.

For Horkheimer's collected works in German see *Gesammelte Schriften*, ed. Alfred Schmidt and Gunzelin Schmid Noerr, 18 vols, Fischer Verlag, Frankfurt, 1987–.

Theodor W. Adorno

(1932) 'On the Social Situation of Music', trans. W. Bloomster. *Telos*, 35 (1978), pp. 128–64. First published in German as 'Zur gesellschaftlichen Lage der Musik'.

(1936) 'On Jazz', trans. J. Owen Daniel. *Discourse*, 12, no. 1 (Fall/Winter 1989–90), pp. 45–69. First published in German as 'Über Jazz'.

(1938) 'Analytical Study of the NBC Music Appreciation Hour'. *Musical Quarterly*, 78, no. 2 (1994), pp. 325–77. Originally written in English.

(1938) 'On the Fetish-Character in Music and the Regression of Listening', trans. M. Goldbloom. In *The Culture Industry: Selected Essays on Mass Culture*, ed. and introd. J. M. Bernstein, Routledge, London, 1991, pp. 26–52. First published in German as 'Über den Fetischcharakter der Musik und der Regression des Hörens'; first published in English in 1985.

(1939/1952) *In Search of Wagner*, trans. R. Livingstone. New Left Books, London and New York, 1981. First published in German as 'Fragmente über Wagner' (partial publication in *Studies in Philosophy and Social Science/Zeitschrift für Sozialforschung* 1939) and in complete book form in 1952 as *Versuch über Wagner*.

(1940/1949) *Philosophy of Modern Music*, trans. A. Mitchell and W. Bloomster, Sheed and Ward, London, 1973. Manuscript 1940; first published 1949 in German as *Philosophie der neuen Musik*.

(1941) 'On Popular Music'. *Studies in Philosophy and Social Science/Zeitschrift für Sozialforschung*, 9 (1941), pp. 17–48. Originally written in English.

(1944/1947) with Max Horkheimer, *Dialectic of Enlightenment*, trans. J. Cumming. Verso, London and New York, 1997. First published in German as *Dialektik der Aufklärung. Philosophische Fragmente* (mimeographed edition 1944; book 1947); first published in English in 1972.

(1944/1981) 'The Schema of Mass Culture', trans. N. Walker. In *The Culture Industry: Selected Essays on Mass Culture*, ed. and introd. J. M. Bernstein, Routledge, London, 1991, pp. 53–84. Manuscript 1944; first published 1981 in German as 'Das Schema der Massenkultur'.

(1944/1951) *Minima Moralia: Reflections from Damaged Life*, trans. E. F. N. Jephcott. Verso, London, 1974. First published in German as *Minima Moralia. Reflexionen aus dem beschädigten Leben* (mimeographed edition 1944; book 1951).

(1949) 'Cultural Criticism and Society'. In *Prisms*, trans. S. Weber and S. Weber, MIT Press, Cambridge, Mass., 1981, pp. 17–34. First published in German as 'Kulturkritik und Gesellschaft'; first published in English in 1967.

(1950) with Else Frenkel-Brunswik, Daniel J. Levinson and R. Nevitt Sanford, *The Authoritarian Personality*. Norton, New York. Originally written in English.

(1953) 'Perennial Fashion – Jazz'. In *Prisms*, trans. S. Weber and S. Weber, MIT Press, Cambridge, Mass., 1981, pp. 119–32. First published in German as 'Zeitlose Mode. Zum Jazz'; first published in English in 1967.

(1954) 'How to Look at Television'. *Quarterly of Film, Radio and Television*, 8 (Spring 1954), pp. 214–35. Reprinted as 'Television and the Patterns of Mass Culture', in *The Culture Industry: Selected Essays on Mass Culture*, ed. and introd. J. M. Bernstein, Routledge, London, 1991, pp. 136–53. Originally written in English.

(1955) *Prisms*, trans. S. Weber and S. Weber. MIT Press, Cambridge, Mass., 1981. First published in German as *Prismen*; first published in English in 1967.

(1959) 'Theory of Pseudo-Culture', trans. D. Cook. *Telos*, 95 (Spring 1993), pp. 15–38. First published in German as 'Theorie der Halbbildung'.

(1962) 'Those Twenties'. In *Critical Models*, trans. H. Pickford, Columbia University Press, New York, 1999. First published in German as 'Jene zwanziger Jahre'.

(1962) *Introduction to the Sociology of Music*, trans. E. B. Ashton. Seabury Press, New York, 1976. First published in German as *Einleitung in die Musiksoziologie. Zwölf theoretische Vorlesungen*.

(1963) 'Culture Industry Reconsidered', trans. A. Rabinbach. In *The Culture Industry: Selected Essays on Mass Culture*, ed. and introd. J. M. Bernstein, Routledge, London, 1991, pp. 85–92. First published in German as 'Résumé über Kulturindustrie'; first published in English in 1975.

(1963) *Hegel: Three Studies*, trans. S. Weber Nicholsen. MIT Press, Cambridge Mass., 1993. First published in German as *Drei Studien zu Hegel*.

(1966) *Negative Dialectics*, trans. E. B. Ashton. Seabury Press, New York, 1973. First published in German as *Negative Dialektik*.

(1969) 'Free Time', trans. G. Finlayson and N. Walker. In *The Culture Industry: Selected Essays on Mass Culture*, ed. and introd. J. M. Bernstein, Routledge, London, 1991, pp. 162–70. First published in German as 'Freizeit'.

(1970) *Aesthetic Theory*, ed. G. Adorno and R. Tiedemann, trans. C. Lenhardt. Routledge and Kegan Paul, London, 1984. First published in German as *Ästhetische Theorie*.

(1991) *The Culture Industry: Selected Essays on Mass Culture*, ed. and introd. J. M. Bernstein. Routledge, London, 1991. Published as a collection of English translations of earlier Adorno essays relevant to the topic.

(1994) with W. Benjamin, *The Complete Correspondence: 1928–1940*, ed. H. Lonitz, trans. N. Walker. Polity, Cambridge, 1999. First published in German as *Briefwechsel 1928–1940*.

Max Horkheimer

(1936) 'Egoism and Freedom Movements: On the Anthropology of the Bourgeois Era'. In *Between Philosophy and Social Science: Selected Early Writings*, introd. G. F. Hunter, trans. G. F. Hunter, M. S. Kramer and J. Torpey. MIT Press, Cambridge, Mass. and London, 1993, pp. 49–110. First published in German as 'Egoismus und Freiheitsbewegung. Zur Anthropologie des bürgerlichen Zeitalters'.

(1942) 'The Authoritarian State'. In A. Arato and E. Gebhardt (eds), *The Essential Frankfurt School Reader*, trans. People's Translation Service. Blackwell, Oxford, 1978, pp. 95–117. First published in German as 'Autoritärer Staat'.

(1941) 'Art and Mass Culture'. *Studies in Philosophy and Social Science/Zeitschrift für Sozialforschung*, 9, no. 2 (1941), pp. 290–304. Originally written in English.

(1944/1947) with Theodor W. Adorno, *Dialectic of Enlightenment*, trans. J. Cumming. Verso, London and New York, 1997. First published in German as *Dialektik der Aufklärung. Philosophische Fragmente* (mimeographed edition 1944; book 1947); first published in English in 1972.

Index

deception 103
decisions 138–41
Dehmel, Richard 87
delusion 129–30, 141
democracy 147, 149–50
demonstrators 147
dependency 66–7, 77–8
Dialectic of Enlightenment 2, 20–1,
    30–1; appendix 27; European
    society 165; revisions 176n1;
    writing of 24, 78, 176n1; *see also*
    'Culture Industry'
Die Hard 137
distraction 138
domination: advertising 115;
    bourgeoisie 66; capitalism 24;
    colonialism 82; competition 117;
    conceptual understanding 42–3,
    72–3; culture 74; culture industry
    75; economic 123; false identity
    78; indirect 25; liberalism 123;
    populism 145; positivism 122;
    propaganda 137; repression 142;
    self-importance 125; sublime 136;
    thought 74; ticket mentality 73
drugs scene 85
Duchamp, Marcel 93, 94; art
    appreciation 93; *Étant donnés* 93,
    97; *L.H.O.O.Q.* 19, 20, 178n10;
    Nude Descending a Staircase 93;
    ready-mades 91, 93; *Sad Young
    Man on a Train* 93; women of
    Dada 96

Eastwood, Clint 81; *Absolute Power*
    27; *Bird* 85, 185n17; President
    films 28, 30
Eco, Umberto 39–40, 180n2
ecologists 158; *see also*
    environmental movement
economic sphere 82, 115–16, 123,
    155–6
educated classes 88, 158–9, 162,
    194n15
'Egoismus und Freiheitsbewegung'
    (Horkheimer) 26, 31, 142, 143,
    190n1

Eisler, Hanns 90
elitism: Adorno 21, 130, 157;
    'Culture Industry' 7; masses 25–6;
    music 69–70; public aloofness
    95
emotion 91–2, 153–4, 182n14
employees: *see* workers
enlightenment 73, 121, 144
'Enlightenment as Mass Deception'
    (Adorno) 24
entertainers 106
entertainment 99–101; comedy 110;
    commodities 76; politics 161;
    television news 28; texts 53–4
environmental movement 162–3; *see
    also* ecologists
Enzensberger, H. M. 101, 102
Ernst, Max 94
eroticism 93, 103, 117
escort agencies 140
European society 165
events in art 88, 91, 92, 135–7; *see
    also* happenings
Everyone Says I Love You 173, 174,
    175
evil/good 142
exclusivity 178n8
executive authorities 77
exhibitionism 97–8
existentialism 87
exoticism 82–6
expendability of individuals 121

fame 20, 127
familiar 83
family as institution 48
fascism 26, 78, 100, 116, 145–6
femininity 54
feminism 139, 158
fetishism 20
fiction: *see* literature
field notes 4–5, 15–16
film: *see* cinema
Fiske, John 188–9n8
A Fistful of Dollars 30
Flusser, Vilém 167
fools 106